EDUCATIONAL THOUGHT

EDUCATIONAL THOUGHT

[Useful for B.Ed. Students and Other Competition Aspirants]

By

Pradeep Kumar Johri

ANMOL PUBLICATIONS PVT. LTD.

NEW DELHI - 110 002 (INDIA)

ANMOL PUBLICATIONS PVT. LTD.
4374/4B, Ansari Road, Daryaganj
New Delhi - 110 002
Ph.: 23261597, 23278000
Visit us at: www.anmolpublications.com

Educational Thought

First Published, 2005

ISBN 81-261-2174-2

PRINTED IN INDIA

Published by J.L. Kumar for Anmol Publications Pvt. Ltd., New Delhi - 110 002 and Printed at Mehra Offset Press, Delhi.

Contents

Part–II : Indian Thought

Preface

Education is a vast discipline and Teachers' Training is a vital part of it. The responsibilities of the educationists and educators are focused on the task of providing better training to the future teachers for their better learning and proper development. Needless to say that this responsibility can only be exercised, if the trainers are equipped with the required knowledge of the subject concerned. That's why it becomes essential for making adequate provisions for each course to the student-teachers or teacher trainees. The present series is designed for providing a solid workable base for all course-papers. It has been prepared strictly according to the syllabus of the B.Ed class, prescribed by the UGC for different universities.

No doubt, there are so many other books on the subject, available in the market, written by worthy authors. However, every writer has his or her own style and way of presentation. The present work also has its own features and characteristics.

In preparation of this series of texts, the editor had to refer to the works of other authors and information sources. The editor feels a deep sense of gratitude for incorporating their ideas in the text. Hopefully, this series would serve as a 'ready to refer' tool for all teachers, teacher-students and others.

—Editor

1

Introduction

For comprending basis of education, educational philosophy and educational thought, one has to understand the fundamentals. There are eight points :

(i) basic concepts of education (ii) philosophy in relation to philosophy, values and education (iii) educational philosophies and thoughts of Indian thinkers (iv) aims of education in an emerging Indian society (v) education with a specific focus on—democratic outlook, human values, health, vocationalisation, modernisation (vi) social agencies of education in Indian society (vii) structure and concerns of modern Indian society like national integration, population explosion, environmental degradation, globalisation and privatisation, social changes, human resource and national development (viii) futurology in relation to education.

The above stated eight dimensions of education in relation to emerging Indian society, must have given a feel about your own country and its people. Besides, you must have understood the social structure of Indian society. Further your attention must have been drawn to new emerging areas of study which seem to be vital in modern times. Study of national concerns and issues must have given you an understanding that a nation can become strong if its people are made aware about emerging them. The purpose of the study is served if you identify yourself will national issues and problems, and as a teacher try to bring out workable solutions for each issue.

Such issues and problems which have inflicted the Indian society need to be studied and researched in order to find solutions thereof.

For undertaking research studies in social and behaviours sciences like education, a researcher needs a strong base for cnducting research. He needs certain basic skills related to processes of conducting research.

In survey studies, a researcher is required to understand the basic terms and steps: involved in the process of research. After having a task analysis related to research may be action research or applied research in education, we need to identify certain skills which are involved. Let us list the skills which are required of an investigator/researcher.

General Skills Related to Field/Practical Work : (i) Skill of sensing a social issue/problem in society. (ii) Defining the social issue in clear terms or language. (iii) State the problem in simple, clear and precise language. (iv) Listing specific objectives of conducting field work. (v) Making hypothesis or formulating research questions. (vi) Planning/conceptualising the action plan, stating sample, tools, data collection, etc. (vii) Collection of data (information—quantitative and qualitative). (viii) Processing data into major and minor categories. (ix) Making tables, diagrams, graphs, etc. (x) Making analysis of data collected. (xi) Interpretation of results. (xii) Bringing out findings of the study in the light of objectives. (xiii) Drawing conclusions from the study. (xiv) Preparing draft report. (xv) Preparing bibliography/references of books, journals, etc. consulted by the investigator. (xvi) Placing appendices at appropriate place. (xvii) Preparing final export with proper binding.

In your course, there are three specific areas where you are supposed to develop skills viz.

(a) Socio-economic Educational Survey (b) Study of Education and Income Patterns (c) Role of Education in Women Empowerment

Let us take one by one these areas and try to identify the type and nature of related skills.

This field of study deals with survey of some area specific. It can be rural area or urban area. Further, we are also to understand the socio-economic and education status of the people.

In such area studies, one is to collect information on three counts:

(a) Social conditions of the people (b) Economic status of the people (c) Educational background of the people.

In order to make a survey of any area viz. village in rural setting, one is to collect data/information about the social life of the people. In this regard, a researcher is supposed to know and collect the following information:

(i) Nature of society-closed/open. (ii) Nature of family-joint/nuclear. (iii) Customs and traditions of the people. (iv) Faith of the people in general. (v) Economic position of the family in a village. (vi) How many persons are working? (vii) Are they doing service or engaged in agriculture? (viii) What is educational background of members of the family?

There are certain behaviours that a researcher is supposed to possess in order to contact people, communicate with them and collect relevant information. It can be through a questionnarie, opinionnaire or interview. Related set of behaviours or skills can be as stated below:

(a) Skill of identifying the issue/problem related to the life of the people (b) Skill of formulating objectives of study (c) Skill of preparing a Schedule/Questionnaire/Opinionnaire (d) Skill of collecting information from respondents or the people (specific category of persons) (e) Skill of communication in order to collect information (f) Skill of processing data (g) Skill of analysing data (h) Skill of interpreting data (i) Skill of drawing out the findings (j) Skill of reporting in writing.

There are two broad aspects which need to be studied viz. education and income patterns. Both education and income patterns are interrelated as each one effects the other. Therefore, a researcher in supposed to establish a co-relation between two factors (variable) i.e. education and income patterns.

In such studies/field work, a researcher is supposed to know the nature of study and type of information to be collected. His attention is to be drawn on these specific areas:

(a) Type of education—academic or professional (b) Level of education (c) Type of profession—unskilled, semi-skilled or skilled (d) Number of persons who are doing a job (e) Nature of job—service, agriculture, labours, etc. (f) Mode of income from various sources (g) Level of income—below average or above average.

There are again some set of behaviours or skills which are needed to undertake a study of the nature stated above. Let us identify some specific skills which are required of a researcher. For illustration, specific skills needed, related to such studies, are as under:

(a) Skill of identifying a problem (b) Skill of formulating a research statement of the study (c) Skill of identifying the components like education and income patterns (d) Skill of preparing a tool for collecting data (e) Skill of collecting information/data related to education and economic pattern (f) Skill of communication with people of different educational and economic background (g) Skill of conducting interview (h) Skill of collecting data (i) Skill of processing data (j) Skill of analysing data category-wise (k) Skill of interpretation of results (l) Skill of drawing conclusions (m) Skill of suggesting type of studies related to the area (n) Skill of preparing a report.

For research or preparing a report, one is to understand the nature and type of area to which a study belongs. The title of this study suggests that education plays a vital role for making women powerful in order to discharge their gender or other roles in society. There are two ways to study this area. They are as under:

(i) Conceptual analysis of education in relation to women empowerment. (ii) Making a survey from the field to infer the contribution of education towards women empowerment.

Before undertaking such a study, it is pertinent to have basic understanding of two concepts, i.e., education and empowerment of women. Education is a term which refers to growth and development of one's capacities-physical, mental, social, emotional, aesthetic, moral and spiritual. In other words, education is a powerful tool, of development of man. The total personality undergoes a change and transforms its to a new state of being.

The empowerment refers to capacity building of a person. It suggests to the development of ideas, thinking abilities, capabilities, skills, values and attitudes of a person. With the development of such faculties and competencies, one becomes powerful.

Woman though occupies an elevated position in Indian society yet for the last a few centuries, her position is lowered and exploited. After independence, when country decided to develop its economy, the role of woman was also seen in proper perspective. It was realised that if women is given her due status, then development activity can be accelerated.

Therefore education of women became a priority area of study and research in this country. The present topic can be taken in the form of writing a paper which needs different set of skills. Skills needed for writing papers are as follows:

(a) Skill of writing a topic/title clearly (b) Skill of defining major/key words in the statement of the topic (c) Skill of formulating of objectives of the paper (d) Skill of tracing relevant information from available literature (e) Skill of organising subject-matter (f) Skill of quoting studies related to area of study (g) Skill of covering possible aspects of the study/topic (h) Skill of drawing models, figures and graphs related to study/topic (i) Skill of drawing conclusions (j) Skill of suggesting related areas/aspects for further study (k) Skill of presenting the complete report.

In the end, it is concluded that whenever a prospective teacher on any topic for simple investigation or writes a paper, first of all he should have broad understanding of the subject matter (content of the paper). After having a grasp over the subject matter, he is directed to select an issue/topic/problem related to what he has read so far.

Part–I
Western Thought

2

Froebel

Kindergarten or K.G is a German word meaning "garden of children". This system was introduced by Friedrich William August Froebel, in short Froebel who had a special love and concern for the children and wanted to introduce a system which could benefit the small children in learning. He was the first to give the call "Come, Let Us Live For Our Children". He exclusively emphasised 'play' as a method of teaching small children, and on their total growth and development. For him, this development is 'intrinsic' and should not be interfered with. For Froebel, teacher was like a gardener who should tend to his garden and create an inducive atmosphere for the growth and development of the plants (children) in his garden.

Educational Philosophy

Froebel's philosophy is the outcome of the great influence of German philosophers like Fitche, Kant and Schelling on him. The following are the main principles of his philosophy:-

Law of Unity: According to Froebel there is one eternal law—the law of unity that governs all things, men and nature. God is the one ground of all things. God is the all comprehending. All things animate or inanimate originate from God. Man and nature are one. They are simply different in unity. All things have come from the Divine Unity (God) and have their origin in the Divine Unity. All things live and have their beings in and through the Divine Unity.

Principle of Development: This principle is based on the first. We are marching toward the same unity. The movement is continuous and upward. Everything is, therefore, changing, growing and marching toward the same unity. Froebel maintained that mind evolves from within. The development of the child can be attained only through development from within. By development, he meant an increase in bulk or quantity, increase in complexity of structure, an improvement in power, skill and variety in the performance of natural functions.

Principle of Self-activity: It is only through self-activity that the real growth and development is possible. Forced activity is artificial and unnatural.

Development through Social Institutions: According to Froebel, the school is a miniature society. The development of the child takes place through the environment of the school.

Basic Issues

Immensely influenced by the German tradition of Kant, Fichte, Hegel and Schelling, Froebel was through and through an idealist who considered child basically a spirit, and believes in an eternal law that manifests itself in everything, animate or inanimate, living or non-living. His philosophical concepts gave birth to the following principles of education:-

Unity with God: Froebel maintains that the aim of education is not to make the mind of the child a jumble of words. He writes, "The essential business of school is not so much to communicate a variety and multiplicity of facts as to give prominence to the ever-living unity that is in all things".

Education through Play: The chief means of education is the child's own activity. Play is an essential factor in the growth of the child. The free and unfettered natural development of the child takes place through play.

Education According to the Nature of the Child: Education should be in conformity with child's nature and needs.

Education through Freedom: The child should be educated in free atmosphere. Freedom means obedience to self-imposed law.

Education through Assistance: The teacher is like a gardener who carefully nurses and protects children in order to secure their full and free development along most desirable lines.

Education through Group Life: Froebel stressed the social aspect of education also. He believed that all social institutions like the home, the school, the church and the state, etc., are the agencies of development of the individual.

Education through Gifts: He devised songs, gestures and construction as the chief means of stimulating the imagination of the child.

Practical Aspects

"Education should lead and guide man to clearness concerning himself and in that to peace with nature, and to unity with God. It should lift him to knowledge of himself to mankind, to a knowledge of God and of nature, and to the pure and holy life" (Froebel). He believed in purity and innocence of child and opened his first Kindergarten at Blankenburg in 1837. He considered child like a plant, tender, delicate and full of immense intrinsic potentialities, just as the plant is in the seed, the man is in the child. He echoes the Shakespearean truism that "Child is the father of man".

Objectives and Motives

According to Froebel, the following are the objectives of education:-

1. Give children enjoyment in agreement with their nature.
2. Strengthen the bodies of children. A healthy mind in a healthy body. A child must grow to his maximum physical potential.
3. Exercise their senses for their optimal sensitivity and perceptions.
4. Awaken their minds.
5. Acquaint them with nature and their fellows.
6. Lead them to unity.

Significant Elements

Self-activity: Froebel stressed that the child should be given full freedom to carry out his activities. The growth of the child is directed by inner force in the child. Education, said Froebel, "should provide for free self-activity and self-determination on the part of the man being created for freedom in the image of God". An Inspector reported about this self-activity—"Self-activity of the mind is the first law of this institution. The instruction steadily goes on from the simple to the complex, from the concrete to the abstract, so well adapted to the child and his needs. He goes as easily to his learning as to play".

The following points should be noted regarding activity-

(a) It should not be vague.

(b) It should be a sublimated or controlled activity.

(c) Social atmosphere is essential in order to secure meaningful results.

(d) Self-activity may take the form either of work or of play.

Play: According to Froebel, "Play is the purest, most spiritual activity of man at this stage... it gives, therefore, joy, freedom, contentment, inner peace with the world". Froebel recognises that play needs to be organised and controlled on definite materials so that it may not "degenerate into aimless play instead of preparing for those tasks of life for which it is destined". There should be rational, conscious guidance. Consequently, Froebel has given seven gifts to children to play with.

Songs, Gestures and Construction: Froebel saw an organic relationship between songs, gestures and construction. He regarded these as three co-ordinate forms of expression in the child. What is to be learnt by the pupil is first expressed in a song, then it is dramatised or expressed in gesture or movement and lastly, illustrated through some constructive work such as paper or clay. Thus, a balanced development of the mind, the speech organs and the hands is aimed at. The three activities provide exercise to the senses, limbs and muscles of the child.

Section of Songs: Contained in his book "Mother and Nursery Songs", they are fifty play songs. The idea to introduce the songs is to facilitate use of child's senses, limbs and muscles, coordination and movement, as well as to familiarise him with the surroundings. The child begins language through these songs. Songs are accompanied by games, e.g. 'Hide and seek'. Songs are also classified to commensurate with the development of the child, and have three parts:-

(a) A motto for the mother.

(b) A verse set to music.

(c) A picture illustrating the songs.

Note: These songs are commercially available in attractive colours, designs and illustrations. Most of the Fun/Nursery/ Preparatory schools are using them though they may not be knowing their origin. These songs are marked by rhyme and rhythm, beat and lilt and, the child loves to move his limbs in appropriate movements that depict the song. For example, a song for drill is:-

Let us have a drill today.

March along grand array.

And whoever steps the best.

Shall be the captain over the rest,

And lead us on our way.

Gifts and Occupations: Materials of activity are carefully graded, and progressively developed so that they lead the child from the activities and thoughts of one stage to another.

First Gift: Consists of six coloured balls contained in a box. The balls are of different colours, and the child rolls them about to play. The rolling ball gives the child an idea about colour, materials, motion and direction. The rhyme accompanying the rolling of the balls is:-

Oh, see the pretty balls,

So round, so soft and small,

The ball is round and rolls each way,

The ball is nice for baby's play.

Second Gift: This Gift consists of a sphere, a cube and a cylinder. These are three things attached to Froebel's grave as they symbolise his system of education. Made of hard wood, the child while playing with these realises the difference between the stability of the cube and the mobility of the sphere, whereas cylinder is both stable and mobile. The child also fathoms the harmonious relationship between various qualities of these articles.

Third Gift: It consists of a large cube which can be divided into eight smaller cubes. This is called the "first building box" and gives elementary knowledge of Arithmetic, e.g., addition and substraction.

Fourth Gift: A large cube which may be divided into 8 oblong prisons. Each of the prisons is twice in length as compared to its breadth. The breadth is twice the thickness. Combined with the Third Gift, this gift helps a child to build various patterns and shapes.

Fifth Gift: Very much similar to the third gift, it consists of a cube divided into twenty seven small cubes, three of which are again divided diagonally into halves and three into quarter. The child can construct many beautiful patterns and forms by combining the third, fourth and fifth gift. This gift is also useful in learning form and number.

Sixth Gift: It is very much like the gift four. It is large cube divided into eighteen whole and nine small oblong blocks. Many designs in forms and construction can be made by the child. It is also useful in teaching numbers.

Seventh Gift: is a set of square and triangular tables made of fine wood in two colours. It provides material for many exercises in geometrical forms and mosaic work.

The Place of Teacher: The teacher is not to remain passive. The teacher has to suggest the idea of occupation when gifts are offered to children. He is also required to demonstrate certain activities to them. He also sing a song with a view to helping the child to form appropriate idea.

Discipline: A teacher has important responsibilities to perform. He has to inculcate sympathetic values like love, sympathy, humility, co-operation and obedience to elders. He has to avoid external restraint and bodily punishment. The child should be made to realise that discipline depends upon his love for order, goodwill and mutual understanding. Froebel stressed that women should be trained for training children at this stage.

Curriculum: The divisions of the curriculum are:-

1. Manual work.
2. Religion and religious instruction.
3. Natural science and mathematics.
4. Language.
5. Arts and objects of arts.

Influential Role

Concept of Kindergarten: "His Kindergarten School was a little world where responsibility was shared by all, brotherly sympathies and voluntary cooperation practised by all". (Hughes).

Great Influence: Kindergarten schools are all over, even in the villages. Every parent seems to be knowing "K.G" school. Froebel exercised great influence in making people realise that the early years of the child are very important for education and, that correct, proper and special type of education should be imparted at this stage.

Importance of Instincts and Impulses: He suggested that the nature of the child be studied and education should be based on this study. That is how 'play' came into the focus of his educational system.

Uses of Senses: His 'gifts' were ideal materials for developing sense. His entire approach was based on the principle of "concrete to abstract".

Occupations: Manual training and "learning by doing" was his lasting and cardinal contribution to education. This is a special kind of education different from the adult education practices which were dull and drab.

Love for the World: Nature study was central to Froebel's system.

The Merits

(a) *Useful for Small Children:* This system is very useful for small children because it is based on their interests and provides for their education in a free atmosphere.

(b) *Importance of the Child:* This is a child-centred system in which the child is granted freedom to do many things that he likes. He is provided with an opportunity for the development of his personality through 'self-activity'.

(c) *Element of Freedom:* There is an atmosphere where the child is free to carry on his self-activity. There is no pressure of the teacher upon the child. He only acts as a guide and not as a director.

(d) *The Principles of Unity or Communion:* This system is based on the principle of unity, based on various experiences. Such attitude leads to realisation of God and His powers.

(e) *Atmosphere where Social and Moral Qualities Grow:* Atmosphere in a Kindergarten school is far different from the atmosphere of the traditional school. It is pleasant atmosphere ringing with freedom that bring about the development of moral and social qualities.

(f) Various gifts provide sensory training.

(g) Inclusion of nature study in the curriculum.

The Limitations

(a) *Philosophy Difficult to Understand:* It is said that the philosophy upon which Froebel based his education system is difficult to understand. This is due to the fact that he has sometimes stretched his principle to a very great extent. He is also symbolic. That is a weakness with this system because the child is not fond of abstract ideas. His learning goes from concrete to abstract and, therefore, to expect the child to grasp abstract out of the concrete gifts is sometimes difficult to understand.

(b) *Too Much Emphasis on Inner-self:* This system lays too much emphasis on the development from within. It believes that the proper development lies in making the inner outer. This system bases its acquirement of knowledge on this process which is not very correct. The real development of the child depends upon his being able to adjust with the environment and atmosphere.

(c) *Out-of-date Techniques:* Songs and the nursery games, which Froebel used in his school, might have been useful for that day and for that atmosphere but they cannot be used in every country, in every environment and in every school. In fact, the songs and the games should change according to environment and needs of the children. This system does not provide for such a flexibility.

(d) *Arbitrariness:* The gifts that are used in this system of education are not based on any reason or principle. Froebel drew a system of philosophy and planned out gifts accordingly. The choice was, more or less, arbitrary. They have also become out of date and useless. Many of the schools have given them up. Really speaking, some new techniques and means should be evolved in order to make this system up-to-date.

(e) *Lack of Correlation:* Subjects prescribed for study in the Kindergarten System do not have any scientific correlation. Nature-study, on which so much emphasis has been laid, is supposed to be taught by 'object lessons'. Today psychological researches have proved that subjects should be taught in correlation with one another, Nature study. Hygiene, History and reading of other subjects should be taught as if they are part of a whole. Froebel did not provide for any such correlation in his system.

(f) *Too Much Emphasis on Social Aspect:* This system lays a good deal of emphasis on 'social unity' and consequently very little has been said about the development of the individual personality of the child. Very little mention is made of the individual differences and their bearing on the education. Today, psychologists accept that children differ from one another and so there has to be difference in their education as well. Every child is to be taught according to his interest and faculties. In Kindergarten system there is no such scope.

While pointing out the defects of the Kindergarten system of education, Dr. James Ward writes:

"The Kindergarten system in the hands of one who understands it produces good results but it is apt to be too mechanical and formal. There does not seem any room for the individuality of a child, to which all free play should be given in the earliest years".

(g) *Specified Social Training:* Social training, that is to be imparted in these schools, is of a specific nature, under specific circumstances. The child is given a specific work to do and that is solely under the guidance of the teacher making him dependent on the teacher.

Life Sketch

Friedrich Wilhelm August Froebel (1783-1852) a German philosopher-educator and founder of the Kindergarten, championed the cause of infant education in response to the inspiration that he derived from the great psychologist Pestalozzi. He ushered in a new era in child education. Today, his Kindergarten System is highly acclaimed all over the world by both educators and parents alike. It is recognised as an effective way to deal with a highly "teachable moment" in the life of the young child.

Froebel was born on 21st April, 1783. He was deprived of parental love and care in his early life—the time when he needed it most. His life presents one of history's strange para doxes that the man whose own childhood was full of tears should bring smiles for the children of the world. In fact, Froebel had to go through a long and tough struggle before he could make his mark and garner life's richest harvest. Being unable to do well at a village school, he started doing odd jobs when he was only 14 years of age.

His wandering spirit was set at peace when he went to Frankfort where he came in contact with the director of a model school. He discovered the real genius of his young man and persuaded him to join his school as a teacher. Froebel gladly accepted the offer. But he felt the need of some professional training and he was attracted to Pestalozzi's school at Yverdum. There he stayed for four years and later on studied natural sciences at Gottingen and Berlin universities. However, the big break came when in 1816 he founded a small school which became a successful institution after 10 years. Now the road to success stretched before him. He achieved world-wide fame when in 1817 he founded his first Kindergarten, an institution for the children of age 4 to 6, at Blankenberg. His Kindergarten ushered in a new era in infact education. Froebel served the cause of education for the remaining period of his life. He died on 21st June, 1852, yet he lives for the children and as it were, continues to pour a silent whisper in the ears of the educators. "Come, let's live for our children."

Literary Stature

1. The Education of Man, his famous work published in 1826, wherein he propounded his Law of Unity and gave expression to his method of educating the children through play way.

2. Pedagogies of Kindergarten. It deals with his theory and practice of Kindergarten.
3. Mother Play and Nursery Songs, containing fifty songs and games as a part of play way education.
4. Education and Development.

The Philosophy

Law of Unity : Froebel believed that there is a Law of Unity which is fundamental Law of Education. Rusk in "Great Educators," emphasised that it was his fundamental law on the basis of which we can understand the educational philosophy of Froebel. In this regard he writes:-

1. Through it we thoroughly comprehend the nature of the child.
2. By it the individual, the child is recognised as the central point of all relations of life.
3. Through it we obtain a true and evident purpose in education and a suitable means and methods for accomplishing this aim.
4. Education founded on this law is practical, since it demands immediate accomplishment and application.
5. Such an education is suited to this practical age, which demands the realisation in life of the highest ideal formulated from experience.
6. Such an education adapts itself to every age of life and every stage in child's development.
7. This education of unification is peculiarly appropriate to an age of isolation, contrariety and individualism.
8. Such an education would make clear in real life, the higher philosophical and ethical thought.

9. Such an education would check the growing proletarianism and the deadening mechanical effect on age of industrialism and unfolds, strengthens and develops the power of the child until it can maintain itself an independent personality since it teaches him how to treat material according to its nature, give to work its high significance as creative activity and cultivates the power of thought and will and of action. Thus it lays the true foundation of character.

Spontaneous Growth : Froebel believed in an internal law which governs all things. He was of the opinion, "Man should become intimate with Nature not in the outer form of her phenomenon but in the spirit of God that lives in her and rules over us. All things live and have their being in and through God." He believed that there is a continuity in the universe. Accordingly a change or a growth is also continuous. It is continuous growth in man and Nature which is reflected through his behaviour. Froebel believed in the theory of organic growth that the seed contains in miniature the whole plant. Similarly all the aspects of knowledge are already is the mind of child. It is this law of growth that plays part in learning or in the field of education.

Froebel considers the education as the growth of the child from within. He considers man as one compassing unity. To him, "It is a development by which man's lift broadens until it has related itself to Nature, until it enters sympathetically into all activities of the society, until it participates in the achievements of the race and aspirations of humanity."

Rules of Discipline

1. Froebel considers that the aim of education is that man only may well understand the idea of unity in diversity. He said that the essential business of school is not so much to communicate a variety and multiplicity of facts as to give prominence to the ever-living unity that is in all things.

2. Education should develop the innate qualities of the child. Child's own activities are the best medium of education.

3. Play reflected the mind of the child and it is considered the free and unfettered natural source of development.

4. Education should be imparted in as atmosphere of freedom.

5. The child should develop his individuality through social atmosphere. All the social institutions like home, school, church are the agencies of education.

6. Education unfolds the innate powers of the child in order to enable him to have a spiritual union with God.

Kindergarten System

Kindergarten is a German word which means 'the children's garden.' To Froebel school is like a garden, where children play and dance like flowers and teacher protects them like a gardener. Child-like a little tender plant grows and teacher makes his efforts to beautify the garden with the proper growth, care and looking after the plants. There is a great similarity between a child and a plant. The child grows because of the tendencies and impulses which are within him and the plant throws out leaves and branches from within according to the seed which is within it. It is this tendency that makes the children and plants of similar nature.

Essentials of Kindergarten

Self-activity. Education is considered a progress of creative development. It is natural for a man to be active and to give expression to his impulses. His spontaneous activity will lead him towards his divine goal. The kindergarten provides opportunities for self-expression. There the entire programme is activity centered. Self-activity is more important than merely activity. Self-activity or self-expression is imparted in three ways—

(a) through songs, (b) through movements, and (c) through construction.

Creativeness. A child is never idle. He is creative by nature. When he is given certain material, he tries to create always new things and satisfies his urge for construction. It is in this way that work is identified with play.

Social Participation. School is a miniature society. What we learn in school influences our behaviour in our later life. The future of the society depends upon the training that we want to impart in schools. The best education of the child is possible in the school where he participates in the maximum number of social activities.

Freedom. Children are always free to work, play, sing or dance in a Kindergarten school. No activity is thrust upon them. They are free to spend their time in a way they like, though they remain conscious about their obligations.

The Songs. Songs have been attached great importance in this system of schooling. Froebel has devised songs for all kinds of activities.

Gifts and Occupations. In order to give proper training to the senses of the child some apparatus (gifts) has been suggested.

1. According to Froebel, school is the nursery of future citizens. Education enables the child to realise the unity in diversity. It trains for cooperative living. It inculcates the sense of socialisation and self-realisation. With this aim, Froebel considers the child as a social being.

2. Child's own activity, instinctive and spontaneous, is the means of education.

3. Play helps free, un-obstructive and natural development. Play is self-active representation of inner necessity and impulse.

4. Education should be in accordance with child's nature and needs and it should be given in an atmosphere of freedom. Here Froebel leads us nearer to modern education or the naturalistic tendencies of education.

5. Froebel, advocated activity method of education. Through play he accounts for various games, such as collection, gardening, building play-shelters and boats etc.

6. Froebel, like Rousseau, was equally alive to the stages of development. Though stages are quite distinct yet they constitute the one organic whole, and perfection in one is a pre-requisite for perfection in the other.

   (i) Froebel regarded infancy as an important stage in the development of the child. At this stage he recommended sensory training through self-activity of the child.

   (ii) In childhood, the development or making the internal external should take place through play. The child at this stage should be allowed free activity to satisfy his natural endowment.

   (iii) Work is the characteristic of the boyhood period. Froebel believed, "If activity brought joy to the child, work now gives delight to the boy." Curriculum in its most formal sense exercises its hold on the educative process. So feeling now gives way to thought and play to instruction. The only difference is that in childhood the pupil imitated domestic activities, in boyhood he imitates neighbourhood occupations. His activities, now, are projects-practical problems demanding co-operative effort and giving intellectual and moral training.

In order to achieve the aim of all-round development of the child. Froebel recommended the following four main division of curriculum:

(a) Religion, (b) Natural Sciences, (c) Languages, (d) Craft and Manual work.

In short, educational aim according to Froebel is the realisation of the Law of Unity through the development of one's mind in accordance with its own inner law being self-active in a free and social atmosphere.

The Ideology

It was very late when the early childhood attracted Froebel's attention. He realised that the pre-school age of the child—this most impressionable, plastic and educationally potent period of a child's life-required the greatest attention if something solid and worthy was to be achieved in education. His early experiences in working with small children convinced him of the importance of pre-school education. It was in 1839 that he conceived the idea of his first Kindergarten which he established at Blankenberg (Germany). This German word Kindergarten, means 'Children's Garden' i.e., a place where children grow up as trees and flowers. This idea has been widely recognised and accepted by almost all the modern educationists.

Functional Side

Froebel's is a miniature State for children where the watch-words are freedom, play and joyful living. Froebel was in favour of spontaneous development of the children through self-expression. The entire school programme is so organised as to give training in self-expression and to make education a joyous experience. No books are prescribed. The learning process is activity-centred. Education is imparted through songs, movements and construction. Whatever is narrated in a song is followed by its dramatisation in movements and gestures. The same is afterwards represented with the help of construction work in blocks, paper clay, drawing or other material. This three-fold procedure stimulates thought, vivifies imagination, trains and co-ordinates physical muscles of hands, eyes, etc. and ultimately strengthens the moral nature of the child. For convenience sake, we may divide the teaching procedure in two parts viz., teaching through songs, and teaching through gifts and occupations.

Teaching through Songs: Songs constitute an essential element of the teaching procedure adopted in Kindergarten. The various songs which Froebel employed for the purpose of teaching are included in Mother Play and Nursery Songs (1843). Froebel regarded these songs as the best means to familiarise the child with his surroundings and to exercise his senses, limbs and muscles. They are also intended to fulfil some physical, mental or moral need of the child. All the songs-fifty in all are connected with some nursery games such as "Hide and Seek" or some trade. The whole atmosphere is intended to be very congenial. It is the teacher who determines the selection and order in accordance with the development of the child. Each song has three parts:

(i) A motto for the guidance of mother or teacher.

(ii) A verse with the accompanying music.

(iii) A picture illustrating the song.

Froebel's Gifts and Occupations: Froebel's Gifts form the basis of the Kindergarten method. These gifts are in the form of educational toys. Froebel devised these gifts for complete education and training of children. These gifts are carefully graded and are to be presented to the child in the definite order. Sphere comes first, followed by crystal, cube, cylinder, etc. The activities connected with these gifts are called occupations. The purpose of these gifts is to train child's senses of touch and sight and to give him an idea of size, surface and number. Occupations connected with these gifts develop skills. Stories, songs and games are necessary adjuncts to these gifts. Froebel designed about twenty such gifts but only seven are now usually called by this name.

It may be pointed out here that in designing these gifts, Froebel incorporated Pestalozzi's idea of 'object teaching' into his own methodology. The only difference lies in the fact that

Pestalozzi used a great variety of objects while Froebel used only a limited range as a means of remote symbolic knowledge suggested by the formal quality of the object or the gift.

The Fruits

First Gift: It consists of six balls of different colours contained in a box. Three balls are of primary colours—red, yellow and blue, and three are of secondary colours—orange, green and purple. The occupation consists in rolling them about in play, accompanied by little rhymes.

Second Gift: It consists of three objects, a sphere, a cube and a cylinder made of hard wood. While playing with them the child notices the differences between their stability and mobility.

Third Gift: It is a big wooden tube sub-divided into eight smaller equal cubes. This gift gives the child a sense of artistic constructions as well as addition and subtraction.

Fourth Gift: It includes a large cube divided into eight oblong prisms in each of which the length is twice the breadth and breadth is twice thickness. With its help the child may construct different designs.

Fifth Gift: It consists of a large cube divided into twenty or twenty seven small cubes. Useful forms and patterns can be constructed with its help in combination with No. 3 and 4 gifts.

Sixth Gift: It has a large cube further divided into eighteen whole and nine oblong blocks. The child can further make different designs.

Seventh Gift: It is a set of square and triangular tablets made of fine wood in two colours. It provides different material for many exercises in geometrical forms and mosaic work.

The above gifts may be used in combination with one another to make various constructions. "By his methodical arrangement of the gifts and occupations," comments Prof. Rusk, "Froebel nevertheless founded a new type of educational institution."

QUESTIONS

1. Briefly discuss the forerunners of early childhood education with special reference to Pestalozzi.
2. What are the essentials of an CEC programme ?
3. "Come, let us live for our children". Discuss.
4. What are the salient features of Froebel's K.G. System ?

3

Montessori

'John Locke's concept of 'tabula rasa' led on to lot of misconception in education as the passivity of mind does not go well with the progressive theories of education. "Going wholly with Locke and to assume that learning is only a matter of intellection and, that learning occurs only neck-up, and the rest of it is an inactive affair, would not be a correct position to take today when education is considered not so much as imparting of knowledge as it is a soliciting or prompting of the student to exert his native potentialities for knowing or learning" (Brubacher). Educational process should, therefore, be activity-oriented where a child learns for himself and has freedom of action and movement. Thus, Activity is one of the general principles of teaching that entails activity in all types of lessons. It is absolutely true of the pre-school teaching programme. Based on construction instinct wherein a child is always busy doing something it is activity-oriented. This activity may be physical and mental. Physical activity means to produce activity in the body organs of the pupil whereas mental activity relates to the exercise of mind. Psychologically, every pupil is temperamentally active. Therefore, activity becomes central to classroom teaching-learning especially for small children. No wonder Froebel and Montessori based their teaching styles on this principle. Amongst the modern and contemporary educationists, John Dewey and Kalpatrick by suggesting the Project Method are advocating the same activity-principle to facilitate teaching-learning.

Great Educationist

The modern school is an activity school which emphasises the creative aspect of experience. These activities provide variety of experiences to the little children and facilitate their acquisition of knowledge, skills and attitudes. An activity may be described as "anything which is carried out with a purpose in a social environment involving physical and mental action."

Such activities help in establishing stimulating environment for creative expression. Children love this kind of a stimulating group environment where desirable social attitudes, useful communication skills, interest and knowledge is acquired and developed. Children, while interacting in a group develop self-confidence and understanding through work and play. It helps break the initial inhibition, diffidence and reservations and helps a child to sort of open up and involve him in the group. Activity, therefore, becomes the crux of a child's initiation into the serious business of learning and socialising.

Children are keen observers of that all goes around. Give them a chance to regenerate such experiences with attention, patience and fun. Fun Schools are the latest in the activity-based schools. These schools create situations in which children learn and enjoy. Teaching and learning are no longer a drudgery nor a grind, it's fun and frolic all the way. It is entirely experience-based, a first hand experience that a child feels on his own pulse.

The Textbooks

Experience curriculum fosters creative expression in learners. Children have varied opportunities to become co-operative and socially creative individuals. Creative expression is the expanding outward manifestation of intense inner emotions and challenging ideas. A rich environment is a potent factor in aiding children to realise their creative potentialities with the teacher as part of the environment. The climate must be democratic, unhurried and informal, charged with a good measure of sympathetic understanding. The imagination of children may be stimulated in various ways as they explore their own daily living and their world-environment.

Practical Aspects

Activities are of three types based on their orientation and purpose:-

(a) *Exploratory:* As the name suggests these activities help explore and to get knowledge. They, are knowledge-getting activities.

(b) *Constructive:* Experience-getting, as experiences are the building blocks of a child's creative and constructive approach.

(c) *Expressional:* Presentation of a child's world-view.

Place of Functions

Activities will vary according to the age group of the pupils. In the elementary school, at the kindergarten stage, activities like singing, dramatising, listening, observing, planning, collecting, talking, experimenting and constructing are useful. The variety of activities grows as children progress in the elementary programme. This may include: painting, drawing, designing, wood carving, writing, composing, dancing, interviewing, acting, reading, map-making and graph-making, field trips, gardening and camping.

It is not always necessary that the activity should be motor or manipulative-it can also be mental. Knowledge-getting activities occupy a prominent place as knowledge-getting is the primary aim of any educational system. Schools are not merely for play and fun. Play, fun and activity are incidental as the main emphasis is on learning. Learning is the end-result, rest is all a matter of ways and means.

Positive Side

(a) Here a group of pupils may be asked to make a study of the various sources of food articles consumed at home by questioning parents, merchants etc. by consulting lables on the foods. The data may be compiled and interpreted by the group.

(b) A committee of pupils may undertake to find out, in a rural area, how many families have members who work also in the city or town part time. In a city, it may be enquired how many people in the local community have come from rural areas and why they have come. With the teacher's help, rough estimates of probable experiences can be made.

Being More Wise

Activities such as excursions, visits, field-trips, etc. provide a rich haul of experience to help a child build-up his own work-experience in which these experiences are the building-blocks.

System at Work

Debates, Talks, Playlets, Roleplays etc. are such activities that engross a child in his presentation. Practical and productive work can help in developing better understanding of almost every subject. In Geography, it may take the form of drawing maps, making models, illustrations, organising excursions, keeping weather records, constructing of appropriate materials scenes from the life of different regions of the world, etc. In History, in addition to the preparation of suitable illustrations of the type mentioned above, they may prepare and stage historical plays-making the costumes, the stage effects, fixing the light, etc., themselves, or co-operatively study local history, or set up a small history museum and in fact take up any project that will bring history to life, etc. In connection with the study of languages particularly the mother-tongue they may undertake to write small write-ups on subjects of special interest to them. The collection of material from relevant sources, its writing, editing, the binding of the write-ups attractively, will be an all absorbing experience for a child who will also learn the basics of group-aims and group-interests.

Corrective Measures

Following activities are suggested to commensurate with the above mentioned three types of activities:-

1. Local surveys and excursion.
2. Hobbies.
3. Debates & Discussion.
4. Dramatisation/Roleplays/Playlets.
5. Mock activities.
6. School clubs and societies.
7. Projects.
8. Competitions.
9. Recreation and cultural programmes.
10. Social service squads.
11. Camping.
12. Write-ups.
13. Games & Sports.

Education should aim at the socialisation of the child. He must be activated to work and live in a group. In modern education creative activities occupy a prominent place so much so they suggest a new approach to school-teaching in which the teacher has a far more creative role to play in that he generates suitable learning conditions so as to achieve desired learning outcomes. Remaining in the background, the teacher leads the child through creative and constructive learning situations.

Education through Games

Play is said to be the language of the child. Due to lack of verbal facility, the child uses his feeling. That is why the gestures and movements of the child while singing nursery rhymes acquire significance. A child would find it difficult to recite such poems while standing still. These movements afford a safe release of physical and mental energy. Same is true of Play which besides releasing physical and mental energy, also provides release of emotional tension and inhibitions.

Play facilitates and encourages sensory and perceptual experience and, within the limitation of individual endowments, lead to the comprehension of the manipulative and constructive possibilities of both animate and inanimate objects.

The meaning of play has significance for the child. Through play he enacts many roles of the adults of his world as he sees them: he casts himself in those roles with which he seeks identification. The child's choice for play is selective and carries emotional components. The emotion may be a positive one of love or a negative one of fear or anger. The child, who assumes the role of the doctor, administering shots, may reduce the fear he feels as the doctor sticks the needle in him. He may be assuming the role of the one he wishes to imitate or he may be passing on his resentment about being hurt or someone he wishes to hurt. Child is learning while playing.

"Play," in the words of Froebel, "is the highest phase of child development-of human development... Play is the purest, most spiritual activity of man at this stage and at the same time, typical of human as a whole of the inner hidden natural life in man and all things. It gives, therefore, joy, freedom, contentment, inner and outer rest, peace with the world. It holds the source of all that is good".

Thus, if play is capitalised in a proper manner, we can help the child to release through play-a natural activity of the child-his tensions, frustrations and fears as well as his joys and hopes. This can only be done if play activity is purposeful and directed. Without rational, conscious guidance, childish activity degenerates into aimless play instead of preparing for future tasks.

Role of Sports

Play being the natural need of the child, Caldwell Cook is the first person, who advocated "way of play" for educating the child. He said, "The core of my faith is that the only work doing is play; by play I mean doing anything with one's heart in it." He taught Shakespearean plays by acting from the text. Difficult passages were never analysed or explained. He criticised "those teachers who insist upon a careful and often prolonged study of all passages which present any natural difficulty". Caldwell Cook believed that proficiency and learning come not from experience, "that good work is more often the result of spontaneous effort, and free interest than of compulsion and forced application". He regarded play as a means of training individuals as individuals and a wonderful technique of making school education interesting, and practical. He asserted, "only that child learns best who learns with interest and with a purpose, and sees significance in what he does". Thus Caldwell Cook introduced a new way in education, popularly known as Playway.

Rules of Discipline

The Playway Method is Based on the following Principles:-

(a) Learning process to be conducted through playful activities.

(b) Atmosphere of freedom without any restraints.

(c) Informal and natural methods to suit the needs and interests of children.

(d) Encourage free expression and provide adequate opportunities for expression.

(e) Enjoyable learning process, active participation and self-learning. Pupils must realise their responsibility for their own progress and development.

Emphasis on play has invited a lot of criticism for this method. Education is a serious business of educating young minds, then why play? Does it not run counter to the basic edicts of education? Education should be a tough process so that one takes it seriously.

Such critics ignore the difference between play and work. Play is a way of teaching, it is not the be-all of teaching. Play is not for the sake of serious task of teaching-learning. Work is paramount but if one reaches there enthusiastically and cheerfully, one should not grudge it. Play makes the serious, dull and drab business of teaching interesting and absorbing. Play does not substitute work. According to Griffith "play is the child's characteristic mode of behaviour" and you are simply capitalising on the innocent nature of the child while basing your education of a child on this principle. As a matter of fact you are taking the child for a ride by capitalising on his characteristic mode of behaviour, in your own self-interest, you want to educate the child, it is your interest, and to succeed in your mission you are taking advantage of a child's innocent nature, without his even being aware of it, and yet you grudge it. Remember Smith Harrison when he said,

"Play is an all-absorbing activity in which initiative, forethought, control and skill can be exercised in full measure", and if that be so, playway is no play, it is an enjoyable way of doing a serious job, and if one can remove or even reduce the drudgery of the classroom in the overall interest of an educational system, it is well worth it. And besides, playway is no easy way, at least for the teacher, whose involvement and anticipation is far more greater than in the traditional way of classroom teaching, "Fun" and "Play" are misleading words as teaching-learning is neither "fun" nor "play"-it is hard, direct and businesslike endevavour. Teaching, as it is, is dull and drab, why make it look dreadful?

The success of playway depends upon the hard labour put in by the teacher. The use of playway can, in no way, be taken as the line of least resistance to which a teacher can succumb but it is a wholehearted application to an arduous task of facilitating the learning process in a natural and interesting manner. Playway, thus, does not lead to soft-pedagogy. Difficult tasks will be there even now, the only thing which is advocated is let difficult things be taught in an interesting manner and let drudgery be made tolerable. The introduction of an element of interest will impart purpose to the work and a purposeful activity is useful and meaningful to the child.

To conclude, we may say that playway aims at making things interesting and meaningful and to do that is a difficult job, it is by no means soft pedagogy.

1. *The Kindergarten Method:* This method of educating children is based upon the play, children are stimulated with an apparatus called gifts, children get the idea of shape, colour, number and weight etc. Froebel emphasises play, song and movement in his method. Children, in fact, learn while they play and sing in a happy atmosphere of Kindergarten.
2. *The Montessori Method:* The Montessori method is nothing but play method. Maria Montessori has given a specially designed didactic apparatus to enable the child to learn the elements of reading, writing and number. He plays with the apparatus and learns to correct himself. There is complete freedom for the child. The didactic material, like the stairs, bars, frames, cubes etc., teach the pupil to be active and learn important concepts while playing with these.

3. *The Project Method:* A project is based on the important principles of spontaneity, purpose, significance and interest. Children take keen interest in the execution of a project. They learn to work as a group: they put in their heart and soul to achieve an objective they had set before themselves. Thus the play spirit pervades the Project method all through irrespective of the specific role a child may have in the group.

4. *The Dalton Plan:* This method gives freedom to the child to organise his time as a whole. There are no restrictions of the time-table periods, a piece of work begun can be finished as a whole and its completion need not be postponed till the next 'period'.

5. *Heuristic Method:* This method places the child in the position of an original discoverer, and an independent engineer. A child pursues an area which he chooses voluntarily and is, therefore, happy in doing it. The happiness is caused by his freedom of action and choice. He feels happy about the results because he identified himself with the activity.

6. *Winneka Plan and Gray System:* The school becomes the hub of children's activities and they learn through play activity.

7. *Basic Education:* India's education philosophers consider the child as the crux of the entire education system. Child-activity and playway approach to teaching-learning is recommended by Tagore, Tilak, Vivekanand and Gandhi besides a host of other educational visionaries. Gandhi's concept of Basic Education is based on the activity principle, and children take active participation in the school activities. Emphasis on art and craft is significant as purposeful and productive activity.

Play principles are widely applied in almost every aspect of a progressive modern school. Administration, management and disciplinary problems are dealt with from the playway point of view. Schools are divided in Houses having different names, colours and flags. Even the staff is distributed Housewise for better control and supervision. A child remains in the House, wears the same colour, and carries the same Flag throughout his entire stay in the school, developing sincere and deep emotional bonds which go a long way in improving the corporate life in a school. Introduction of Students Councils, Prefect System, Monitors, Houses on Duty on important school functions, Excursions, Participation in inter-house and inter-school academic and sports competitions, N.C.C., Scouting, all are manifestations of the play-principles in general School life. There is no limit to this application, it all depends on the ingenuity of the school administration, Faculty and the Students' Body.

1. *Teaching of Language:* Dramatisation of interesting episodes, excerpts and plays can be usefully fused in day-to-day teaching of language; Mock pronunciation and spelling drills and competitions; framing of sentences, Quizs; Discussion; Short talks (lecturettes); Story-telling may be used effectively in a language class.

2. *Social Studies:* Dramatics, Pageants, Tableau, Graphics especially Cartoons and Posters; Student-made models; Pictures, 3-dimensional presentations like Dramas; Historical recordings of major political, social and military events, should be used to the maximum to make teaching-learning interesting and enjoyable.

3. *Mathematics:* Collapsable models, cubes giving geometrical concepts, number and arithmetical functions with the help of beads, charts, drawing, chalkboard etc, can be successfully used for developing mathematical concepts.

4. *Sciences:* Most of the science teaching is activity based, add a little fun to it and children would look forward to science classes with eagerness and anticipation. Let them handle the equipment under your remote presence and supervision. Let them learn to apply their mind.

Bright Side

1. Play is a wonderful motivator, creates interest and involvement, and helps a child to get attuned to the serious school activity in a joyful manner.
2. The combination of work and play, freedom and restraint develops in a child the habit to learn on his own and be on his own.
3. Play encourages self-advancement and self-discipline through self-education. It is completely activity based and child-centred hence, psychologically sound.
4. Harmony between play and work, keeps the child absorbed in what he is doing and there are no distractions.
5. It is the best way of learning without taxing the young minds, is natural and fully activates all the senses, hence, playway is in line with the principles and maxims of teaching, therefore, psychologically, socially and logically sound.

Life Sketch

Maria Montessori was born at Chiaravalle the province of Ancona (Italy) on 31st August, 1870. Maria Montessori was the first woman in Italy to be honoured with the degree of Doctor of Medicine in 1896. Yet another ten years were to elapse before she could discover her great mission in life, the mission of an educator. The real opportunity to complete this noble task came to her when she was appointed the directress of a State school for mentally deficient children. Continuously for two years, each day from 8 a.m. to 7 p.m., she worked with the children; and then at night she would sit late making notes, tabulating, comparing, analysing and reflecting, and preparing new materials, "Those two years of practice", she once remarked, "are indeed my first and only true degree in pedagogy." The remarkable results shown by those children convinced her that her methods would set free the normal children's personality in a marvellous and surprising way.

Once the beginning was made, there was no end. She worked and the world followed her. The pilgrimage of her life was complete. Destiny brought to an end her long and self-sacrificing labours on behalf of the child on 6th May, 1952 at Noordwija-on-sea in Holland. She is no more, yet she lives in the sense and joyful atmosphere which emanates from thousands of happy children in every part of the world.

She has written a number of books on education-'The Discovery of the Child,' 'Education for a New World,' 'The Secret of Education' 'Child Training,' 'The Child's Place and Education,' 'Reconstruction in Education,' What You Should Know about Your Child,' 'Montessori Method' and 'The Advanced Montessori Method.'

The Ideology

Modern psychology has contributed a lot to education. Montessori bases her ideas upon the training of senses and advocates love and affection for children. She says, "If a new and scientific method of teaching is to arise from the study of individual, such a method must occupy itself with the observation of free children." She is of the opinion that the new method of teaching children is a reaction against the collective teaching of children. Thus she individualises and psychologises education. Her system of education is said to be based on the following principles:

The Principle of Development. Education has been regarded as a process of Development. This development is from within. Montessori says, "The child is a body which grows and a soul which develops. We should neither mar nor stifle the mysterious form which lies within those two forms of growth but we should await the manifestation which we know will succeed another." Again she writes, "If any educational act is to take place, it will be only that which tends to help towards the complete unfolding of the child's personality." In her opinion education unfolds what is hidden inside the child and a teacher is a guide for that.

The Principle of Individuality. Montessori is of the opinion that each and every child has his own peculiar aptitude, interest, capabilities and he reveals these specified qualities and powers in his own way. Every child is unique and higher individuality should be left to develop spontaneously. Therefore, it's undesirable to adapt similar methods of teaching for all the children and to give the same mental food to them. Generally the collective handling will crush the individuality of the child.

The Principle of Freedom. Based upon the idea of development and the separate individuality, the concept of freedom has been accepted. Freedom is the fundamental right of each human-being without any difference of colour, creed, class, age or sex. The future development is hidden in his nature by birth, then he is to be given freedom to unfold his potentiality freely. She says. "The school must permit the free, natural manifestations of the child if he is to be studied in a scientific manner."

Principle of Self-education. Child should not be forced to learn. He is to be given freedom as individuality is to be respected. He is to learn by instinct. Here the idea is that the teacher is to provide opportunities, environment and tools and apparatus. On the basis of different activities he will learn and never forget such a learning.

Principle of Learning by Insight. Since child is to be provided proper environment and apparatus, he gets stimulus and reacts accordingly. Psychologists have accepted this S.R. Theory as the action of outside and the reaction of inside which is equal in potency. The child looks around him and acts by using his insight or inner urge. She writes, "It is necessary to offer those exercises to the child which correspond to the need of development felt by his organisation." In this way it is for the tutor to provide suitable toys and apparatus which is needed according to the physiology and mental development of the child.

Principle of Sense Training. She made experiments with the feebleminded children and got success in improving them by giving training of senses. By providing a large number of toys depicting different colours and producing different sounds, she could make the children learn to differentiate different sizes, different colours, different levels of surface, different sounds and different types of articles. This was based upon the concept of audio-visual education. When she successfully made experiments on such children, she turned her attention to the young children and successfully experimented that children learn more and quicker with the help of tins and apparatus because they appeal to their senses.

Principle of Motor Training. Children by treatment and nature are active. It is a wrong concept to expect children to be disciplined like wooden toys. It is the duty of the teacher to provide necessary but useful activities for them where they get opportunities to move their limbs. It has been commonly said that an idle child is a devil because the very nature of the child is to be active. If no reasonable interesting and useful activity is provided to the child, he may do whatever chance may provide to him which may be on any side of the social norms.

The Fundamentals

Dr. Montessori believed that "Education is the active help given to the normal expansion of the life of the child." That is why the important principle of her system of education was "Liberty in Environment". "My method", said Montessori, "is established upon one fundamental base-the liberty of the pupils in their spontaneous manifestations." Secondly, Montessori believed in 'development from within,' that must lead to the development of the child from within. So she explained it by saying it that the child by its very nature is 'capable of spontaneous organic development.' She said: "If any educational act is to be efficacious, it will be only that which tends to help towards complete unfolding of the child's individuality."

Thirdly, she laid stress on 'development of individuality.' According to her, "His own self-development is his true and almost his only pleasure." It is on this point that the Montessori system is severely opposed to class teaching class as unit of teaching. The fourth principle is the "Principle of Auto-education." Individuality of the child best unfolds itself through self-education. The constant interference from the teacher kills the child's initiative and does not give him that pleasure which he will otherwise receive from auto-education. He moves at his own pace and learns in his own way. The didactic apparatus as devised by Montessori is meant to overcome the inadequacy of the child in self-direction and self-correction.

Fifthly, "Sense Training" is an important feature of the Montessori system of education. Dr. Montessori believed that properly developed and properly trained senses facilitate the educational growth of the child. Sixthly, there is the "Principle of Motor Efficiency". Motor efficiency is complimentary to sense-training. Again, Montessori believed that "Individual Development must lead to Social Development." She was conscious of the fact that social development and social efficiency of the child is as much important as his individual development. Her 'Children's House', calls for certain basic social needs which are important in special behaviour. The discipline which pervades in the prepared environment is both individual and social. Dr. Montessori indicates the importance of child's social needs when she writes: "The discipline to which the child habituate himself here is, in its character, not limited to the social environment but extends to society." The very idea of planning individual child-in the unit of teaching-the unit of organisation-is to prepare him for a wider social environment in which he is to justify his existence later.

Functional Side

The Plan of the Method. The Montessori Method as advocated by Dr. Maria Montessori came into action in a prepared environment which she called 'The Children's House.' The prepared environment of the House is prepared in such a way as to provide an atmosphere of freedom and choice to the child to enable him to develop himself in the best possible manner. The Children's House, as we name a Montessori school, is a many-roomed school with a nicely, laidout garden. The spirit that prevails in the Kindergarten-Froebel's 'Children's Garden' is also not missing. The equipment in the rooms is especially designed to arrest children's interest and to motivate them to work on the apparatus meant for educating them. The nucleus of the school is study room with attached smaller room where children have their lunch, take rest, engage themselves in manual work, and fulfil their other day-to-day needs. In fact, a Montessori school is a real centre of life and activity and work.

Thus the plan of the Montessori method involves all these consideration which characterise a child's life. Besides, the above environment of the Children's House, the plan of the method centres round three major types of activities which are:

(a) Exercises for practical life.

(b) Exercises for sensory training.

(c) Didactic exercise for teaching language and arithmetic.

Exercise for Practical Life. The main purpose of various exercises for practical life is to render the school true to life—not a preparation for life, but life in itself. The various types of exercises may be enumerated here:

(i) Taking care of one's own self is the first phase of daily life. The children are given training in personal hygiene. They are taught to wash their own hands, brush their teeth, clean their nails, comb their hair, keep their dress neat and tidy, polish their shoes, tie their laces, fasten their buckles, and so on. The young ones are also trained to take care of their surrounding. They are taught to sweep their rooms, dust and clean their furniture especially meant for their use, and also handle it with care and without the assistance of elders. The children learn to arrange things in the House in perfect order without making any noise.

(ii) The Montessori Method also makes a provision for formal gymnastic exercises to help the child in developing co-ordinated physical movements. The gymnastic exercises are especially designed to suit children's needs. From the physical point of view children are not 'littlemen'. They need exercises different from those meant for grown-ups. There is provision for special types of apparatus for the purpose of these exercises. For instance, there is the 'Little Round Stair' which consists of a wooden spiral stairway with a balustrade on the side. The children habituate themselves to ascending and descending stairs and thus learn to balance themselves. Certain rhythmic exercises without music are also provided for.

(iii) The children are also given practicc in hand work. The exercise meant for this purpose are in clay modelling, making of tiles and bricks with the help of simple moulds.

Exercises for Sensory Training. Dr. Montessori attached special importance to training the sense of the children. According to her, sensory discrimination is more important than reasoning and thinking, as self-education is possible only through the development of senses. She believed that physical and intellectual development is also associated with sense-training. She devised finally graded material for this purpose. A few examples are given below:

(i) Sense of Touch is developed with the help of rectangular blocks or table with rough and smooth surfaces varying in smoothness. A highly polished surface or a sand paper surface may also be used.

(ii) Sense of Hearing or Sound is developed through musical bells, metal discs and music charts, each given a sound varying tune as well as in character. Boxes full of pebbles may also be used.

(iii) Sense of Colour is imparted through coloured cubes, prisms, and rods pink, brown and green, alternating red and blue rods and coloured tables, etc. Graded series of coloured words may also be used.

(iv) Sense of Size is trained with the help of series of wooden cylinders varying in height only, in diameter only or in both dimensions at once. Wooden blocks of varying sizes and rods of regularly graded length may also be used.

(v) Perception of Form is imparted with the help of geometrical insets in metal or in wood. There is a prism, a pyramid, a sphere, a cylinder, a cone etc.

(vi) Discrimination in Weight is taught with the help of wooden blocks similar in size but varying in weight.

(vii) Discrimination in Temperature is taught by enabling the child to wash his hands alternately in hot and cold water or by planning his hands on bowels full of hot and cold sand or with the help of small metal bowels with caps.

Exercises meant for sensory training, especially for visual sense, training, work through three steps, namely, association, recognition and recall.

Association: The children are shown two colours, and the teacher pointing to the two says, "This is red", "This is blue."

Recognition: The teacher then gives the command 'Give me the red, give me the blue'. The children get a chance to differentiate between the two.

Recall: The teacher afterwards asks "What is this?" (showing one) "What is this?" (showing other).

It may be pointed out here that the steps are identical to those involved by Seguin, and the procedure is the one used by Preyer and Baldwin.

Didactic Exercises. The third type of exercises involving the use of didactic apparatus are designed to teach Writing, Reading and Arithmetic. These exercises were included in the system of a later stage. A brief account of these exercises may be given here:

Teaching of Writing. In Montessori's system, writing precedes reading for, according to her, the latter involves superior intellectual activity and the former involves merely muscular skill which is an easy process. Moreover, she believed that while the teaching of writing is in progress, the teacher should examine the individual who writes and not the writing. Her system of writing consists of the following three steps:

Recognition of the Forms of Letters. The children are made to pass their fingers over the letters of alphabet cut out of the sand paper and pasted on card-board. The children practise this act later on with eyes closed. Thus the children learn to recognise the letters not by visual analysis and retained by visual imagery but by tactical and motor experience and grapho-motor imagery.

Learning of Phonetic Sounds. Now the children repeat the first and at the same time keep pronouncing the sounds which these letters represent.

Control of Pen. It is taught by the use of a metal frame and an inset. They drew lines round the frame with a coloured chalk, repeating same act be placing the metal inset.

Teaching of Reading. Reading, according to Montessori, is not mere "barking at print." It is, as she believes, a transmission of ideas. To quote her, "Until the child receives a transmission of ideas from the written word, he does not read." The reading material consists of slips of paper or cards on which words and phrases are written in large script. The start is made with those cards which contain names of familiar objects. Once the child is able to read correctly, he is asked to repeat "faster." This reading of word-cards is followed by reading of sentences, describing some action or expressing some command. This involves mental reading followed by the action represented in the sentences.

Teaching of Arithmetic or Counting. The method of teaching counting, not being very original, involves the old way of teaching by means of coloured beads, numerical rods, wooden spindles, sand-paper numbers, simple boxes, etc. The device that is generally made use of is the long stair. This consists of ten rods, the first being one metre long and the last only one tenth of it. Each rod is conveniently divided into portions of one decimetre each, and each portion, painted red and blue. By manipulating the rods all the four fundamental rules of Arithmetic can be learnt. The graphic signs for the numbers are cut in sand-paper and the pupils are taught to associate the numbers with their graphic forms.

Teacher's Role. According to Robert R. Rusk, "The Montessori Method necessitates the employment of teachers who are possessed of a training in child psychology and in its application to young children." In the Montessori system, the most important function of teacher is to observe the psychological and individual development of the child and to develop his psychic activity. The teacher is an active observer, a guide. That is why Montessori prefers to call a "directress" about whom it has been well-pointed out: "Instead of felicity of speech she has to acquire the power of silence; instead of teaching she has to observe; instead of the proud dignity of and when claims to be infallible she assumes the vesture of humility." The Montessori directress is a doctor, a scientist and a worshipper, all in one. She is expected to watch the child's progress like a Scientist, she should be humble like a worshipper in the presence of the children and she should deal with the situation like a doctor. The whole programme is to be so devised as to fit in with the child's needs. There only lies the teacher's expert guidance and excellent organisational ability.

Concept of Discipline According to Montessori. Montessori like other modern thinkers advocated free discipline and self-discipline. Child must be allowed to enjoy freedom. Virtue is self-regarding. There is no need for external imposition. The child must be kept busy. Teacher as directress must be disciplined herself.

Negative Side

Critics are not all praise for Montessori system. They criticise Montessori system on the following counts:

1. Didactic materials used in the system give only one sided knowledge. The mental development is only one sided.
2. This is a system developed by working on dull and handicapped children and not useful for normal children.
3. While playing with various implements, the children are not allowed to talk amongst themselves. This is not a good feature and does not add to self-expression.
4. It is not psychological to train only one sense at a time.
5. The didactic material is costly. Ordinary schools can't providc this.
6. Social co-operation is not developed. The child is busy in his own activity.
7. The system is based on faculty psychology. Only one sense is trained at a time. Faculty psychology is rejected.
8. This system is sheer wastage of time. Too much time is consumed in teaching to little.
9. Suitable teachers for the system are not available.
10. Imagination development in children is ignored.

Motives and Purposes

Madam Montessori gave the following aims of education:

Adjustment with the Immediate Environment. This means that the child should be so educated that he can adjust with his parents, brothers and sisters, classmates, playmates and so on. That child has to adjust himself in school as well as in home.

Development from Within, not from Without. Through education, the child's inner development should also be possible. He should develop his own ideas, thinking, feeling towards good or bad vice or viotic, right or wrong.

Unfolding Hidden Powers of the Child. Through education the child gets guidance from the teacher for his inner hidden traits. The teacher can read to which way the child should go and the way in which he would he successful. The inner qualities of the child are unfolded in the school and these should be guided by the teacher.

The Experiments

Madam Montessori has given the following exercises for practical life.

(i) Taking care of one's own self is the first phase of daily life. The children are given training in personal hygiene. They are taught to wash their own hands, brush their teeth, clean their nails, comb their hair, keep their dress neat and tidy, polish their shoes, tie their laces, fasten their buckles, and so on. The young ones are also trained to take care of their surrounding. They are taught to sweep their rooms, dust and clean their furniture especially meant for their use and also handle it with care and without the assistance of elders. The children learn to arrange things in the House in perfect order without making any noise.

(ii) There is provision for formal gymnastic exercises to help the child in developing coordinated physical movements. The gymnastic exercises are especially, designed to suit children's needs. There is provision for special type of apparatus for the purpose of these exercises. The children habituate themselves in ascending and descending stairs and thus learn to balance themselves. Certain rhythmic exercises without music are also provided for.

(iii) The children are also given practice in hand work. The exercise meant for this purpose are in clay modelling, making of tiles and bricks with the help of simple moulds.

Status of Teacher

In the Montessori system, the most important function of teacher is to observe the psychological and individual development of the child and to develop his psychic activity. The teacher is an active observer, a guide. That is why Montessori prefers to call a "directress" about whom it has been well-pointed out: "Instead of felicity of speech she has to acquire the power of silence; instead of teaching she has to observe; instead of the proud dignity of and when claims to be infallible she assumes the vesture of humility." The Montessori directress is a doctor, a scientist and a worshipper, all in one. She is expected to watch the child's progress like a scientist, she should be humble like a worshipper in the pastime of the children, and she should deal with the situation like a doctor. The whole programme is to be devised as to fit in with the child's needs. There only lies the teacher's expert guidance and organisational ability.

In Montessori Method teaching of counting, not being very original, involves the old way of teaching by means of coloured beads, numerical rods, wooden spindles, sand-paper numbers, simple boxes, etc. The device that is generally made use of is the long stair. This consists often rods, the first being one metre long and the last only one-tenth of it. Each rod is conveniently divided into portions of one decimetre each, and each portion, painted red and blue. By manipulating the rods all the four fundamental rules of Arithmetic can be learnt. The graphic signs for the numbers are cut in sand paper and the pupils are taught to associate the numbers with their graphic forms.

Reading and Writing

Madam Montessori designed Didactic Apparatus for teaching, reading, writing and arithmetic. The teaching of writing precedes the teaching of reading.

Writing. It is taught by enabling children to recognise the forms of letters. Children pass their fingers over the letters of alphabet cut out of sand paper. They learn to recognise the letters by tactical and motor experience. They learn phonetic sounds. The control of pen is taught by the use of a metal frame and in set.

Reading. It is taught with the help of material which consists of paper or cards on which words and phrases are written in large scripts.

Arithmetic. It is taught through coloured beads and simpler boxes. Use of a stair with ten rods is also made.

System at Work

Dr. Maria Montessori's (1870-1952) great love and affection for children, keen sensitiveness, artistic imagination, exceptional sympathy for children, gave a special slant and perspective to the theory and practice of early childhood education. An Italian by birth she became one of the prominent international educationist, and originated the system of education called Montessori Method.

The Development. As an idealist she had great faith in child's innate and inborn tendencies and potentialities, and therefore, believed that education of a child is from within, and is the complete unfolding of child's individuality. What a child needs is a suitable environment in which he may grow and develop his potentialities. Education, therefore, is intrinsic.

Doctrine of Freedom and Liberty. This principle is based on the previous one. Since Dr. Montessori has started with the assumption that the child's future is destined at the moment of his or her birth, she or he should be given ample opportunity for the development of the inner faculties. This means that the child should be given freedom and that is perfectly justified. In a democratic set-up, this is a fundamental right. That is why Dr. Montessori said, "The school must permit the free, natural manifestations of the child if he is to be studied in a scientific manner". She also believed that discipline must come through liberty. This was so because she had her own concept of discipline as well. In her own words:

"Freedom does not consist in having others at one's command to perform the ordinary services but in being able to do these for oneself in being independent of others".

Growth of Individuality. This principle is based on the belief that child manifests his individuality in his natural and spontaneous manner when he is left free. Therefore, the child must be left free to let his individuality grow. The teacher should try to help the child in the right manner. While giving this help and advice, the teacher should know of the physical development as well as psychological development of the child. Unless the teacher is intimately connected with the child, he cannot give proper guidance.

Self-education/Auto-education. Montessori has shifted the emphasis from teaching to learning.

She believes that self-education or auto-education is the only true education. She advocates that the child should remain undisturbed by adult interference. She has devised the didactic apparatus which attracts the attention of the children. It keeps them busy spontaneously. It leads them to learn the power of movements, reading, writing and arithmetic etc.

Principle of Sense Training. Montessori asserts that our senses are the gateways of knowledge and therefore on their training and development depends the acquisition of knowledge throughout life. She pointed out that the senses are very active between the age of 3 and 7 and that a lot of learning takes place during this period. She advocates that the sensory training is the key to intellectual development.

Principle of Motor Efficiency or Muscular Training. She has also attached importance to the muscular training as a part of the early education. She believed that muscular training facilitates other activities like writing, drawing, speaking etc. She takes muscular activity as purely physiological in character. She stresses that running, walking etc., all depends on muscular training.

The Teacher as the Directress. She replaces the word 'teacher' by the word 'directress' as she thinks that the function of the teacher is to direct and not to teach. Her motto should be, "I must diminish to let you grow".

No Place for Fairy Tales. She would like to banish fairy stories from the curriculum of young children since these tend to confuse children and hinder them in the process of adjusting themselves to the real world.

No Material Rewards and Punishment. According to her, incentives are unnatural or forced effort and the development that comes with their help will also be unnatural.

Role of the Teacher

"The Educator" says Montessori, "must be as one inspired by a deep 'worship of life'."

Teacher as Gardener. She thinks that a teacher should care for the child like a gardener who cares for the plant so that the natural growth of the child is properly guided and aided in the process of unfolding itself.

Knowledge of Each Child. The teacher should have an intimate knowledge of the mind and character of each individual, She should keep the physiological records of each child's development, his weight, height and other measurement.

Doctor-cum-Scientist-cum-Missionary. In the words of Montessori the Directress should be partly doctor, partly scientist and completely religious. Like doctor she should avoid scolding or suppressing the patient and should be sympathetic. Like a scientist she should wait patiently for the results and should conduct experiments with her material. Like a religious lady she should be there to serve the child.

Faith in the Personality of the Child. She should allow the child to grow according to his own inner law. Her business is to provide for suitable environment. She should provide children with suitable opportunities to think for themselves.

Moral Qualities. "Virtues and not words are the main qualifications of the Directress". She must acquire moral alertness, patience, love and humility. She must banish anger which is a great sin and which prevents from understanding the child. The soul of the child, which is pure and very sensitive, requires her most delicate care. Her motto should be "I must diminish to let you grow".

Various Functions

There are three types of exercises that are provided in the children's school:

1. Exercises in practical life.
2. Sense training exercises by use of didactic apparatus.
3. Didactic exercises for teaching language and arithmetic.

Exercises in Practical Life: According to Dr. Montessori these exercises are called exercises in practical life because in the children's house real everyday life is called, one in which all which all house work is entrusted to the little ones. The little ones execute with devotion and accuracy their domestic duties. By doing so they become singularly calm and dignified. The students are required to sweep their rooms, dust and clean the furniture and arrange it as they like. They learn dressing and undressing and washing themselves. They are expected to hang up their clothes tidily. They lay their tables. The children take turns in various household duties. They learn by imitation to overcome their difficulties in the process. "Enthusiasm and delight, fellow feeling and mutual aid are characteristics of the children learning the jobs". The students learn how to wash their hands. They learn how to use wash stands with small pitchers and basins. Children learn how to use their own soaps and towels. They learn how to comb their hair, cut their nails and brush their teeth.

The main purpose is to give children training in self-reliance and liberty and also to be independent.

Motor Education: These practical life exercises are considered to be very helpful for motor education. Muscular education is imparted in connection with the movements of walking, sitting and holding objects. The care of child's own body, managing the household affairs, gardening and manual work and rhythmatic movements provide motor education. Children also learn how to walk in straight lines and to balance them properly.

Sensory Education: Madam Montessori, like Rousseau, Pestalozzi and Froebel stressed that the senses are the gateways of knowledge. She attaches more importance to sensory training than even to reasoning and thinking. Various materials are employed to develop sensory training.

Reverence for Small Children: To Madam Montessori "the child was God. Her school was the temple". She writes, "To-day there stands forth one urgent need the reform of methods in education and instruction and he who struggles towards this end is struggling for the regeneration of man". The method as suggested by Montessori gives an important place to the child.

Scientific Bases of the Method: The method is based on scientific grounds. Madam Montessori was a scientist and she applied scientific principles based on experience and observation and not upon prejudices.

Montessori Method: Her method is a reaction against collective teaching.

The Comparison

Kindergarten	*Montessori*
1. Based on philosophical back-ground. Froebel was a philo-sopher who got interested in education. To understand his educational principles one has to understand the philo-sophy he subscribes to.	1. Based on scientific back-ground. Maria was a doctor and a scientist. Her principles are clear cut.
2. Development of imagina-tion/ storytelling.	2. No place for fairy tales.
3. Social development; students are encouraged to work in a group/social matrix.	3. Too much stress on the deve-lopment of individual.
4. Classroom, formal teaching.	4. Self-learning; no time table; learn to one's own conve-nience.
5. Sense training through 'gifts' which are graded and are in a set order.	5. Sense training through dida-ctic apparatus which differs qualita-tively from the 'gifts' of Froebel.
6. Emphasis on playway.	6. Self-corrective apparatus to be used in a specific way. Hence, very little scope for play.
7. Importance of Manual activi-ties like gardening, nature study, clay modelling, plasti-cene, etc.	7. Emphasis on daily life routine activities e.g. washing, dusting, cleaning, sweeping etc. A forerunner of modern day "socially useful and productive work" (SUPW) movement
8. Teacher as a leader.	8. Teacher as a director who has little involvement in child's work, is rather remote super-visor.
9. Easy application.	9. Apparatus is indispensable.
10. Not a detailed system.	10. Detailed system for teaching of three Rs. i.e., reading, writing and arithmetic.

Individual Teaching: Individualism is the keynote of the educators who want to give education in an atmosphere of complete freedom. In her method discipline is that of self-control and self-directed activity.

Sense Training: The Montessori method aims at educating; the children through the sense training. It is based upon the maxims 'proceed from concrete to abstract', 'from general to abstract'.

Unique Method of Reading and Writing: Special importance to the learning of writing has been provided in her method. She takes to consideration of the muscular movements in the process of writing property graded and correlated exercises for reading and writing are provided.

Learning through Living: She has provided practical exercises in her school which enable children to learn good habits of cleanliness and others. The students learn the lessons of dignity of labour and self-help by attending to their needs themselves. Many practical lessons are provided.

The Limitations

Mechanical and Artificial Nature of Didactic Apparatus: Too much importance has been given to the didactic apparatus. The critics argue that the apparatus handcuffs both the teacher and the pupil. The pupil is expected to do different types of exercises with the help of the apparatus and the teacher also has to teach through the didactic apparatus with the result that the free expression of the children is limited and so the work of the teacher. The apparatus is unreal and unnatural.

More Emphasis on Biological Aspects and Less on Psychological: The teacher in this system keeps special care in keeping records of the height, skull and limbs of each individual child. She does not observe temperament and other emotional traits.

Didactic Apparatus means the teaching Equipment that help a child learn by physically manipulating it. It was evolved by Mm. Montessori for her 'Children's Houses'.

This Apparatus consists of:-

1. Three sets of solid insets.
2. Three sets of solids graduated in sizes and containing:-
   (a) Pink Cubes.
   (b) Brown Prisms.
   (c) Rods: These rods are green in colour and alternately in red and blue colour.
3. Various Geometric solids like prism, pyramid, sphere, cone, cylinder etc. These refer to geometrical shapes.
4. Tables of rectangular shape and different sizes with rough and smooth surface. These refer to type of tactual experience.
5. Small wooden tablets of various weight to develop concept of weight.
6. Collection of various tuffs.
7. Two boxes each containing 64 coloured tablets.
8. A chest of drawers having plane insets.
9. Three series of cards with geometrical forms on paper pasted on them.
10. A collection of closed boxes cylindrical in shape. They are called 'sounds'.
11. Pink Tower.
12. Series of music bell.
13. Alphabetical letters made of wood for children to have a feel of them, and also to pronounce them.

The Comparison

1. Importance of Nursery/Pre-school education.
2. Development from within.
3. Conducive Environment.
4. Affection for the child.
5. Sense Training. Point of Contrast

QUESTIONS

1. What are the major views of Montessori on early childhood education ? How did these views creep into her methodology ?
2. What are the salient features of Montessori system ?
3. Write a detailed note on research on early childhood education.

4

Rousseau

We generally initiate various issues of education with reference to the existing and / or desirable educational practices, but soon find ourselves stuck with some sort of philosophical problems choking our ingress into the dynamics of the educational theories and practices. For example, "in the social context of education, we considered political theory; in the aims of education, value theory; in curriculum and method, knowledge theory (Brubacher) leaving us to ponder if there were other possibilities including that of the "role of educational philosophy," wherein each current of thought leaves its mark and impact on the succeeding deliberations. Some of the educational philosophers who delved into this contemplation with effect are discussed in the following sections. What stands out significantly is that each one is convinced about the solution conceived by him.

Life Sketch

Rousseau was a naturalist and it reflected in his concept of education. He was against the artificial and hypocritic atmosphere of his times. He was against the conservative and so-called scientific education of his times because it was man-made. He was of the view that everything that is natural is good but as soon as it reaches the hands of man it is spoiled. It was because of this that he believed in imparting education to children in the atmosphere of nature. He, in other words, wanted to make nature or naturalism as the basis of education. It was he who first said that children should be imparted education according to their natural capacities and capabilities. Back to Nature or Follow Nature were the slogans introduced in the field of education by Rousseau. According to him education should be capable of guiding the natural qualities and requirements of the child. He did not believe that education should aim only at imparting instruction or information or making the child the store-house of knowledge. He also believed that education cannot be acquired from outside.

The Ideology

"It (Education) is the development of child's natural powers and abilities. That is why he has given out three sources of education—Nature, Man and Things or Objects.

Education by nature, according to Rousseau, means development of various faculties and organs of the body of the child in a natural manner. Such a development cannot take place unless the teacher is well aware of the natural faculties of the child. In order to be the master of these faculties, he has to study the nature of the child, "the child is a book which the teacher has to learn from page to page." A child should not be taken as a mini adult.

The Capacities

According to Rousseau, the proper development of the natural faculties of the child cannot take place unless the love for nature is inculcated in him. He should not only be told about the facts of nature but made to study the things given out by nature.

If education is imparted in the natural ways, the natural man will grow. This natural education does not mean that he should be educated only about social life or institution. With these, the man that will grow, will not be the natural man. It has been rightly said, "Natural man is not the savage man but the man governed and directed by the laws of his own nature rather than those of the social institutions.

Rousseau was of the view that the education from men and things must be subordinate to that from nature. He preferred the education from the nature because this education brought about the development of the natural powers, emotions and reactions more naturally. Emotions, natural powers and reactions are more dependable agencies or foundations of education. Actions that grow or are based upon these things are more suitable than the experiences that the child gains from the association of society or other things. That was why he thought that education should aim at giving facilities to the child to grow according to his natural tendencies and internal feelings. Nature was more dependable and friendly.

Aims and Purposes

1. As asserted by Rousseau, "The process of education should facilitate the development of the child's innate powers and capacities. It should not confine the child to the acquisition of knowledge only." If education is not capable of bringing about the purposeful development of the natural capacities of the child, it will be no good. According to Rousseau, "Emile should be imparted education to be able to live and survive. He should be made man first and then anything." To live is not merely to breathe, it is to act, to make use of our organs, senses, our faculties and all those parts of ourselves which gave us the feeling of our existence." He also said that Emile should be taught to be able to take up some occupation or vocation in life. Here has said "To live is the trade I wish to teach him."

2. With this aim in view, Rousseau laid down education for Emile according to various stages of his development. Education, as suggested by Rousseau, aims at the development of the child's physical as well as mental personality in a rational and natural manner.

3. Rousseau was of the view that children should be given sufficient opportunity to acquire present happiness in accordance with their natural tendencies, desires and interests. In "Emile", he writes:

"Father, why roll these innocents of the joys which pass so quickly? Why fill with bitterness the fleeting days of childhood which will call your children to him.... Let them rejoice in the joy of life, so that whenever God calls them, they may not die without having tasted the joy of life."

Basic Principles

It has already been said that Rousseau worshipped nature and naturality and tried to propagate Naturalism in the field of education. He was against the conservative or conventional education as no good because it was man-made and artificial. All the things created by nature are beautiful and pure. Following points may be noted to understand the educational concept of Rousseau:

1. Rousseau recommended the education of child in the atmosphere of nature. This was the first meaning of nature.

2. He was the first to suggest that education should be based on nature, natural capacities and instincts of the child. This was the second meaning of nature.

3. Again, he was the first to suggest that a teacher before imparting education should study the nature or the natural capacities of the child. This view of Rousseau proved to be a boon as it made education child-centred.

4. Today education is child-centred. We frankly say that we educate the child and not the subject-matter or anything else. But it was Rousseau who first introduced this idea into the field of education. Munroe accepted this contribution of Rousseau and said that according to Rousseau the entire education of the child should be according to his nature, capacities and his natural desires and disposition.

5. To give importance to the development of the sense organs and to provide for their proper development in education is the contribution of Rousseau. He said "Our first teachers are our feet, our hands and our eyes."

6. He was the first to introduce the psychological tendencies in the field of education. He said that the educators should realise the capacity of the child and only then provide for his education. A child of a tender age should not be loaded with books and other tedious material. The burden of the education should be in conformity with his age and physical and mental capacities. It was here that his education for various stages of the child's development comes into picture.

7. He wanted to introduce the idea of complete freedom for the child. The views of John Dewey that the child should be left free to educate himself, had their roots in Rousseau.

8. He talked of woman education but believed that education of woman should aim at making her ideal house-wife.

9. He did not believe in imposing on the child anything from outside. On the other hand, he said that 'it is the development of the child's natural powers and abilities from within that constitutes education."

The Textbooks

Though Rousseau has not set forth definite principles for teaching different subjects at the different stages of Emile's education yet the discussion contains many valuable suggestions in regard to curriculum. He might not have talked about curriculum directly but, of course, talked about it in his own way. He has set forth curriculum for various stages of child's education. We will discuss it under the following headings:

For Infancy-We have already said that Rousseau did not prescribe teaching of any subject at this stage of the child's development. He said that the child should be, first of all, made healthy and strong. His sense organs should be trained. That will be the ideal education at this stage. According to Rousseau "The only habit the child should be allowed to contract is that of having no habits."

For Childhood-Rousseau has suggested the choice of the studies on the basis of negative education. Positive education, according to Rousseau, lies in imparting physical education to the child through a set of exercises that are meant for the training of the senses. He believes that if senses are not properly trained, the education would have no value. For this stage Rousseau has talked of negative education which means that no set pattern of gymnastic exercises should be provided for the physical development of the child. On the contrary, he should be left free to develop his organs and take the exercises of the senses.

In accordance with this principle, Rousseau suggested the maximum possible freedom of physical movement, simple diet and light clothing. There should not be any verbal lessons for him. They should also not be taught language, history or geography. He said that reading is not the course of childhood and so he has not provided for any book at this stage. He has, of course, provided for instructions in order to let the child acquire moral values. But these instructions are not to be given by any outside agency. They are to grow out of the actions of the child himself.

For Boyhood-Rousseau has said that Emile by now would have acquired the development of the bodily organs and he should now be given knowledge. He is now grown and is equipped to be taught physical sciences, language, mathematics, manual work, a trade, social relations, music and drawing. The teaching of the drawing is meant to train his eyes and muscles while the teaching of the physical sciences will help inculcate in him heuristic attitude. Trade or manual work is to be taught as it will help to develop his power of judgement and reasoning and cultivate in him the habits of cleanliness, neatness, accuracy, precision and work. For this, he has suggested carpentry and making of scientific instruments. He provided for the teaching of social relations because it will help child know the reciprocal duties of man, the need of co-operation in life and the economic dependence of man on man in today's social set-up.

For Adolescence-Rousseau provided for religious and moral education at this stage. He said that Emile at this stage should be imparted moral and religious education.

Moral Education, according to Rousseau, lies in the child's learning the following things:

(i) his relations with his fellow men; and

(ii) acquisition of moral qualities like generosity, benevolence, kindness, sympathy and service.

Here, again, Rousseau suggested that this education should be imparted not through instructions but through activities and occupations. Besides moral education, Emile (child) at this stage has to be taught history, religious education aesthetics, physical education and sex instructions. For all these subjects he has specific aims. For example, history is to be taught for the service of moral instructions. He also recommended teaching of geography for Emile.

As has already been suggested, the child at this stage is to be taught aesthetics for the cultivation and improvement of his tastes, physical education is to be taught so that his body grows healthy and he would be able to undertake heavy responsibilities and work. Sex education will help him to avoid falling into bad company and safeguarding against vices. He will also be able to learn the secret of the creation of the world and practise celibacy.

While explaining the ideas of Rousseau with regard to the education of Adulthood, Munroe writes:

"Now the youth is to be educated for life with others and is to be educated in social relationships. Love for others becomes the controlling motive, emotional development and moral perfection, the goal."

Instructional Approach

As Rousseau was essentially a naturalist, the method of teaching that he suggested reflects his philosophy or naturalism. He emphasised that the child should be given an opportunity to learn by direct experience of things and the method of teaching should be based on the principle of learning by doing. He has said that whatever a boy learns by doing is stable and permanent. In his own words, "Teach by education whenever you can and only fall back on words when doing is difficult question." It is because of this view that he suggested that Emile should learn by experience rather than from books as he disapproved the idea of using books in childhood.

Significant Elements

Dislike for Rote Memory : Rousseau disliked learning by rote memory He believed in the development of the child's sense of good and bad rather than rote.

Heuristic Attitude Methods : He advocated the adoption of heuristic method which places the child in the centre and in the position of a discoverer. The child is to be given an opportunity to resort to practical methods and experiment with the apparatus that he made himself or invented. He was in favour of applying this principle to the teaching of Mathematics, History, Geography,

Social Relations and Morality. While talking about moral education he laid more emphasis on the acquisition of moral virtues by the child than telling him what to do in a specific manner. He said that "It is by doing good that one becomes good; occupy your people with all the good actions that are in his reach; let the interest of the pure always be his; let him assist them not only with his purse but his personal education; let him serve them, protect them and considerate to them his present and his time; let him be their advocate: he will have nobler employ." Similarly, he suggested that Emile should learn about social relations by actually visiting the shops and factories where he shall have an opportunity to see people working together according to their talents and opportunities for the production of the industrial goods or mechanical arts.

Rousseau did not specifically lay down the principles or method of teaching as such. But these things are contained in his work 'Emile'. It was he who contributed to the use of 'Laboratory Method'. 'Heuristic Method', and 'The principle of Learning by Doing' and 'Learning by Sense Experience'. All these methods were suggested by Rousseau in 'Emile' and they have stimulated the thinking of most of the modern educators.

Child to be the Centre of Education Methods : Rousseau talked less about the teacher's exposition and more about the learning experiences of the educated. That is why he did not like the idea of teaching the child through instructions or didactic style of the teacher and said "I like not explanation given in long discourse; young people pay little attention to them and retain little of them. The things themselves! the 'things themselves'; shall never repeat often enough that we attach too much importance towards; with our chatterange education we make nothing but chatterange."

In regard to discipline in the education, Rousseau raised the slogan Leave the Child Free and "There should be Absence of Restraint for Emile." He was of the view that natural capabilities of the child would have their natural development only in an atmosphere free from restraints. External restraints retard the natural growth of the personality of the child. It was because of this that he suggested that punishment will not lead to the correction of the child because he does not know what is good and what is bad as his reasoning power has not developed. On the other hand he was of the opinion that the child should be left free to have the natural punishment that he shall gain out of his own experiences if he did anything that is against the law of nature. His views are contained in the following words: "Children should never receive punishment as such it should always come as a natural consequence of their fault." Dewey exploited it fully.

He advised the teachers not to impose moral instructions or discipline from above because anything that is imposed from above does not really go home. He believed that child is essentially good and interference from outside will only harm him. He should be given education in a natural atmosphere free from evil things and he shall learn good things and grow into a good or natural man.

Role in Education

Rousseau was a great thinker of his time and his views have certainly influenced education in many respects. Emile contains some of the wonderful principles and passages, which educationists look up to, even today for guidance and inspiration. Influence of Rousseau on education is evident in three ways—(a) Psychological, (b) Scientific, and (c) Social.

Psychological Tendency : Psychological tendency in Education it is the contribution of Rousseau. He considered education as a "Natural Process" and, therefore, laid stress on educating children according to their natural tendencies. It was on account of this that he placed the child in the centre of education. He does not give importance either to the teacher or to the curriculum. In olden days it was believed that child is meant for education. But Rousseau brought about the change in this concept. Now it is being believed that education should aim at the development of the natural tendencies of the child. The teacher should try to understand the child and then only educate him. This brought about the introduction of the educational psychology and so psychology was applied to the field of education. Pestalozzi Herbert and Froebel are the other thinkers who also made their contribution in this respect.

Scientific Tendency : Use of scientific tendency in education is another contribution of naturalism. It was only on account of Rousseau's movement that scientific tendencies were given importance in education. He (Rousseau) drew the attention of people toward the observation of nature and utility of the science and not remained confined to book reading or verbal instructions only, the child should be given opportunity to observe various facets of nature. With this movement, study of natural sciences, Botany etc., got a place in the curriculum. These ideals have influenced many educationists. Amongst them Spencer and Huxley are more important. If scientific tendency has any importance in education today, the credit very much goes to Rousseau and his treatise "Emile."

Social Tendency : The movement of Individualism has been introduced in education by Rousseau. He was a great individualist and it was only on account of his individualism that the boy was recognised as an individual and education was given on the basis of individual differences. It was on account of Rousseau that it was recognised that education should aim at the development of the natural faculties of the child. If on the one hand he was a great individualist, his views also led to the prevalence of social tendency in education. In "Emile" we find the seeds of human welfare. He has very clearly talked about co-operation, sympathy and working together. He has also tried to make the child well at vocation so that he may be able to earn his livelihood. These things do have a social importance. Today great emphasis is laid on social tendencies in education. Vocational training is considered essential and moral education is as much important. Working together or doing things in co-operation has a very valuable place in education and are there only on account of 'Emile'.

Not only restricted to these areas, Rousseau has influenced education and his impact is clearly visible in other respects as well. In regard to method of teaching he laid emphasis on imparting education according to natural faculties of the child ushering in new techniques of teaching and education. Education according to natural tendencies, Education through Activity, Heuristic Method, Project Method, Dalton Method etc. having roots in Rousseau developed in due course. It is also said that Boy Scout Movement, has to a very great extent, been influenced by naturalism in education.

The Impact

Influence of Rousseau on education is evident even today. If it is accepted that the child should be imparted education, treating him a child and that conservatism should have no place in education, it is all due to Rousseau. If we talk of teaching of vocation or craft to children, the credit again goes to Rousseau. He also laid emphasis on educating the heart along with mind and hands. In fact, he brought about a new revolution in education.

Although naturalism started with a very useful movement in education, yet its influence was not very quick, especially in Europe, France and England were considered to be centres of learning in those days and were not prepared to accept Rousseau's views. Schools there went on in their old ways. English people did not like this movement in education because they thought it was not practical. Man is by nature conservative and is not prepared to leave what he has been following for a long time and that is true of educationists as well. On the other hand, Rousseau was considered to be an enemy of church as well as rich people. It were these two institutions that dominated education in France as well as England and therefore, his views were not acceptable to them. Germany was the first country to follow the idea of Rousseau. Schools were reorganised according to his views. It was since the middle of the 19th century that Rousseau and his views found place in education of others countries.

Along with certain qualities, naturalism has certain defects also. First of all, the word Nature does not carry a uniform meaning. Rousseau himself has used the word in many respects. Secondly, it has given great importance to the natural tendencies of man but neglected the spiritual qualities. According to naturalist, the aim of education is quite ordinary, neither high nor attractive. Even Rousseau's Negative Education is not free from defects. It does not seem to be very wise to leave the child completely free and let him grow without any check or restriction and in complete absence of any verbal instructions. This is true that the child can acquire education by self-experience but he requires proper guidance at every step. In the absence of this, he is likely to drift toward some wrong direction. On the other hand, it is also not correct to keep the boy away from the society. By nature, the child learns by imitation. He can get this opportunity only in society. Kept away from society, he will have little opportunity to imitate. Besides this, by nature, the child has certain social qualities. They are equally natural. Love and affection can grow only in society. Here we find certain contradictions in the views of Rousseau himself. Yet in spite of all these defects, naturalism influenced education to a very great extent.

Past Experience

Jean Jacques Rousseau was son of a poor watch-maker. He was born in France in 1712. His mother died while young and his father remarried. Rousseau mourned the loss of her mother by saying, "I lost my mother, her life, and my birth was the first of my misfortunes." He grew up to be a man of romantic temperament. He used to read love letters of his stepmother which she used to write to his father while away to her parents sitting by the side of his father. Rousseau was ultimately taken care of by his aunt. Rousseau's father was totally ignorant in the art of rearing up children.

Rousseau had very little formal education. He used to be busy almost whole of the day playing pranks on ladies of the village. He was in that sense a very naughty student and full of mischief. At the age of 12, he was appointed as an apprentice to an engineer. He did not like that. At the age of 15, he was sent to the priests for his father wanted him to be a priest but Rousseau was disgusted with the life led by the priests then and he ran away from the church also. He did various jobs in various capacities ultimately taking to tutorship.

Rousseau read all sorts of books. He was fond of music. He loved nature passionately.

The Philosopher. J.J. Rousseau had an oscillating personality. He had abnormal awareness of sex and was a little neurotic. He packed off his own children to Foundling Hospital (orphanage) despite the protests of his wife and his own presence. He during his youth also crossed Alps on foot and thereby came across Nature and developed his love for nature. He was moved then by the corruption in society. He wrote much. His books and writings were in fact responsible for revolution in France. He prompted people to revolt.

His important writings are in shape of books:

1. The Confessions of J.J. Rousseau.
2. Social Contract.
3. Emile or A Treatise on Education.

His books still show us light and are a source of inspiration and for centuries to come, such like books will not be having their parallel.

In 1778, Rousseau died in the streets of France. Though we call him as father of modern educational theory and practice, yet at that time he was called various names and allowed to rot. It is also said that Rousseau's philosophy is contradictory in nature.

Educational Philosophy

Rousseau emerged as a revolutionary philosopher. Whatever he thought and wrote was as a reaction to the hypocrisy and corruption and formalism prevalent during those times. He felt disgusted with that social order. He was a champion of Naturalism, Natural state, Natural man, Natural civilization. He wanted us to go back to Nature. That was his slogan. His beliefs and his philosophy can he read in the following quotations taken from his famous books:

From Emile, "All things are good as they come out of the hands of their Creator, but everything degenerates in the hands of man." This means that essential nature of child is good and it is only we who corrupt the child. 'We' here means society. To quote from Social Contract, "Man is born free but everywhere he is in chains." This means that social institutions tend to curb the freedom of man. He revolted against the established mores. That was why, he raised the slogan of 'Return to Nature' as stated above.

We would like to explain these concepts of Naturalism, Natural state, Natural man and Natural civilization a little more.

Naturalism. A school of thought where Nature is the final reality. Here Rousseau did not believe in the artificialities of life.

The term naturalism has been variously used and many brand names have been given to philosophical views that come under this banner. We have Scientific Naturalism, Biological Naturalism, Psychological Naturalism and Romantic Naturalism. We are concerned with Scientific Naturalism which means Mechanical Nature of the world. It starts with external nature and tries to fit man into the picture of the universe as painted by science.

Biological naturalism explains man as the highest form of life—the last word in evolution.

Natural State. Natural State is the state of goodness of man. Man as he is born is good but he degenerates in the hands of society. 'Return to nature' means back to natural state—the state of innocence and goodness. Artificialities of life has to be removed.

Natural Man. By the term 'natural man', Rousseau did not mean an uncivilized person. In fact, by this term, Rousseau means that person who acts according to his own nature-original nature-and is not compelled to follow social restrictions. It is very difficult to understand human nature.

Natural Civilization. It means that way of life which is based on original nature of man—the man who acts according to his own inner feelings and natural tendencies.

Rousseau was also champion of dignity of man. He also gave to us the concepts of Fraternity, Liberty and Equality.

Rousseau was essentially a naturalist. He is discussed as a naturalist or believer in Naturalism. The main tenets of naturalism are:

1. Belief in nature—Return to nature.
2. Belief in science—Naturalism in which Rousseau believed is simply a generalisation of science.
3. No faith in soul or spirit or divine.
4. Belief in heredity and environment. Both are important.
5. Child is born good. It is the society, that makes him bad. This is the belief of Rousseau.
6. All knowledge is gathered through senses. Rousseau believed that senses are the gateways of knowledge.

Influential Role

Whenever we talk of education-it means aims of education, method of education, content of education, concept of discipline and role of the teacher etc. These are various aspects which comprise the subject of education. A particular individual's philosophy affects or influences these aspects of education and gives twists to his educational philosophy. The same applies to J.J. Rousseau also. Let us see that.

The Perception

For Rousseau education is not merely imparting information or storing knowledge. It is development of inner powers of the child. Rousseau makes his point clear when he says that there are three sources of education, namely.

(i) Nature

(ii) Men

(iii) Things

Nature. Education from nature means spontaneous development of our endowments and faculties.

Men. Education from men means getting socially developed and influencing our social contacts and various groups.

Things. Education from things consists in acquiring knowledge and information through contact with physical surroundings and our experience of dealing with things. Education from Nature is supreme and superior. Education should be considered as "the process of development into an enjoyable, rational, harmoniously balanced, useful and hence natural life."

On Aims. "In the natural order of things all men being equal, their common vocation is manhood. To live is the trade I wish to teach him. On leaving my hands, he will not, I grant, be a magistrate, soldier or a priest. First of all he will be a man"—Emile.

This means that education should aim at making man a full man so that he is able to lead a full and rich life. Such like men will also be an asset to the society. Education thus aims at reforming society also. Return to Nature does not mean living as in nature but reforming the society, making it decent, free from corrupt practices and not that man should become a savage and return to deserts and forests. It is living according to rational principles. Rousseau's Education aims at giving up fit and healthy individuals who may face and change the corrupt environment. It is a case of survival of fittest in bad environment and hence building of body and stamina.

In a nutshell, the educational philosophy of Rousseau aims at:

(i) Making a man full man so that he is able to lead a rich and full life.

(ii) It also aims at reforming society.

(iii) Education should make a person physically fit.

(iv) We should not hasten the development of man. Let him develop at his own natural speed.

(v) And lastly to develop the power of self-expression.

Only Rousseau gave us naturalistic curriculum. He was interested in the nature of the child and his natural development. He said that for the first 12 years, there, should be no formal teaching and no formal schools. It is also known as a period of Negative education. Rousseau accordingly kept those subjects in the curriculum that suited the nature of the child. He divided the developmental stages as:

(i) *1-5 years: Infancy:* Characterised by years habit and training of emotions.

(ii) *6-12 years: Childhood:* Characterised by training of senses and discipline by natural consequences.

(iii) *12-15 years: Boyhood:* Characterised by utility and training of intellect.

(iv) *15-20 years: Adolescence:* The stage of morality and moral education.

(v) *20-25 years: Adult:* The stage when one is ready to take responsibility and be a father.

In the light of this division, he fitted his curriculum accordingly. Formal education, to repeat once again, is to begin only at the age of 12. Up to the age of 12, the child is to learn from his family.

According to Rousseau, there are three phases of education-natural or negative; the social or moral and the civic or political.

In the light of this division of stages and phases of education, Rousseau recommends the inclusion of physical exercises. The emphasis is on building the health of the child. These also include games. Man gets social and moral training by participating in common games. He also emphasises the inclusion of those subjects which will give him civic training.

Not much has been talked by Rousseau on intellectual training. His practical education.

Rousseau stands for sciences and diversified courses.

The Experiments

Education, according to Rousseau, should be free and there is no such thing as teaching profession. No formal teaching provide only direct experience to the students. This way learning will not be so boring. While 'teaching' or providing experience, however, the interests of child be considered. It is a sort of Heuristic method that he advocates.

Rousseau's method of teaching is direct experience or self-experience. Rousseau says, "Give your child no verbal lessons; he should be taught by experience alone. Teach by doing whatever you can; and only fall back on words who is doing it is out of question."

(i) The students can also be given direct experience of social life. This can be done by organising the school as a free natural society. School self-government can teach students their rights and duties as citizens.

(ii) And when students learn by direct experience, their senses are fully made use of. Rousseau wanted the maximum utilisation of senses.

(iii) Text books are advocated only at higher levels of education.

Rousseau believed in discipline by natural consequences. To quote him, "Children should never receive punishment as such—it should always come as the natural consequence of their fault." 'He must never act from obedience, but from necessity.'

The Other Side

The chief distinguishing factor which makes Rousseau stand out as distinct from others is his concept of idea of 'Negative Education' upto the age of 12. He by this does not mean that deliberate attempts made not to educate the child. He only suggests that there should be no conscious effort to teach a child. Let the child learn himself by his own experiences primarily from home. Let him be trained physically and also sharpen his senses. To him good physique is a must. It is most important thing and this will develop by letting the child roam. Even after the age of 12, in positive education, importance of physical education has been stressed by him-'A feeble body makes a feeble mind.' All wickedness comes from weakness. It is also time for exploring the neighbourhood.

By Negative education he means perfection of bodily organs and not premature attempts to mature mind.

Any way, Negative education consists of:-

(a) No textbooks or book learning.

(b) No formal teaching.

(c) No restriction-discipline by natural consequences.

(d) No saving of time. Rather, let us lose time.

(e) Direct and indirect moral education is also prohibited.

(f) No examinations.

(g) Lastly, no sticking to formal methods of teaching.

(h) Protest against habit formations.

(i) No social education.

Women's Education

In his earlier writings Rousseau advocated that women were equal to men and they should get the same education. Later on, he appears to have been offended by them and became critical of them-even started them calling names such as 'decoration pieces' or 'charm of drawing room.' He insisted, however, that if society is to be strong, family life must be good and free from vice. Family life will be good, if husband and wife performed their functions nicely and individually. He also said that home life will be good, if woman or wife has a subordinate position to her husband. Further he realised when his Emile grew up and needed suitable companion. Accordingly the education of women be such that would make them healthy, attractive, expert in household affairs, capable of bearing children and be of use to men and please them. Rousseau, infact, was awfully orthodox. He condemned the move of higher education for women. He said, "A woman of culture is the plague of her husband, her children, her family, her servants-everybody." You may criticise him on this as the idea is not appealing to us today but that was Rousseau—the romantic.

Child's Importance

The entire discussion on various aspects or faults of education should convince one that the child occupies a central or key place in Rousseau's scheme of things. Education should suit the nature of the child. The child is good, he should be respected, the child should be left free. Discipline should be by natural consequences and the child should enjoy unlimited freedom, no punishment should be given to the child. What does this aims at? That Rousseau is all for the child as a child—not as an adult in the making. Child enjoys the central place. His personification of child as Emile further lends credence to this belief. Child is the centre of all education. Due place and recognition are given to a child.

The Pioneer

The following points will convince us that Rousseau is indeed the father of modern educational theory and practice. We fully agree with the statement:

1. Rousseau gave to us the importance of stages in the development of child. Each stage be treated separately and due consideration be given to the characteristics.
2. He believes in the spontaneous unfolding of child's capacities. This we have started following.
3. The entire scheme of education is child centred. The child is not to be treated as a miniature adult.
4. He stressed the importance of physical education and sense training. We are now laying due stress on it by adding games period in the regular school Time Table and also by launching movements such as National Physical Efficiency Drive.
5. We have become considerate towards children. Corporal punishment is rarely used. Discipline is maintained by appealing to the child.
6. Diversified curriculum has been introduced to suit the interests of the child. Recognition of individual differences is there.
7. The idea of Learning by Doing has been introduced. It also gives him direct experience. Learning by doing is also in agreement with psychology of the child-he likes to be active. Our basic education is based on it.
8. Even aims of education stand modified. We teach children to think of present and live it well rather than think of future. Rousseau said, 'To live is the trade I wish to teach him.' We are following him to a large extent in our schools.

The Assessment

Briefly, J.J. Rousseau stands criticised as under:

1. Rousseau's personality was very offensive. He annoyed people in his life time.
2. It is also said that Rousseau was not a very original person. He borrowed ideas from people like Locke and expressed these in his own words.
3. Rousseau's educational philosophy as expressed in his book Emile is full of contradictions and inconsistencies. Rousseau used to contradict his own statements. Even his schemes of education are negative as opposed to positive.
4. Giving too much freedom to the child is bad. What do you say?
5. His attitude was anti-social. He considered society to be bad. In fact every society is not bad. We cannot isolate an individual from society.

One sunny October after-noon in 1749, a slender, darkly handsome man strolled along the Paris Vincennes post road glancing through his paper. Suddenly, his eyes riveted on an announcement that the Academy of Dijon was offering a gold medal for the best essay on the theme "Has Progress in the arts and sciences purified or corrupted morals?"

All at once, it seemed to the stroller that he had been preparing from childhood to answer just that question. Inspiration came in a flash: "Crowds of vivid ideas thronged into my mind", he would write later. His theme would be, "Man is naturally good and social institutions alone have rendered him evil".

His essay, 'Discourse on the Sciences and the Arts,' not only won the prize but marked a turning point in Western political thought. It also catapulted the writer, Jean Jacques Rousseau, into the forefront of European philosophers.

Democracy, rights of the individual and just government—all these and many more basic and sometimes contradictory issues facing us today can be linked directly with the writings of the Genevan who died some 200 years ago. He sowed the seeds for so much of society's subsequent evolution and revolution that one editorialist commemorating the anniversary of his death recently stated: "Had there been no Rousseau, we would have been impossible."

At the time he wrote his first Discourse, Rousseau, then 38, was still almost unknown, struggling to make ends meet as a tutor, music copier and music teacher. Yet, he was intensely ambitious and convinced of his unique qualities.

He was to seize on the principle weakness of the Eighteenth Century Enlightenment: its emphasis on pure reason to oppose the absolutist regimes of the time. He preached reliance on feeling or conscience to bring about revolutionary changes. Nature was the source of the all truth, and he felt there was morality in a mountain lake than in all the world's cathedrals. As a promoter of the "natural man," he believed that originally man was a creature of good instincts that had been perverted by an acquisitive tyrannical social order.

Meaningful System

Long before the ecologists, Rousseau was warning against the excess of science and the degradation of cities. Urging teachers to use persuasion rather than coercion he set his stamp on all subsequent education. Most important of all and running like a central thread through all his work was the nagging question that has preoccupied men ever since Rousseau formulated it: how to reconcile the interests of society and those of the individual citizen? His late biographer Jean Guehenno wrote that for two centuries Rousseau had embodied "the state of man in the modern world."

During that time, virtually every one who has yearned to transform society has found justification in Rousseau. His writings were a source of inspiration for both the American and the French Revolutions. The Declaration of the Rights of Man, adopted by the French Constituent Assembly on August 26, 1789, echoed Rousseau's "Social Contract" when proclaiming that "the purpose of society is the common good", and "sovereignty resides in the people". The same principle has weighed in the founding of the United States. While violent revolutionaries from Robespiree to Lenin have invoked his elusive notion of the "general will" in defence of tyranny, Rousseau has appealed as widely to believers in peaceful moral change. Goethe revered him, as did Tolstoy.

In 1978, on the 200th anniversary of his death, international seminars were devoted to Rousseau, new biographies were published, he was the subject of television plays and panel discussions. He was again considered current in his writings, he forecast the pitfalls of a consumer society, the turmoil of great cities and the ruinous burden of armaments. In France alone some 150 scholars are presently researching aspects of Rousseau's thoughts.

5

Dewey

Life Sketch

John Dewey was a climatic figure in American philosophy. He gave to us new idea and those ideas shook the world. He gave to us new and revolutionary ideas. Dewey also gathered all the confusing impulses, all the varied but partial insights, and reduced them to coherent synthesis, to a systematic and well ordered world view.

John Dewey's boyhood was as plain, as average, and as middle class as his name. He was born in Burlington, Vermout, in 1859, the year Origin of the Species was published. He attended local schools and in later memory criticized the abstract content of instruction and recalled his own lack of interest. His school years were not that stimulating. He did not become intellectually stimulated until his senior year at the University Vermout, when he became enthused over the courses in physiology and psychology. Even after the beginning, his intellectual development was slow. He was almost forty years old before he worked out the main doctrines of mature philosophy. Yet his growth was steady.

He slowly built on his past constantly revising where necessary but never quite relinquishing anything. For this reason, his youthful Vermout years were of vital importance. He never repudiated most of the values of his childhood. Instead he correlated them with a new knowledge of man and his environ-ment a knowledge never possessed by his less sophisticated forebears.

Dewey remained a nominal Christian until his thirties. As he developed his own philosophy, he simply dropped the vague symbols of Christianity. He also displayed a sharp distaste for supernaturalism.

After completing his undergraduate work at Vermout, Dewey taught for two years in a Pennsylvania High School. There he continued his interest in philosophy and wrote articles. Dewey enrolled as a graduate student of philosophy at John Hopkins in 1882. He was a symbol of a new generation of American scholars. At Hopkins, he was disappointed at the lack of philosophic content in his minor subjects. He was unimpressed by Charles S. Peirce also who taught mathematics and logic. He was greatly impressed by G. Stanley Hall who taught psychology. Dewey was a superior graduate student, completing his doctorate in 2 years. At the urging of Morris, the University even had him teach an undergraduate course. Morris then invited him to Michigan as an instructor. He remained there for about 10 years. At Michigan, Dewey wrote his publications, soon established him as one of the prominent advocates of the then prevalent idealism.

Dewey's years at Michigan paralleled the rapid growth of anthropology as a new and influential academic discipline. Constantly, Dewey turned to anthropologist for information on other cultures and incorporated this material into his philosophical criticism.

In 1894, Dewey moved from Michigan to Chicago. He stayed there for 10 years. In this decade, he finally completed the outlines of his nature philosophy and cooperatively expressed it in 1903 manifest of his Chicago school studies in Logical Theory.

At Chicago, he married Alice Chipman, herself an able educator. They had six children, four of them survived.

At Chicago, Dewey also established and directed an experimental elementary school, perhaps the most significant educational experiment in American history.

In one of the few embittered and personal controversies of his life (over educational theory), Dewey resigned his position at Chicago. The following year he began his long career at Columbia University, remaining a professor until his retirement in 1930, and a revered friend and adviser until his death in 1952.

Published Books

1. Democracy and Education (1916).
2. Human Nature and Conduct (1922).
3. Art as Experience.
4. Logic—the Theory of Inquiry.

He married a second time at the age of 86 and adopted two more children. His letters even in the last two years, revealed a mind that was still curious and acutely critical.

Educational Philosophy

Concept of Reality (Metaphysics). Nature was the ultimate term in Dewey's thought. It encompasses all reality. Only in human organism has nature attained some awareness of itself. Thus, any general statement about nature has to be limited to the evidence provided in human experience. On the basis of this evidence, Dewey says that nature is a flux of events in time. All events are temporal exist in relation or in interactivity with other events and are thus conditioned. But events often exhibit some order and stability as well as spontaneity and novelty. Neither complete anarchy nor complete necessity characterize nature.

Change is basic but, varies tremendously in tempo, permitting enough stability for getting a bearing and thus effecting desired controls and enough uncertainty and instability to allow such guidance and direction.

Nature is defined also as a completed or fully rational deterministic structure or as completed anarchic flux.

Any understanding of Dewey's concept of nature must be supplemented by his concept of experience. He had greater respect for experience which precedes any knowing, which is simply had, which is simply irreducible what it is. It is the existence which always precedes essence. Experience involves an inter active or to use Dewey's choice term a trans active relationship between a sentient organism and its environment, "an environment that is human as well as physical and includes the materials of tradition and institutions as well as local surroundings." This experience continually leads to modification of behaviour.

Dewey not only stressed the qualitative aspect of experience, but he also stressed that nature is ordinarily encountered in gross, macroscopic forms, and in large, qualitatively unified situations. The gross subject matter of experience may be classified as Mental or Physical.

Dewey always rejected a materialistic interpretation of nature. To him Nature is more than materialistic account.

In order to understand nature, you must know language. Language is man's supreme tool. All other tools are dependent upon language. In language he attached great importance to meaning. Meaning are as real as any other aspect of nature.

Status of Individual

Man is to be understood in social context. He has natural inclinations but these must be ensued for the welfare of the society. He believed man to be active and his education has to be actively centered. Man is growing organism.

He has strong faith in the power of man. Man will have to make his own path for development and progress. He will have to be experimental for this purpose. He will have to depend upon his creative thinking. He had strong faith in the power of man. He says that man will have to make his own path for development and progress. And for that creative intelligence is a must for man.

Brain and Wisdom

Dewey's theory of knowledge is based on organic evolution of man. He points out that human mind is an organic natural development in meeting the various practical and social situations of life. The employment of mental powers help men in overcoming difficulties and desiring satisfaction from activities of daily existence. Mind includes its triple aspects-thinking, feeling and willing. Knowledge is not different from mind, ideas are only modes or activities of the mind. They are developed or retained by the individual to keep him control the objects of environment.

Dewey further points out according to Dr. R.N. Pani, that knowledge is not prior to action as it is generally understood, rather it is product of action. Action first knowledge later. An example: A child puts his triggers into fire, it burns. The experience of burning sensation prevents the child from coming too close to fire. Thus learning takes place and knowledge is desired from activity.

Knowledge and action are closely interrelated. Moreover while action gives birth to knowledge modifies further action. They are interconnected.

One of the most crucial aspects of Dewey's view of knowledge was his continuous insistence that cognitive (activities of the head, existentially true or false) propositions are instrumental and not initiative. They are means for guiding process of change in nature and are adequate or valid if they succeed in doing this. Knowing was always the issue with Dewey. Knowledge constantly directs and order the flow of events. Knowing here is not merely accepted knowledge but discovering something new. That was experimentation and experience.

Norms and Traditions

His concept of values was entirely different from the traditional concept. According to Dewey ideals and values of life are not predetermined and fixed. Values are not static. Values change. Truth is a value. Truth also changes. That which is true is useful and that which is useful is true. Values of life are man-made and change according to change in circumstances, times and places. As such, human life is a laboratory where in each individual indulges in ever new experiments and experiences according to his mental capacity to explore, investigate and search out relevant ideals and values. In the light of changing nature of values, even God is not absolute and infinite. To Dewey, God and soul are not immortal. Things are in a change of flux. This is the view of Dewey on values.

The Ideology

Concept of Education. Dewey was one of the founders of pragmatist philosophy. Its educational implications are as under (Dewey's view is discussed).

Education, according to Dewey is necessity for life. Education is very important activity of society and it results from participation in the activities of the society. It is the process of reconstruction or reconstitution of experience giving it a more socialised efficiency. According to Ganid and Sharma, it is a process and consists of "the acquisition of characteristic social activities, responses and modes of conduct that make the child human and at the same time individual."

According to Dewey, education has two aspects:

1. Psychological.

2. Social efficiency.

We cannot ignore any of these, otherwise we shall have to face the consequence. Psychologically, we understand the natural inclinations, interests and capabilities of the child so that we may prepare suitable curriculum for his development.

Social outlook means creation of useful social environment which is in concurrence with social conditions. Both individual and collective methods are to be employed. But for this, according to Claube, it is necessary to know the social conditions.

Aims of Education. Dewey is a pragmatist philosopher. His concept of values is that values are not static and permanent. Pragmatism also believes in it. Aims depend upon values or values determine aims. If there are no static or permanent values, it is implied that in Dewey's philosophy of education, there are no fixed aims of education. Values change. Aims change. But then education for what? The end of education, according to Dewey, is more education. Dewey says, "The process of education has no end beyond itself, it is its own end, the educational process is one of continuous reorganising, restructuring and manufacturing-there is nothing to which education is subordinate save more education." The end of growth is more growth. It is creation and recreation of values.

The Curriculum. Dewey's concept of curriculum is as broad-based as the concept of democratic education. Curriculum is as broad as life. It is experience based curriculum. "The scheme of a curriculum must take into account of the adaptation of studies to the needs of the existing community life, it must select with the intention of improving the life we live in common so that the future shall be better than the past."

Curriculum is utility oriented. Science gets prominence in it.

Method of Teaching. Dewey talks of teacher and taught relationship in the field of education. In the light of his philosophy, the teacher will have to bring changes in his work. He should not consider himself superior to the child. Natural talents of the child should be stimulated. The teacher also know that students differ.

If children work according to their interests and aptitudes, there will not be any problem in the school.

When children complete one programme (popularly called project), the teacher should help them decide the next. It is possible that children are so much motivated by the activity that they themselves propose the next activity. The entire programme of the school should be determined according to the proposal of the students. Students stand enriched. This teaching method is called Project method. Kilpatrick is another supporter of this method. Project method includes both individual and collective plans and programme. Collective plans develop feeling of cooperation in children. So provide experiences. Experiences are provided by the project method.

Discipline. Discipline is defined by Dewey as the proper use of one's energies and powers. Once an individual becomes interested in an action, he becomes disciplined. Discipline involves use of power avoiding wastage of energy, determining what is to be done and what is to be avoided.

"Discipline is positive. To cow the spirit, to subdue inclinations, to compel obedience, to mortify the flesh, to make the subordinate perform an uncongenial task-these things are, and are not disciplinary according as they do or do not tend to the development of power to recognise what one is about and to persistence in accomplishment."

Four great thinkers have had a special impact upon American education. Pestalozzi's educational concepts greatly influenced the American, Charles Sheldon, a firm believer in humane discipline. At his school at Oswego, New York, Sheldon emphasised the importance of object lessons and contact with nature. He showed how instruction must start with simple concepts and be based upon correct sense perceptions.

Herbert's influence reached the United States through the work of the McMurrays. In 1892, a National Herbartian Society was established. It changed the methodology of education and emphasised history, geography and social studies. Its formal technique was challenged by Dewey, who believed in a more elastic methodology in education.

Froebel had great influence on Mrs. Carl Schurz, who established a kindergarten, based on his ideas, in Wisconsin. Elizabeth Peabody established the first English speaking kindergarten in Boston in 1860.

Another educator who exerted a strong influence, especially upon progressive education, was the Italian educator, Maria Montessori. Like Froebel, she stressed the natural goodness of children. To her, freedom was a cardinal goal of education. She believed that children should proceed at their own pace and that coercion should always be avoided. The individuality of the child was to be safeguarded. She summarised her ideas by the statement: "My method is established upon one fundamental base-thé liberty of the pupils in their spontaneous manifestations." To Montessori, no intellectual progress could be achieved without training of the senses.

Fundamental Issues

1. Dewey was influenced most strongly by the theory of evolution. Thus he approached education from a biological perspective. To him, the scientific method had meaning not only in the laboratory, but also in the school room, which was to be guided by the spirit of tentativeness. Dewey believed that knowledge is power and that it has to be used experimentally for the benefit of mankind. The seeds of his ideas can also be found in Rousseau, Pestalozzi and Froebel.

2. Another fundamental idea in Dewey's philosophy of education is his concept of the mind. Man's mind is not a static entity, a thing-in-itself; it is part of our evolutionary development, it is tool of adjustment. He called his own philosophy instrumentalism to indicate his concern with methodology.

Aims and Goals

According to Dewey:

"The function of education is to help growing of helpless young animal into a happy, moral and efficient human being."

Dewey did not believe in circumscribing education by certain aims. He believed that education should aim at the stimulation of the child's powers through the social medium. Since the interest and the capabilities of the children differ from child to child, the education cannot grow according to set aims. This will hamper the proper growth of their personality. It should only aim at the growth of the innate nature of the immature child as to help him to be able to live up to the social standards and the demands that are made on him. In other words, it should aim at social efficiency.

The aims of education can be divided under two heads—(1) Individual, and (2) Social.

Individual Aims : Following are the individual aims of education:

(i) Education should help an individual to establish those principles and standards that are of immediate importance and value to him.

(ii) To equip the individuals as be to able to test the truth and the utility of these values and standards through experiment and examination.

Social Aims : In order to be able to bring about social efficiency, the education should have the following qualities:

(i) *Economic Efficiency:* It should be able to equip the child to earn his livelihood.

(ii) *Negative Morality:* It should be capable of making a child of leaving those standards and wishes whose satisfaction may hinder the economic efficiency of others.

(iii) *Positive Morality:* It should be capable of stopping the children or individuals from trying to satisfy those desires and wishes whose fulfilment will directly or indirectly, disturb the social business.

School as an Enlarged Family: Dewey did not believe that school should be isolated or cut off from the family. It should preserve, continue and re-build the activity with which the child is familiar at home. It should be like an enlarged family in which the child should continue to perfect and improve what he has learnt at home with, of course, better equipments and more scientific guidance. School should be natural extension of home.

Vocational Education: Dewey believed that in schools children should be taught at least one vocation which may be helpful to them in their actual life in earning their livelihood. These vocations should be in accordance with the requirements of the society. Teaching of these vocations has a social utility also. It leads to creative and individual balance in the child. Their preservation power increases and the constructive tendency develops. It also leads to their interest in the society and will encourage them to work in co-operation with others and, if required, even collectively.

Moral Education: Dewey was also a believer of moral education. He thought that it should be important to children but not in artificial way as we generally do in schools. He thought that it should not be in the form of a separate lesson but through 'social and conjoint activities'. The best and deepest moral training is precisely that which one gets through having to enter into proper relations with others in an unity of work and thought.

School should be the Reflection of Society: Dewey believed that there is no definiteness or unity in the requirements and needs of the society. They change according to the situations. The society is also not very definitely conscious of its needs and requirements. An ideal school should help the society to achieve this consciousness. In other words, it can be said that it has to guide the people to have a clear and definite understanding of the needs and requirements of the society. It is these needs that the school has to cater to. This, in other words, means that the school has to provide for certain ideas according to which people will determine their needs and requirements. But these ideas too cannot be isolated from the life of the society; they have to grow out of it.

In his book, "Democracy and education" he has determined that the main aim of education is the development and preservation of democracy. This can happen only when people get education in the democratic way of life. This education can only be imparted by the schools and so they have to reflect a living atmosphere of the democratic way of life.

Instructional Approach

Ideas of Dewey in regard to the method of teaching are reflected in his works entitled 'How We Think' and 'Interest an Effort in Education.' Here he has said that the best method of teaching or education is that which is based on learning by doing. These activities should form a part of the life. The method should aim at co-ordinating the subjects with the activities and life. Child, according to Dewey, is the centre of education and it is his interest in the faculties that matter most to him.

Dewey has accepted the same thing in the following lines:

"The genuine principle of interest is the principle of recognized identity of the proposed line of action with the self that it lies in the direction of agents in self-expression." In other words, Dewey believed that self expression of the child should be related to the activities that he takes up in the school.

Project Method, which is identified with the method of teaching enunciated by John Dewey, was introduced by Kilpatrick, one of the famous followers of John Dewey. It is believed that the ideas of John Dewey in regard to the method of teaching are reflected in this particular method.

It is correct also because the plan of this method was originally drawn by John Dewey in the following words:

"..... first that people have a genuine situation of experience, that there be continuous activity in which he has interests for its own sake, secondly that a genuine problem develops within this situation as a stimulus to thought, third that he possesses the information and make the information needed to deal with it, fourthly that such solution occur him which he shall be responsible for developing in an orderly way, fifth that he has opportunity and occasion to test his ideas by application to make their meaning clear and discover for himself their validity." (Democracy and Education.)

Keeping in view the aforementioned ideas we can say that a good method of education should have the following steps:-

(a) The initiative should be with the children. They should propose what they actually do.

(b) Then they should be allowed to do only those things which help them build certain attitude.

(c) Only that learning should be allowed which is necessary for the proposed activity.

(d) Lastly, these activities should be properly guided so as to add to 'the subsequent stream of experience'.

These are summed up in the following 5 steps required for a method of teaching that John Dewey would propose:

(i) Activity

(ii) Problem

(iii) Data

(iv) Hypothesis

(v) Testing.

The Textbooks

Like the school and education, Dewey has no rigid views about curriculum. He believed that curriculum should reflect the social life of the child and his activities in society.

Basing his ideas on these things, Dewey has laid down the following principles in regard to the curriculum:

1. *Flexibility:* The curriculum should be flexible. It should not be pre-determined. It should be determined on the basis of the interest and experiences of the child and should be in accordance with the 'social requirements.' For a child, at an elementary school, the curriculum will be different from that of a child at the secondary school.

Curriculum at the elementary school should be based on the four-fold interests of the child as envisaged by John Dewey, "Four interests are paramount-interest (a) in conversation and communication; (b) in enquity and findings; (c) in making or construction; and (d) in artistic expression."

2. *Based on Experiences:* The curriculum must follow the "progressive organization of knowledge consisting of educative experiences and problems."

The curriculum should be so organised that it should enrich the experiences already acquired and the problems should be so set that they serve as a stimulus to the learner to add new experiences and ideas to the already existing ones. These new experiences and problems should grow out of the old ones and that is how the process should go on. Educative experience for John Dewey has a special significance. According to him, it is like a creative activity which leads to further experiences. It not only modifies the existing experiences but also affects the subsequent ones. This educative experience should be above all and the books, teacher, apparatus etc. are subordinate to it. Socio-economic conditions are taken into consideration while framing the curriculum.

3. *Organisation of the Subject:* Subjects in the curriculum should be organised according to their utility. But it is not possible to give a definite order to these subjects as their utility cannot be predetermined. Dewey's philosophy is that the knowledge acquired beforehand does not matter very much. It has to be based on the child's own experience and, therefore the importance of the subjects has to be determined in the process of life.

This is what he said in the following words:

"It is futile attempt to arrange subjects in an order beginning with one having least work and going to that of maximum value. The only maximum value that can be set up is just the process of living."

According to Dewey, neither any subject is important nor secondary; neither any futile nor important. Activities are directed by the problems of the actual life from the curriculum. He has himself said. "Men's fundamental common concern centre about food, shelter, clothing, household furnishing and the appliances commended with production, exchange and consumption."

4. Curriculum to be determined according to Instincts and Natural Capacity—According to Dewey, the curriculum should be constructed while keeping in view the innate tendencies, interest and capabilities of the child. As already stated, it should be based on present experiences. Different subjects should be drawn out of the day-to-day life and each subject be naturally co-related. They should not be taught as if they are independent studies, but in a way as to look a part of the entire process which keeps the life going. Subject matter of the curriculum should also be co-related with the actual life of the child.

Status of Teacher

What is the actual place of teacher in education has also been discussed by John Dewey. Unlike Rousseau he does not shut his eyes completely from the importance of the teacher in education. He gives an important place to teacher in his education. He treats the teacher to be the servant of the society whose duty is to lay foundation of a good social life. Therefore, the teacher should create such an atmosphere in the school that may lead to the development of the social personality of the child.

While presenting the view of Dewey in this connection, G.S. Puree writes:

"The teacher is to be a friend and a guide to the child. He is not to transmit any information or knowledge to his pupils, but he has only to arrange the situation and opportunities which may enable them to learn."

While talking about the importance of the teacher in education Dewey has said that if activities in the school are organised according to the natural interest of child, there will be no problem of discipline.

He was very much dissatisfied with the concept of discipline prevalent in his times. He has laid stress on the social discipline. He was of the view that the individual capabilities of the child can develop properly only in the society and, therefore, his conduct and discipline should be developed while keeping in view the requirements of the society. In order to maintain discipline, the school should try to create a social atmosphere. If children are allowed to take part in the collective and cooperative activities in the school, their impulses will get refined and a new type of discipline will come into being.

In other words, it can be said that Dewey believe in a discipline which emanates from the co-operation in the social life. "Out of doing things that are to produce results, and out of doing in a social and co-operative way, there is born a discipline of its own kind and type," was the real view of discipline presented by John Dewey. He thought that such a discipline will bring about character-building and training which cannot be achieved by force or imposition from outside or instructions from authorities. He also believed that all the activities of the child-intellectual, moral, social and physical can be disciplinary in effect if they are carried out in co-operation and with a definite purpose.

The teacher has to provide the proper environment that will enrich the child's experience and encourage him to perform his activities purposefully and in a co-operative manner. This will lead to development of the social attitude, social interest and habits and social will.

Dewey does not belittle the importance of order and calm in the class. On the other hand, he believed that such an atmosphere is congenial for the smooth working in the school. But this thing is to be a means and not an end in itself. He also believed that such an atmosphere will result from the proper atmosphere and work.

In short, it can be said that the main purpose of discipline according to Dewey is the cultivation in the people of social attitudes, social habits and ideals of co-operative conduct through the conjoint activities in the school which has to be organised like a community or society.

QUESTIONS

1. What is the status of John Dewey among great educationists ?
2. What are Philosophical Notions ?
3. Explain Theory of Knowledge and Mind.

6

McLuhan

A discussion of the philosophies of education would be incomplete without reference to the unique contribution of Marshall McLuhan and his observations on the effects of the media on man. A contemporary thinker, and a prolific writer, Marshall McLuhan has made a study ot the psychic and social consequences of technologies and media. In many respects, Marshall McLuhan's observations are comparable to those of Mahatma Gandhi, who in the 1930's was concerned about the effects of industrialization on India.

Mahatma Gandhi's Basic Scheme of Education was designed, among other things, as an attempt to overcome the pitfalls of industrialization, in the educational sphere. In All Men are Brothers Gandhiji writes: "I would categorically state my conviction that the mania for mass production is responsible for the world crisis. Granting for a moment that machinery may supply all the needs of humanity, still it would concentrate production in particular area, so that you would have to go about in a round-about way to regulate distribution".

Again, relegating a minor role to literacy in education, Gandhiji writes in his Autobiography, "By education, I mean an all-round drawing out of the best in child and man, body, mind and spirit... Literacy is not the end of education, not even the beginning. Literacy in itself, is no education."

Marshall McLuhan has devoted his book The Uutenberg Galaxy to an elaborate exploration of print culture and literacy in the western world, and the consequences of these on man's sensory life. He is an outspoken critic of literacy and mechanical industrialization which, he points out, are the products of the Gutenberg era of print, of Cartesian dualism, and of Newtonian physics. Modern man, according to Marshall McLuhan appears to have become merely a machine for the production and consumption of goods. He may be literate but he is not sensitive, nor truly educated and cultured in the fullest sense of the word. He may be logical and rational, yet he is often without real feeling and emotion. Mahatma Gandhi, in his Autobiography writes, "High thinking is inconstant with a complicated material life based on high speed imposed on us by mammon worship."

For teachers and educators in India, making a study of the applicability of Mahatma Gandhi's educational ideals and the adaptability of his Basic Scheme of education to the contemporary scene, a consideration of the effects of print culture and industrialization and the rigidity that these have imposed on thought and action, in the western world, according to Marshall McLuhan, would be highly relevant.

Not only industrialization, but mass production, and the distribution and sale of goods through advertising have been the subject of thorough analysis and comment by Marshall McLuhan. One of the outcomes of the Second and Third Five Year Plans in India has been the rapid growth of industrialization, and the production of goods for internal consumption as well as for foreign export. According to him, advertisements are not visible or audible but exert an influence as though by E.S.P. at a distance. No educator in India, has considered nor exposed the subtle and pervasive effect of advertising on young and tender minds, and the teacher has not noticed the competition of the advertisements in the educational process. The Mechanical Bride and Culture is Our Business expose the subtleties of advertising and their effects on society as envisaged by Marshall McLuhan.

Marshall McLuhan's observations, although paradoxical in nature, and made in a satirical vein frequently, point out that the media are not an unmixed blessing, and have a tendency to devour mankind by their psychic effects. He urges an education in perception and awareness, in order that mankind may survive their consequences. While Gandhiji was concerned about the role of education based on the economics of material poverty, McLuhan bases his observations on education and the role of a teacher in an affluent society. Like other great teachers of bygone ages, he searches beneath the surface of things and looks beyond apparent reality into the future, in his discovery of signs and signals to warn mankind. His warnings regarding the nature and the power of media are prophetic in nature and have, in many instances been substantiated by recent events. Some of Marshall McLuhan's suggestions regarding education embodying his philosophy, as gleaned from his works are given in the following section.

Educational Philosophy

His diagnosis of the present malaise in education is related to the general chaos and confusion experienced in modern life, and may be stated briefly as follows :

(1) Our educational system is outmoded. It is geared to vanishing values and old print technologies. It represents the mechanical age which gave us mass education, the age in which matter and man were manipulated; metal machines and men became parts of a great social order. Education, therefore, became part of producing people who could meet the needs of an industrial society. Compulsory education came to mean the exploitation of manpower for performing the ordinary tasks of trade and commerce, the production and marketing of goods.

(2) Most classroom teaching in schools is based on 'print' culture and the book. Teaching is visual and fragmentary, it does not attract or interest the young; they do not react to it, since they belong to the electric era which has left the age of print literacy behind; they want involvement and stimulation of all their senses, and not education that is visual and in isolation.

(3) Set patterns of educational requirements are imposed on the young; those who learn facts faster and better are considered superior. Competition still remains the main factor in mass education. Examination grades are used to categorize a person as superior or mediocre. There is no place of those who do not fit into the rigid pattern, and not much room for originality, or creativity in the regimented pattern of teaching, learning and assessment, in the majority of schools.

(4) The young today, feel bored in schools, because most of them were brought up viewing T.V. from their cradle. They are used to an environment in which there is involvement, depth, action and sensory stimulation; hence the classrooms where the lecture method interspersed with a few "audio-visual aids" now and then, fails to hold their attention. The linear logic of doing 'sums', or of tracing cause and effect in history or science leaves them untouched and uninterested.

(5) Children today gain information and learn much more outside than inside the classroom. Their education begins outside the schools and remains outside, mostly; it is acquired through television, radio, stereo, movies and tapes. They are wide awake and fully responsive to whatever they experience through these media, unrestricted and uninhibited in regard to the time, place, manner and content of learning.

(6) The child, who enters, the elementary school on the first step of the ladder of our educational system, is

really no longer a child; he has outgrown his childhood, for, from his cradle onward, he had experienced, along with all the adult members of his family, the horrors of war and violence, the hypocrisy and sham of politicians, rioting, arson, looting, assassinations, space travel, moon landings, sex stimulation, besides news of the world generally. He has experienced as much as adults through television, radio, movies and stereo. The elementary school curriculum in general therefore, is utterly remote and removed from his needs.

(7) The information available in all fields today, is greater than it has ever been before. With the present modes of instruction, which are linear, logical, visual and fragmentary, it is impossible to present such a vast amount of information to students. Information in textbooks becomes out of date almost as soon as it is published, because it increases hourly and many changes occur in all fields. Reliance on printed material alone for information, in teaching, is restrictive, apart from being out of date. The young today are alive and alert to happenings through the other media, and are often repelled by the efforts to educate them through outdated printed matter, inside the classroom.

(8) There is an absurd proliferation subjects in schools and colleges. Knowledge has been compartmentalized, and sheer specialism results in instruction by "specialists" who have little or nothing to do with knowledge in its broad sense, since they are only concerned with their own limited subject areas. The young enthusiastic learner, unaware of this narrow fragmentation in learning fields becomes confused, and soon loses interest and 'gives up'. If he has any questions, he does not know which specialist to turn to for guidance. A unified approach to knowledge is sadly lacking in our centres of learning; they appear to have become dehumanized.

(9) Just as the teaching of reading is standardized in schools, whatever the student reads is also standardized. It seems the printed page of a book is the example of a rigidly organized classroom in which the seats are all fixed in rows, the children learn the same topic at the same time, the teacher in front, and the children in rows in front, like the rows of printed lines on a page. This rigidly stirs rebellion within the children.

Aims and Objectives

(1) Liberal education is of utmost necessity in this age of automation, an education which enables the youth to participate in society in an imaginative way. An education which encourages encyclopedic learning obtained through the electronic media of programmed learning, of teaching machines, films and tapes, is advocated by Marshall McLuhan.

(2) The oral tradition of speech, of rhetoric and eloquence should be preserved, in education. An orchestration or harmony of touch, taste, sight and sound can be achieved through emphasizing words and oral learning; the oral presumes a listener and an audience, the printed, an individual's reading in isolation.

(3) The best education is that which develops critical awareness in growing minds and curbs placid and passive acceptance of factual data whose sources we imbibe without criticism.

(4) Education should provide a protection against "media fallout", which means the ill-effects of uninhibited utilization of television and other modern media. It should help them to become masters rather than slaves of the media.

(5) Instead of our goals being an interest in subjects of the curriculum, teachers should attempt to learn about the

media themselves, the pupils can be made to realize that the media have the power to devour our precious heritage of culture and values. We should aim educational efforts towards the prevention of media from swallowing our literary and cultural heritage.

Approaches and Syllabi

(1) The 'implosion' in education means, that the curriculum instead of exploding into a large number and variety of subjects, demands a growing and expanding in wards; there should be an expansion of learning in depth. Instead of teaching many different subjects, a structural study of learning and of knowledge itself, a knowledge of the world and of life itself should be introduced in schools and colleges, in a unified form.

(2) In order to cope with tremendous amount of knowledge available in the world today, the schools should enable the young to have free access to it and to utilize it However, this is impossible under the older analytic methods, because of the sheer quantity of knowledge. The only successful method of teaching, when the amount of knowledge to be acquired is so vast, would be that of pattern-recognition, through the Gestalt approach, and the unified field frame of reference, in which a person interacts within a field of psychological forces wherein memories, anticipations and purposes are included.

(3) If we wish to change the methods of teaching from the older techniques of emphasis on book learning and the visual approach, we should make use of television. Merely putting a television in the classroom is of no value whatsoever, what is needed is the conscious planning of elaborate educational programmes for the varying levels of requirements in each broad area of study. The close inter-relationship between geographical

facts, biological and anthropological studies, sociological and historical evidence and the overlapping between all areas of knowledge should be brought out through all sensory modes in television programmes so planned.

(4) Learning is accelerated through the use of the newer media, two-year olds, have learnt languages through the provision of a proper environment and use of media. Similarly Physics and Mathematics, as well as many other subject areas may be learnt speedily at a very early age by young children through the sensory field approach which comes through television, video tapes, recordings and similar media.

(5) By creating a favourable environment in learning such as Skinner created in Walden II, education need not become the painful experience it is, at present, for the young New horizons should be created and the frustration and failure of present-day educational methods avoided, involving the emotions of the learners in the learning process.

(6) Grasp and apprehension by students, in the process of learning may be stimulated by a unified sensory experience of what is being taught. All the senses will be involved in this experience and this experience can be translated into any other form of experience. Such a technique in teaching is a matter of using rationally. Real understanding of what is taught can best be brought about through electronic media which have the power of bringing about an interplay of the senses.

(7) A great revolution in teaching can be brought about by a very wide use of Telstar, teaching machines, programmed instruction and television on a massive scale. Teachers should do all they can to utilize these to the greatest extent with relevance to their teaching-learning situation.

(8) A rich oral and auditory heritage of music, drama, poetry and classical literature from cultures all over the world is made accessible to us through the media of tapes, recordings, films and movies. These are invaluable for use in education. They can be used in conjunction with printed books, paintings sculptures and other visual means. A combination of these forms of learning can bring about a new hybrid of learning, in the classroom. Such a creative use of media in the development of a hybrid innovation in the classroom will be much like that Erasmus achieved in the sixteenth century, for this pupils, in the classroom. The existing oral method was combined and used with the newly invented printed book. The rich heritage of music was thus preserved by printing it from the Elizabethan age onwards.

(9) There needs to be training in perception given in schools, a power developed which can enable one to see below the appearance of things. For example an advertisement, unlike a book is the conscious work of many intelligent minds, it is composed like a mosaic and has an iconic appeal, by glamour and repetition; the advertisement as it were does the work of brainwashing. Education should develop among the young and old alike, a resistance to the pressure that the advertising media, on television, or radio or in the newspaper or journal, exert on one's individual thought and opinion. Training in perception in the typographic is imparted in schools; Marshall McLuhan recommends that training also be imparted in the perception of the graphic and the photographic. Along with this, the power to discriminate between good music and the alluring sounds of the singing commercial with its glamorous action appeal, are also needed, in education today.

(10) The new technology, according to McLuhan, requires a new kind of education to enable us to use it. At the

same time, it also creates and provides the teacher and pupils with the means of obtaining this new kind of education. The new educational media require the teacher and pupils to master their new languages, these languages are rich and meaningful and have to be used in the process of education. They are also to be learnt through observation, perception and practical use of the new media themselves. For example, a poem, a novel or play may be studied and experienced through all the different media, the book, the radio, the movie, stereo and television, and comparison as well as contrast between the presentation and its resultant effect studied. The biases of each medium can then be discovered by studying some more instances of a similar kind.

(11) For real learning to take place, Marshall McLuhan says that environment should be free, the pupils should be able to move around freely from one room to another, and from one building to another, to learn what they please, and when and how they please. Learning thus becomes an exploration and a discovery, a process of play and of pleasure. The teacher will be responsible for the effectiveness of how and what the pupil has acquired in the process of learning,

(12) By developing the perceptions and critical awareness in children, the mass media will not have any destructive influence on their sensibilities. Their consciousness will be strengthened instead of being benumbed by the effects of the media as they are in the present times.

(13) A teacher can always use a painting or a poem in the same manner as one can use a teaching machine. Comparison and contrast of the values and ideas, intensity and insight that go into the composition of a painting or a poem can bring about a training in observation and judgment in art as well as in life McLuhan believes that the artist and the poet have a great awareness of the challenge as well as of the threat

that the electronic technologies pose to man kind. As such, their works have an importance in the teaching-learning process in schools.

(14) Art should be taught to all pupils at all levels, but not as a separate subject. To classify art as a subject, according to Marshall McLuhan, is to separate it from the other activities of mankind, because art has taken on a new meaning in this space age of information.

Role of Teacher

(1) According to Marshall McLuhan, if there is any real concern about the preservation of some of the finest and most beautiful contribution of civilization today, then teachers, scholars, intellectuals, instead of hiding in the 'ivory towers' of exclusiveness and isolation, should come out and attempt to understand and exploit the new electronic resources. Instead of allowing the electronic technologies to master and guide the thoughts and actions of people and to destroy the cultural heritage of mankind, teachers and scholars should control them and use them for the benefit of mankind. Marshall McLuhan illustrates this idea graphically in "Counterblast" as The Ivory Tower Becomes The Control Tower Of Human Navigation.

(2) The resources of the electron in media such as televisions, movies, recordings, video tapes, computers make it possible for a great deal of learning to take place for the young, outside the school. The educator may feel that he is being pushed around, or in fact pushed out of the picture, in relation to the education of the child with the school. Besides this, politicians, businessmen and other people with vested interests, also seem to have taken over the educational programmes, and exert an influence over young and old alike through the mass media. It appears, these days, in Marshall McLuhan's opinion, that mammoth

educational programmes, both national and international are being carried on by interested parties, sometimes using dubious means, and occasionally even by war and violence. Under such circumstances, the teacher feels discouraged and helpless. The only remedy is that the teacher should enlarge his role and attempt to reach out and exert his influence far beyond the walls of the classroom and the school.

(3) The teacher has to be a devoted and a dedicated person, one who knows his place and function in society. He has no personal, social or commercial ambitions, and places his personal desires behind, because he is involved and interested in his students. He is loyal to his profession. Teachers, artists and poets are the antennae of the race. They can understand the present and interpret the future. The power of human navigation should be in their hands, and they should be able to steer the path towards survival of the human race.

Leaving Midway

(1) To keep the drop-out within the school, means to involve his whole being, to give him interplay, to make him an explorer, a researcher, and to let him hunt through the new world of electronic environment provided in the school. Let him work alone or in groups seeking solutions to living problems, problems that perhaps have never been solved before or which may never have been recognized as problems before.-

(2) The student who gets flunking grades frequently becomes a dropout. He is out of touch, he cannot fall in line with other students, mass-education in which he has no individual identity has created a sense of loneliness and alienation within him. In such a case, the educator should set about the exciting work of creating a completely new kind of learning environment

in which there will be no drop-outs. Students, instead of being expected to sit rigidly according to "classroom seating plans" which are fixed for them, will be allowed to move about freely from class to class, room to room, through halls and corridors and on campus in search of knowledge and learning which is really discovery, play, research on an individual or group basis, as the student himself desires. He will have the use of electronic devices, tapes, recordings, video tapes, computers, microfilms to assist him, as and when he wishes to utilize them.

(3) In order to make education relevant to the young and to prevent them from becoming drop-outs, the impersonal and dehumanizing atmosphere of educational institutions should give way to one which is geared to their needs and problems. The long, hard road to obtaining a degree, and its alternative the draft card, both create desperation, conflict and alienation within youth. An educational system in which there is an in-depth approach to learning, a revolution in attitudes between the teacher and the taught, a recognition of the sensibilities is what is urgently needed.

QUESTIONS

1. From a reading of the 'Gutenberg Galaxy and Understanding Mediatry' to some of Marshall McLuhan's observations on the various technologies.

2. How would you interpret Marshall McLuhan's statement "The Medium is the Message?" Has it any relevance for the teacher?

3. To what extent can Marshall McLuhan's observations on the media be applicable to Indian conditions?

4. Briefly outline McLuhan's observations on education. Would any of them be useful to you as a teacher?

5. What is the role of the teacher, according to McLuhan? Is his picture of the teacher in any way similar to that of the Indian guru?

6. How do the electronic media affect man and society, in McLuhan's view? What are his suggestions regarding their use by the teacher?

7. Construct, if possible, an imaginary dialogue between Mahatma Gandhi and Marshall McLuhan, on education.

8. Keeping McLuhan's contribution in mind, write a description of Basic Education in the Electronic age.

9. Could a proper system of education help the executive from becoming a drop-out? How do you envisage this education?

10. Offer your comments and criticisms on the educational television programmes in Indian schools, and suggest some measure for enhancing their educational value.

11. Describe "education outside the classroom" in the case of the Indian student. What is the role of the movies in this education?

7

Annie Besant

Annie Besant came from an aristocratic English family. Her father was a mathematician and a classical scholar who studied philosophy. His mother was Irish, and very religious. Annie Besant had a good education from the earliest years. She read many books on religion and philosophy from her father's library. She married a clergyman, but had many doubts about the beliefs of the Christian church. After some years, she left the Christian church and become an agnostic and a Free Thinker. She joined a Socialist group and worked among the poor in the slums of London. She supported the demands for higher wages by the lower working classes. She was attracted by the teachings of Madame Balavatsky, founder of the Theosophical Society in London and become its member. Annie Besant supported the movement for the Status of Women in England.

After 1893, she made India her home. She came to India as a leader of the Theosophist movement and founded many schools and colleges on its principles, in India, She also wrote many books and pamphlets on religion, socialism, politics, education and the status of women, both in England as well as in India. During her many and fruitful years of service in India, Dr. Besant strongly supported the movement for independence, and took an active part in the freedom movement from her headquarters in Adyar, Madras.

Dr. Besant loved India. Her respect and understanding of India's religions and cultural heritage was profound. She studied Hinduism and delved deeply into its philosophy. She wrote many books and brochures on Hinduism.

Dr. Besant's support of India's national aspirations and struggle for freedom evoked much opposition from her English countrymen, but she regarded India as her adopted homeland. She strongly criticized the conduct of the British in India and openly defended India and Afghanistan against the oppressive policies of the British.

Annie Besant died in 1933, after leaving an indelible mark on India education, the fight for women's rights as well as on India's aspirations for freedom.

Faith in Faith

True religion, according to Annie Besant consists not only in one's feelings towards God but also in performing duties towards our fellow-men. A morally good man who does not believe in God at all, is in a far higher state of being than the man who believes in God and is selfish, cruel and unjust.

Theosophy : the Concept

Every great religion has two parts—a spirit and a body—so has Theosophy. (1) Knowledge of God—(2) Dogma and rites. Knowledge of God is known as Brahma Vidya and belongs equally to all great religions of the world—Hinduism, Christianity, Islamic Sufism, Judaism. No man is truly a theosophist unless he has a direct knowledge of God, which he may arrive at through any religion, or by his own earnest efforts to seek the truth.

Theosophy emphasises (a) The Unity of God who is the universal source of all existence; and (b) Universal brotherhood of man.

Theosophical Morality

Annie Besant believes that the ethics of philosophy are not formulated into any code, they consist of the highest and purest teachings of world's noblest saints, prophets and founders of religions. All that is sweet and most lofty in the world's Bibles, and all that is most inspiring and ennobling of the philosophers of all countries and religions of the world form the ethics of theosophy. If man lives by the highest principles that he can grasp, he becomes capable of appreciating the sublime. The theosophist looks up to the examples of Christ, Buddha, Rama and all great leaders. He strives to become like them.

Educational Philosophy

Dr. Besant's educational philosophy is based on the Theosophical Ideal of Education—Each child should receive an education suited to develop his particular and individual faculties. Such an education should be imparted which will make him useful as a citizen in his community and his country.

Aims and Goals

Education should draw out the child's capacities, and develop and train these capacities so that he becomes a healthy and useful member of a civilized society.

The object of such an education is:

(1) To train the body in health, vigour and grace, so that it may express the emotions with beauty, and the mind with accuracy and strength.

(2) To train the emotions to love all that is beautiful

(3) To sympathise with the joys and sorrows of others and to inspire to serve others until we love our elders as our parents, our equals as our brothers and sisters, and youngsters as our children.

(4) To find joy in sacrificing for great causes for the helpless, and compassion for those who suffer.

(5) To train and discipline the mind in right thinking, right judgment and memory.

(6) To subdue body, emotion and mind to Spirit.

In short, education should make man a good citizen of free and spiritual commonwealth of humanity.

Annie Besant divides the period of education in life, into three parts, to each of which appropriate attention should be paid.

Various Stages

First Period : 1 to 7 Years

(1) The Physical health and development of the child's body should be the chief concern of parents and the teacher. The child's entire future depends on the care bestowed on the child during the first seven years of his life. Nothing in later years can fully make up for insufficient food, or insufficient light, exercise and sleep, during this period.

(2) This is also the period for cultivating observation, for training the sense into alertness, accuracy and grasp, for training hand and finger skills of memory—especially the word-memory which is very quick and retentive in childhood. Nursery rhymes remain in the memory for life. Rhymes and poems employing succession of events, names or dates learnt in childhood, are never forgotten.

No abstract reasoning processes should be forced upon the child during this period. His attention should be directed to observation of sequences of facts but not the logical processes. The brain cells are not sufficiently inter-related to make any train of reasoning intelligible and there is no object in memorising logical sequences which are not understood by the child.

Second Period : 7-14 Years : Education in this period should be chiefly directed to the development and training of the emotions, and thus to the building of character. Histories consisting largely of biographical stories of great men of varied types, saints heroes, martyrs, political, artistic, literary leaders in every department of human life—these should inspire enthusiasm and shape the ideals of developing boys and girls. In this way character will be built and the channels of right emotions will be prepared. Thus when the great emotional rush which follows the attainment of puberty is upon the youth, that rush will find channels ready to receive it, to render it uplifting and beneficent, instead of degrading and mischievous.

Third Period: 14-21 Years : This should be the time of intellectual development of hard and strenuous mental labour. The reasoning faculty should be thoroughly trained by logic and mathematics. Specialization in some areas should prepare the youth for his future career.

The Textbooks

First Period: 1-7 Years : Tales of noble deeds and heroism should be narrated from the earliest days. Emphasis on health, physical dexterity and skills; nursery rhymes, cultivation of word-memory. Observation of sequences of facts, love of beauty arousing of sympathy for the poor and helpless.

Second Period : 7-14 Years : History and Biography, Geography, Physiography, Physics, Chemistry and Geology should be taught. Practical and laboratory work in the sciences should be included. Algebra, Geometry and Arithmetic should occupy an important place in the curriculum at this stage.

Third Period: 14-21 Years : Since this is the period of the rapid intellectual development, Logic and Mathematics should be taught intensively. The sense of duty to one's fellowmen should be taught through Civics and Social Studies. Sciences such as Biology, Physiology and Psychology should be mastered. Literature, Philosophy, Economics should occupy an important place. Various aspects of the Arts should also be included in the curriculum. Specialization in some chosen field should prepare the student for his future career in life, during this period of his education.

Propagation of Faith

Should begin with easy stories in the child's early stages of education and pass on to Metaphysics in the later years in all of the three stages, being adapted to the intelligence and understanding of the student.

Health Care

Should be all-pervading, and should be adapted in theory and practice to the physical development and needs of the growing pupil in all the three stages.

Education for All

Annie Besant writes "I look forward to a time when every child shall receive, in the national schools, the elements of a literary, scientific, artistic and technical education. No boy or girl should leave the school ignorant of our literature, or of the wonders of science. He should delight in beauty. He should also learn some definite means of bread-winning, let it be tailoring, cookery or carpentry or any trade or profession. Every pair of hands should be able to do at least some one thing well by which an honest living may be earned."

Pioneering Role

(1) Dr. Besant loved India. Her respect and understanding of India's religions and philosophies was profound. She wrote many books and pamphlets on Hinduism, as well as text books for students in Physics Chemistry, Biology and stories from the Mahabharata, as well as narratives of heroic deeds for children to read.

(2) Dr. Besant's support of India's national aspirations led her to encourage and support many innovative educational efforts. She founded many schools and colleges. The Central Hindu School and College was founded by her in 1398 in Benares. It later became the Benaras Hindu University. She also founded the Theosophical Institute at Adyar, Madras, among many others.

(3) Not only did she start the Central Hindu School and College at Benaras, she organized its debating clubs and many sports organizations. She was an excellent teacher and educational administrator, who set high standards for other teachers and organizers around her. She was admired and loved by her students and colleagues for her dedication and efficiency in educational endeavours.

(4) She took a firm stand against Child-marriage which was widely prevalent in India at that time. Students were discouraged from marrying while they were still studying, and they and their parents were made to realize that the students were not mature enough to assume adult responsibilities.

(5) She gave speeches on nationalism, freedom and social reform in schools and colleges as well as in public. This made the students realize their responsibilities to live and work for a free India.

(6) Annie Besant was an ardent promoter of Women's Education in India. She organized many groups to strive

for the furtherance of girl's schools and colleges in many parts of India where facilities did not exist, and girls and women were neglected. She worked to raise the status of girls and women through education.

(7) Due to Annie Besant's pioneering work in education, many communities, Parsi, Muslim,Christian, Arya Samaj, DevSamaj, Brahmo Samaj and others started schools for their youth on modern lines. She inspired a great deal of enthusiasm for education in India at a time when the British neglected educational betterment and expansion to fit the needs of the country, in their schemes.

(8) Dr. Besant was a strong advocate for vocational education in schools. By the end of schooling, every pupil should have learnt some trade or craft: carpentry, cooking, tailoring or any useful skill or vocation, to enable him to earn a living, at any stage in his educational career.

(9) Annie Besant strongly believed and preached that there is no such thing as racial superiority. The white races and the so-called higher castes of people are not in any way superior to other people. Domination by races and castes of people over others is totally unjustified. All people in the world are endowed with intelligence and ability, regardless of race or caste. All have a right to educational opportunity, and the amenities of life. There should be free schools established for universal free and compulsory education in India. No one should be denied the right to education, and upward mobility.

Books to Credit

While in London, Dr. Annie Besant wrote several books and pamphlets on Population, Physics, Physiology, Biology, Socialism, Status of Women.

In India, her publications include:

Education as a National Duty (Benaras, 1903)

The Education of Indian Girls (Benaras, 1906)

Principles of Education (Madras, 1915)

Education for the New Era (London, 1919)

Theosophical Education Report (Madras, 1917)

Some Lessons from the Mahabharata (Benaras, 1899)

Sri Ramachandra, the Ideal King (Benaras & London, 1901)

Hindu Ideals (Benares & London, 1904)

Sanatana Dharma: An Advanced Textbook of Hindu Religion & Ethics (Benaras, 1904)

The Universal Textbook of Religion and Morals (Adyar 1914-1915, 3 vols.)

Lectures on Political Science (Adyar, 1919)

Legends & Tales (London, 1883)

Civilization's Deadlock and the Keys (London, 1924)

Kamala Lectures: Indian Ideals in Education & Philosophy, Religion and Art (Calcutta, 1925)

World Problems of Today (London, 1925)

India Bound or Free (London & New York, 1925)

Belief in Indian Values

1. Annie Besant loved India. Her respect and understanding of India's religious heritage and culture was profound.

In an article INDIAN UNREST (London, 1910) Sir Valentine Chirol wrote "No Hindu has done so much to organize and consolidate the movement of revival as Mrs. Annie Besant, who in her Central Hindu College at Benaras, and her Theosophical Institution at Adyar, Madras has openly proclaimed her faith in the superiority of the whole Hindu system to the arrogant civilization of the West. Is it surprising that Hindus should turn their backs upon our civilization, when an Englishwoman of highly trained intellectual power comes and tells them that it is they who possess and have from all times possessed the key to supreme wisdom—that their gods, their philosophy, their morality are in a higher plane of thought than the West has ever reached?"

From this passage, we may gather that Annie Besant had two chief lines of approach to the re-awakening of India and the achievement of Independence: (1) the Religious (2) the Educational.

2. Annie Besant gave lectures and supported the Independence movement and criticized the British openly regarding their policies in India. She was opposed strongly by the British, in India as well as in England, for her critical views.

3. She was the founder of the All India Women's Conference, which attracted many Indian women, and because a strong force for women's education, Child Marriage Bill, the Sharda Act, and many other reforms affecting women and children. She was a pioneer who started many of the reforms that have given women the equality of status and rights which they enjoy today.

4. She brought about a revival in the study and application of Hindu philosophy and culture at a time when these were fading. She writes "I set myself toward showing the insufficiency of materialism as an answer to the problems of life and the immense superiority of Hinduism as a philosophy encasing an all-embracing reverence, and a science of Yoga. All these were an open road to the invisible to the ancient Rishis of India

and the East, to the saints of Christendom, to the Wisdom which included, all religions and excluded none.

5. Annie Besant lived and worked in India during the period when Dr. Rabindra Nath Tagore, Sri Aurobindo Ghosh and Mahatma Gandhi were carrying on their revolutionary ideas and ideals in the social, educational, religious and political fields. She supported their cause, and furthered their aims by her great work and noble example. She had the same great zeal and missionary endeavour for social reform, educational expression and India's freedom, as these great national leaders had.

QUESTIONS

1. What are the aims of education according to Annie Besant? How does she propose to achieve these aims?
2. "Dr. Annie Besant paved the way for many educational reforms in India." Elaborate this statement with specific instances.
3. Describe the contributions of Annie Besant to education in the later nineteenth century in India.
4. In what way did Annie Besant support the movement for the revival of Indian culture?
5. The permanent mark on Indian education made by Annie Besant would be—

   "Complete and expand the ideas that occur to you."

8

Whitehead

Dr. A.N. Whitehead was an Englishman, an educator, philosopher and mathematician. He studied philosophy, theology and classics at Cambridge and was appointed lecturer in Mathematics at the University. In 1924 he was appointed as a professor of Philosophy at Harvard, U.S.A. Bertrand Russell was his most famous student and together with him, he wrote Principles of Mathematics. He also wrote many other well-known works: Science and the Modern World, Process and Reality, Aims of Education.

Educational Philosophy

His philosophy has been called realistic and idealistic. Actually it is an active philosophy of process in which he tries to show the relationship between man and his environment—natural, social and spiritual. He claims that matter is alive and in process. He writes "The doctrine I am maintaining is that neither physical nature nor life can be understood unless we fuse them together as essential factors in the composition of "really real" things. There is a unity..... of the body—and soul into one person... Philosophy begins in wonder, and at the end when philosophic thought has done its best, the wonder remains."

Aims and Motives

According to Whitehead, education is the art of the utilization of knowledge. From the very beginning of his education, the child should experience the joy of discovery. The discovery which he has to make, is the general ideas which give an understanding of that stream of events which pass through life, which is his life. Whitehead's whole idea of education lies in the process, and methods of educating the pupil. The curriculum is not just subjects, but the manner in which it is implemented.

Practical Aspects

According to Whitehead, there is one subject matter for education and that is "Life in all its manifestations." He criticizes the traditional school for teaching ideas without meaning or application and says "Education with inert ideas is not only useless, it is above all harmful. What education has to impart is an intimate sense for the power of ideas, for the beauty of ideas, and for the structure of ideas, together with a particular body of knowledge which has peculiar reference to the life of the being possessing it."

Education is Culture and culture is an activity of thought and receptiveness to beauty and humane feeling. Scraps of information have nothing to do with it. A merely well-informed man is the most useless bore on God's earth. What we should aim at producing is men who possess both culture and expert knowledge in some special direction. "The race which does not value trained intelligence is doomed", he writes.

Education is to be imparted according to the child's readiness and stages of development.

Different Phases

The process of mental development is essentially periodic and there are three: the stage of romance, the stage of precision, the stage of generalization.

(i) Romance is the first apprehension of vividness, of novelty—the child's first contact with knowledge-through observation and experience of the world and objects around him, (ii) Precision in the stage of grammar, language and science, where width of relationships is subordinated to exactness of formulation, and (iii) Generalization as a synthesis. A return to romance with the advantage of classified ideas and relevant techniques; the final success of precise training. Education should repeat these cycles.

Curriculum—Whitehead advocates that (1) each school must develop its own curriculum, and that (2) the sequence of subjects shall be determined by the readiness, interest and abilities of the learner and the use which he will make of it. It is not true that the easier subjects should precede the harder. On the contrary, some of the hardest must come first because nature so dictates and because they are essential to life, the first intellectual task which confronts an infant is the acquirement of spoken language.... We should cease to talk nonsense about postponing the harder subjects. (4) There is not one course of study which gives general culture and another which gives special knowledge. The subjects pursued for the sale of a general education are special subjects, specially studied/On the other hand, one of the ways for encouraging general mental activity is to foster a special devotion. You may not divide the seamless coat of learning. (5) Let the main ideas which are introduced into a child's education be few and important, and let them be thrown into every combination possible. The child should make them his own and should understand their application now in the circumstances of his actual life (6) Theoretical ideas should always find important applications within the pupil's curriculum. This is not an easy doctrine to apply, but a very hard one. It contains within itself the problem of keeping knowledge alive, of preventing it from becoming inert, which is the central problem of education.

(7) Instead of teaching unity we subject children to isolated subjects like Algebra, Geometry, History—should reform their teaching. First we must make up our mind as to the quantitative aspects of the world that are simple enough to draw up the curriculum in Algebra. Graphs, maps, curves of history, study of instalments, village and town surveys these should make dull subjects into living experiences worth learning. (8) The ultimate aim of the curriculum in education should be the acquirement of STYLE. It is the most useful attainment. It pervades the whole being. The administrator with a sense of style hates waste, the engineer with a sense of style economises his material, the artisan with a sense of style prefers good work. Style is the product of careful specialist and study, is the ultimate morality of mind.

Scientific Education—A scientific education is mainly training in observing natural phenomena and in knowing and deduction of laws of the sequence of these phenomena.

There are many types of Natural phenomena and one, two or three of these can be studied at a time, because science is such a vast subject. The peculiarment of a scientific education should be that it bases thought upon first hand observation. First hand knowledge is the ultimate basis of all branches of science.

Vocational Training

In technical education we chiefly utilise knowledge for the manufacture of material products. Such a training emphasises manual skill and the coordinated action of hand and eye, as well as judgment and control of the process of construction. Judgment requires knowledge of these natural processes. Hence technical education requires scientific knowledge.

Technical education is not merely connected to science, it may be education for an artistic craft in which aesthetic appreciation and creativity are needed as well. However concreteness is the strength of technical education—abstract or vague ideas about what is to be produced, will not do. A rounded technical education, with broad as well as specific objectives can be imparted from the ages of 13 to 17 years, oral the middle and senior stages of schooling. By the age of 17 or 18 years, the student with a technical education should have a technical training and skill to make him useful to the community.

Technical education, however, is doomed if we consider it as a system of catching children young and for giving them one highly specialised manual aptitudes. Technical training should be broader than the ultimate specialisation. It should give them the power of adaptation to varying demands to suit the needs of society and the nation. The skills learnt should be flexible.

In considering the curriculum in Technical Education, Whitehead states that we should be guided by the principle of coordination of studies. The intellectual studies most closely related to manual training are various branches of science. More than one branch of science will be included, since scientific studies cannot be narrowed down to one branch alone.

Technical studies will require:

(1) Geometrical Techniques, (2) Mechanical Techniques, (3) Physical Science, (4) Biology, (5) Chemical Techniques, (6) Commerce, (7) Social Sciences.

For example, Carpentry, Steel-making, Plastics, Artistic Crafts, all require knowledge of geometrical techniques as well as Physics. Agriculture requires Biology and Chemical techniques. Cooking and Food Catering requires Biology, Physics and Chemistry.

Teaching Process

Whitehead has thrown light on many aspects of children's education and methods of teaching.

(1) Apprehension of general ideas, intellectual habits of mind and pleasurable interest in mental achievement can be taught by no form of words, however, accurately adjusted. All practical teachers know that education is a patient process of the mastery

of details minute by minute, hour by hour, day by day. There is no royal road to learning through generalizations. We must prepare ourselves to teach slowly, patiently and very carefully. (2) Do not teach too many subjects at a time, and what you teach, teach thoroughly. Do not teach dull facts and dates. Whatever interest can be attached to subject-matter, should be evoked here and now. The mind is in a perpetual state of activity, delicate, receptive, responsive to stimulus. So the powers of mind must be utilised in whatever is being taught (3) In scientific training the first thing to do with an idea is to prove it—by prove, is meant to prove the worth of the idea. Now an idea is not worth much unless the propositions in which it is embodied are true. Accordingly a teacher should realize that an essential part of the proof of an idea is the proof either by experiment or by logic, of the truth of the propositions. (4) We have to remember that the most valuable intellectual development is self-development. Teachers should stimulate the pupils to think over what is taught and to develop their own individual thoughts and ideas over and above those. Spoon-feeding should be avoided. (5) About formal discipline, Whitehead remarks that the mind is never passive and must be sharpened—whatever values the teacher wants to inculcate must be taught here and now. Value education cannot wait, and must be introduced early. Discipline must begin at the earliest stage. (6) There should be a balance between training the intellect and the character, by combining and balancing the subjects we teach and the attitudes we inculcate in children. (7) There is no conflict between a liberal and a technical education. There is no adequate technical education which is not liberal, and no liberal education which is not technical. For true education must impart both technique as well as intellectual vision. Education should be so imparted by the teacher that the pupil should turn out the pupil with something he knows well and can do well. (8) Teachers should keep their imagination alive, and teach the subjects with imagination and creativity. Routine and repetition of the usual methods should be changed imaginatively, so that the pupils should also grow into imaginative creative and thinking beings.

Evaluation and Measurement

Whitehead criticises the prevailing system of external examination of pupils very strongly. According to him (1) pupils should not be subjected to any system of external examinations. "Uniform external examinations are deadly. They kill the best part of culture. We are dealing with human minds, not with dead matter." (2) He says that no educational system is possible unless every question directly asked of a pupil at any examination is either framed or modified by the actual class-teacher in that subject. The external examiner may report on the curriculum or on the performance of the pupils, but never should be allowed to ask the pupils any question which has not been strictly supervised by the actual teacher. "No system of external examinations which aims at examining individual scholars can result in anything but educational waste", he writes. (3) Frequent tests and assignments designed by their own teachers, is the best for educating pupils. One big schedule of examinations does not have any educational value. It cannot encourage or assess curiosity, judgment, power of mastering a complicated tangle of circumstances. In short, a big schedules examination cannot measure the values or attitudes encouraged and evoked through classroom teaching, and must be abandoned in favour of informed short tests and practical assignments.

Regarding Inspection he thinks that it is the schools and not the pupils in the classroom who should be inspected.

Educational Administration

Whitehead is a forerunner of many modern ideas, which are in vogue now. Long ago, he said that each school should grant its own certificates and diplomas to its students, based on its own curriculum. The schools should be treated as individual units, and should be expected to maintain their own high standards.

Stature as Educationist

1. Whitehead is the forerunner of many educational reforms and movements, which are based on his

educational philosophy. According to him education is a process and education is what goes on in the classroom.

2. Real education is education for life and is not based on inert ideas acquired through study of subjects.

3. Subjects have no meaning unless they are taught in a connected manner relating to life situations.

4. Discipline cannot be taught separately. It must begin with intellectual discipline and mastery, in the classroom. The best discipline is self-discipline.

5. The educated man, according to him is a man with the power of thought, judgment, finer feelings and humanity. One who can apply all these to life situations.

6. He spoke out strongly against External Examinations and Inspection of pupils in the classroom.

7. He advocated that schools grant their own certificates and diplomas. Outside bodies should not certify students on the basis of examinations.

QUESTIONS

1. Discuss Dr. A.N. Whitehead's views on education. Do you have some measure of agreement with him on any of them.

2. Why does Dr. Whitehead speak out against external examinations? What are his reasons for advocating that schools grant their own certificates and diplomas?

3. Compare and contrast Dr. Whitehead's educational ideas with those of any educator of that time.

4. What are Dr. Whitehead's views on curriculum and the methods of instruction?

9

Marx

Karl Marx, the propounder of Communism was born in 1818 in Germany. He died in 1883 in London. He wrote "Das Capital' which laid the foundations of a Communist state. Interestingly, the founder of Communism did not stay in any Communist stray.

Let us have a look at his teachings.

Nature of Man. Marx's basic beliefs about the nature of man, include the following:

1. Man is a purely material being with a natural origin and destiny.
2. Man is not composed of body and mind or body and soul, mind is simply a complex function of the material body.
3. Man possessed no personal or individual freedom but finds his freedom in following the collective will of the people.

4. All knowledge of man's nature is derived from scientific sources. Philosophy and theology yield no valid knowledge about man's essence.

5. The science of man is included in the science of society.

On the basis of the above principles, it is clear that the Marxist view of the nature of society, determines what the nature of man should be. Individuals by themselves are of no significance, groups are more important.

Concept of Knowledge. The nature or origin of truth are not major problems. Knowing does not consist in an apprehension of the thing in itself but rather as a grasp of the thing as it exists for us. In the process of acquiring knowledge, man is simultaneously changed by the knowledge acquired. True knowledge of the world then, consists in more than a comprehension of isolated facts. To understand the world, the knower must perceive the relations which exist among the things of the real world and between himself and these external objects. Therefore, the Marxist theory of knowledge is neither realistic nor idealistic, but a mixture of both. Hence in Marxism, truth is not objective or absolute, it is a relative experience, which does not have set laws. There is a priority in Marxism on the scientific method of knowing. Knowledge gives power. Lenin believed the only path to truth is science, which holds the materialist point of view.

Values in Marxism. A person must be given moral training to subordinate all his interests, desires and actions to the service of the Communist State and the people, and this is possible only by inculcating certain specific values among the school children.

The Ideology

(a) *Respect for Public Property*-Teachers should uphold the principle by using stories from history, but above all by example. The teacher must strictly enforce that the child must not harm others by breaking any rules regarding respect for public property.

(b) *Respect for Authority*-It is another moral principle which children must learn early in life. This respect is not to be based upon fear of punishment, but rather the child should learn to respect the authority of the teacher and others because these people have been helpful, understanding, fair and firm.

(c) *Patriotism*-The development of a good moral character is an essential part of the Marxist education. These virtues must be expressed in an unwavering devotion to one's country. This devotion begins with love of parents, relatives, friends, the local community and then the government and the thinkers and leaders of the State—Marx, Lenin, Stalin and others.

(d) *Love and Respect for Parents, Elders and all Workers*-Patriotism is based upon the immediate attachment to parents, friends, relatives and local environment. But the love of persons is a value worth cultivating for its own sake. Stalin insisted that "people are the most valuable and most decisive capital." Education should play an important part in fostering love and respect for people. Children should be taught these noble sentiments through literature, good example and the practice of manners expressed in word and deed. This is the true essence of the basic values.

Another aspect of developing respect for persons, whether old or young, should be respect for truth and hatred of lying. From early childhood, children should learn to tell the truth and never cheat or lie, not only because these acts harm others, but because they destroy a person's integrity.

(e) *The Common Good*-The common good is ranked very high in Marxist philosophy. There is public ownership of all land, resources and instruments of production, housing, recreation and education. This is achieved through comradeship, friendship, sharing, co-operation, discharging social obligations. Respect for school property, group work and play, co-educational projects are all aspects of working for the common good.

(f) *Discipline*-In the Marxist system, discipline is a most important virtue. The school must insist on discipline not only because it is necessary for life.

(g) *The Value of Labour*-In Marxism, the true value of any object is to be measured by the amount of human labour which has been performed in its production. Labour is not to be regarded as something distasteful or unpleasant. On the other hand, labour is to be considered an expression of the highest aspiration of a human being. Labour is a matter of "honour, glory, valour and heroism". It gives man the opportunity to serve his fellow men, thus promoting the common good.

Motives and Goals

Under Marxism, the ultimate purpose of education is to strengthen the State and the building up of a classles society. This central aim provides the rationable for the curricula and the teaching methods in the schools-while teaching, the teacher must have the following goals in mind:

1. The development of knowledge in the academic area such as mathematics, sciences, foreign languages and history. Knowledge is not to be imparted or acquired for its own sake, it has a social purpose—namely the service of the state.

2. Encouraging competence in vocational fields, specially in scientific technology and in agriculture and technical trades.

3. Development of good health habits.

4. Respect for public property.

5. Development of habits of industriousness and persistence in learning.

6. Development of initiative and courage.

The Curriculum. The doctrines of Marxism are studied at all levels of school and university, as also the history of the Party and the contributions of the leaders of the State. Political economy and political education are very important subjects. Mathematics and the Sciences as well as scientific and technological education are introduced from the very earliest years at school. Geography, Biology, Geology, Astronomy, Languages and Literature are taught in the first ten years of school. Youth education and organizations provide life education and life adjustment training and experience. Humanities, arts, aesthetics are also taught, the performing arts are entirely cooperative and not competitive as sports, drama, music.

Educational Agencies. The State is the sole agency of education. There are State-sponsored nursery schools in all cities and villages where very young children of nursery age can be admitted. Mothers are encouraged to participate in productive work and labour. Mothers also actively participate in political life. These nursery schools assume the responsibility of the family in providing food, shelter, exercise and the general physical environment of home for the child. The central authority for all education is the State, which has absolute power and control of all schools. There is no decentralization of school administration or educational planning and curricula. The methods of instruction, text-books and evaluation systems are all centrally controlled and administered by the State.

There is free and compulsory education for all at all levels, and student can go to university depending on his ability, or go to technical or trade school.

The Advantages

1. Equal educational opportunities for all.
2. Free education at all levels.
3. Love of labour, hard work and respect for elders and respect for property are inculcated through education.
4. Patriotism, cooperation and sharing are instilled through education.

5. Discipline, hard work and persistence are regarded as virtues to be learnt in schools and by example.

6. Nursery and adult education are available freely to all.

The Limitations

1. Education is centrally controlled by the State in every way, hence the district or area has no say in the matter. No consideration is paid to local needs and demands, in curricula, or teaching methods.

2. The curriculum is rigid and centralized, as are the textbooks, teaching methods and evaluation techniques. There is no opportunity for the teacher to use his or her own initiative or creativity in planning, in teaching methods, evaluation etc.

3. There is an over-emphasis on scientific technology, mathematics and technical trades from the elementary school onwards. Individual creativity in fine arts is not emphasised.

4. There is an absence of academic freedom for teachers. Individual initiative is not encouraged.

QUESTIONS

1. What are Marx's basic belief ?

2. Explain the Concept of Knowledge.

3. What are the advantages of Marxist System ?

[illegible]

Nursery and [illegible]

Limitations

1. [illegible]

2. [illegible]

3. [illegible]

4. [illegible]

QUESTIONS

1. [illegible]

2. [illegible]

3. [illegible]

Part–II
Indian Thought

10

Tagore

Education has been defined as a consciously controlled process whereby changes in behaviour are produced in a person, and through him in a group. It is a gradual adjustment of the individual to the spiritual possessions of the race. Hence, education is considered to be normative in that it explores various aspects of human personality so as to prescribe a generally suitable and acceptable programme of learning which should be conducive for the attainment of its objectives and goals. However, there has been a continuous change in the nature, extent and import of these objectives which are inversely related to the meaning and reality ascribed to human nature and to the environment in which education takes place. Hence, education is in dire need of some sort of a philosophy which may provide it with direction and roots, stability and purpose.

Life is dynamic, it is a continuous change. Since education invariably occurs in a social matrix, it also acquires the same characteristic. The ideals of life are eternally at variance, due to contemporary socio-economic conditions and political ideology, and their conflict, for whatever reason, reflects itself in educational theories. Hence, as long as life is what it is, in all ages the singular aim of education had been to educate man to achieve his complete self in accordance with the concepts prevalent from time to time. Education, therefore, is a means to achieve functions of philosophy.

As the field of education has been possessed by respective philosophies as the final means of shaping the young minds toward attainment of prescribed goals, education, in this sense, is an offshoot of philosophy and it translates those desirable objectives through its inherent processes and spells out means for doing so. Ross speaks of this "inevitable tendency of the philosophers to turn into educationist" as the great philosophers of all ages and of all countries, have also been great educators. This is but logical because if one does not preach his own philosophy who else would, and the best means of preaching one's philosophy is to ensure it as an instrument of human regeneration.

Rabindranath Tagore based his philosophy of education on human regeneration. The main tenet of his philosophy is the ultimate affinity between man, nature and God. His educational philosophy is an attempt at self-realisation by means of communion with nature and God. He lays special emphasis on education as a means of self-realisation which consists in the realisation of the universal soul in one's self. According to him the fundamental purpose of education is not merely to enrich ourselves through the fulness of knowledge but also to "establish the bond of love and friendship between man and man". The spark of divinity that Tagore saw in man lends a special significance and import to his philosophy of education as it singles him out as a visionary who had his feet planted on firm ground. His philosophy is as much relevant today as it was during his time: it is a philosophy of love and compassion responsive to human hopes and despair. It is a philosophy of man in search of himself in this myriad of wonderland called universe. Man is not only the centre of this edifice but is the "measure and the sanction of all things". Tagore believes that the chief end of human life is to work for happiness of man upon this earth within the confines of nature which is his home. His philosophy of education is an elaboration of this central theme and provides ample opportunities to reconcile and resolve apparent anomalies in our day to day life. Tagore is a champion of humanity, of human values and ideals. His philosophy of education aims at producing enfranchised citizens who may hold their heads high without any fear in their hearts.

Pioneering Role

Rabindranath Tagore was one of those contemporary philosophers of education who may be called a humanist in the most strict sense of the term. His humanism is not naturalistic but is integral to the tradition of Indian humanism. His philosophy was cosmopolitan humanism of which his theory of education was a direct corollary.

Aims and Purposes

The aim of education, according to Rabindranath, was self-realisation. He was a great poet and a saint who through his imagination and insight, realised the universal soul within himself and in Nature. This realisation by every one, according to him, was the goal of education. Self-realisation means the realisation of the universal soul in one's self. Man's aim in life is to achieve this status, a process which, cannot be realised without education. Education, therefore, is integral to life. In the absence of education the individual will be deprived of self-realisation. Rabindranath did not find any incompatibility between thought and life, philosophy and education, both are inversely related and are inclusive of each other.

Rabindranath believed that every one is potentially divine and every one can realise this potentiality. Man has a spark of divinity in him which inspires him for self-attainment, self-realisation, the realisation of his true nature. Education should, therefore, provide opportunities to harness these innate potentialities. His philosophy was influenced by the great Indian traditions contained in the Gita and the Upanishads, though

Rabindranath had the added advantage of familiarity with the educational ideas prevalent in the West. Therefore, like other Indian humanists, he synthesised the ancient Vedic traditions with the modern western scientific attitude in formulating the goals of education.

Defining the aims of education Rabindranath said "the fundamental purpose of education is not merely to enrich ourselves through the fulness of knowledge but also to establish the bond of love and friendship between man and man." This shows the humanistic aim of education in his philosophy. His approach to ultimate reality was integral and therefore he believed in an inner harmony between man and nature, and nature and God. The trinity of man, Nature and God is in fact the three dimensional view of the same reality. In man again, the physical, the mental and the spiritual aspects are equally important and are internally related. Rabindranath, therefore, believed in multisided education with physical, intellectual, moral and religious overtones. He condemned the system of education "which partially exercised the intellect only to the entire neglect of the body." Education of the body in the real sense, according to him, "does not exist in play and exercise, but in applying the body systematically to some useful work". Thus, one of the aims of education, according to Rabindranath, is physical development and he gives it a special treatment and import.

Evolution and Growth

It was quite natural for Rabindranath to emphasise the role of games in the school education. Pointing out the value of physical activities in the children's education he said "even if they learnt nothing they would have had ample time for play, climbing trees, diving into ponds, plucking flowers, perpetuating thousand and one mischiefs on Mother Nature, they would have attained the nourishment of the body, happiness of mind, and the satisfaction of the natural impulses of childhood". It is the active process of familiarisation with nature, a sort of feeling it on their pulse, that is so central to his educational system. The physical fitness is the first cardinal principle in the child's development, which is possible through intimate contact with Nature.

As a poet Rabindranath well realised the life-giving value of Nature's contact with man. About this he said "I speak in very moderate terms: seven years till then let the child have nothing to do with clothes and shame. Till then let nature alone conduct the indispensable education of the savage. This is particularly relevant for the educational institutions in our society. Almost all contemporary Indian philosophers of education including Gandhi, Vivekanand, Dayanand, Aurobindo and Tagore point out the importance of setting educational institutions in natural environment so that the educands may learn by their touch with Nature. Rabindranath translated his faith in Nature by setting up his three institutions, Shantiniketan, Vishvabharti and Sriniketan in similar atmosphere.

The Cultivation

Tagore lays equal emphasis on the mental aim of education. He was critical of the prevalent system of education which laid sole emphasis on bookish learning. Condemning this tendency Tagore said "we touch the world not with our minds, but with our books. Intellectualism takes us away from nature and creates a schism between man and man as we know only the people of the books, not those of the world.. Intellectual aim of education should be the development of the intellectual faculties such as logical thinking, critical appraisal and assimilation, sharpening of sensibility and imagination. Thinking and Imagination are the two faculties which should be developed through education as they are vital for adult life". The emphasis on the education of sensibility rings a familiar note contained in the philosophy of another great poet, John Keats who drew inspiration from the immortal system of Immanual Kant who made sensibility and imagination central to his critical philosophy.

Rabindranath criticised the prevalent system of education which puts unnatural premium on memory and cramming with too little left for thinking and imagination. He said "since childhood, instead of putting all the burden on the memory, the power of thinking and the power of imagination, should also be given opportunities for free exercise."

"True education consists in knowing the use of any useful material that has been collected to know its real nature and to build along with life a real shelter for life". Education should facilitate assimilation of culture so that the educand, by means of education, is able to use it in his interaction with the environment. Explaining this aim of education, Rabindranath said "if we believe that the chief aim of education for an Indian is to initiate into the unique pursuit of infinite, then we must constantly remember that neither the education of the senses nor that of the intellect, but the education of feelings, that should receive the place of honour in our schools... our true education is possible only in the forest through intimate contact with nature and purifying austere pursuits".

Particular Objective

Tagore's approach toward aim of education was realistic. He was, however, not favourable to utilitarian aim of education which has permeated the present day philosophy of education. He objected to the imposition of the British system of education on India which has damaged the body structure of the Indian system of education to such an extent that in spite of concerted efforts since Independence nothing much could be done to minimise its influence on the ethos of Indian intelligentia. Tagore said "knowledge has two departments: one pure knowledge, and the other utilitarian knowledge, whatever is worth knowing is knowledge. It should be known equally by man and woman, not for practical utility but for the sake of knowing... the desire to know is the law of human nature."

But Rabindranath did not ignore the earning of livelihood aim of education. He appreciated the practical bias in the western system of education. Though he did not want to make education as an instrument or means for earning livelihood alone, he admitted that bread earning is a necessary part of any sound goal of education. Therefore, he said that from the very beginning such education should be imparted... that one may know what mass welfare means, and which may facilitate earning a livelihood. He emphasised that the real aim of education is to develop man and woman who may be able to fulfil the needs of the country; "one of the main aims of education is to prepare the individuals for the service as future citizens by equipping them with such skills that enable them to take up their appointed role, as well as to foster socially desirable attitudes. Tagore, however, did not give as much importance to utilitarian aim of education as was done by Gandhi who considered education as an insurance against unemployment and exploitation.

Novel Concept

Tagore's philosophy of education cannot be understood without understanding his metaphysical theory which revolves around the concept of Cosmic Man: a vision, a poet's dream which Tagore cherished and lived by. Referring to Cosmic Man as the ultimate reality Tagore said "truth is the infinite pursued by metaphysics, fact is the infinite pursued by science, while reality is the definition of the infinite which relates truth to the person. Reality is human: it is what we are conscious of, by which we are affected, that which we express". The Cosmic Man, is known by individual not by his reason or logic but through direct realisation, a sort of communion. In the words of Tagore "Reality, in all its manifestations, reveals itself in the emotional and imaginative background of our mind, we know it, not because we think of it, but because we directly feel it. It is not banished from our conscious mind". This further affirms Tagore's emphasis on the feeling aspect of human experience. He considered man more central to the scheme of things. Man is more than reason, a soul, a spirit, a finite-infinite being, an angel who seems to have lost his wings, and is now in the process of becoming.

The idea of Cosmic Man is in conformity with the message in the Gita: the message of Vishvaroopi Darshan. The cosmic man is at the back of all movements, all change, all order and system in the universe: he is the measure of everything and is central to all movement. The relation between him and Nature is panentheistic which finds meaning in the concept of God. Cosmic Man includes both Nature and God. Rabindranath admitted "I have never looked at God, Man and Nature as problems which can be considered in isolation from each other. I could never conceive of their occupying watertight compartments". Cosmic Man lives even in the humblest person, therefore, even the lowliest of the low should not suffer from personal and social neglect. The worship of the poor is the direct corollary of Tagore's vision of the Cosmic Man. He said "He is where the tiller is tilling the hard ground, where the path maker is breaking the stones. He is with them in sun and shower, and His garment is covered with dust (and sweat). Put off your holy mantle and like him come down on the dusty soil". That work is worship, was an essential tenet of Tagore's Cosmic Man, and he lived by it.

Concerning the metaphysical problem arising from assigning personality to the ultimate reality, it should be remembered that for Rabindranath personality is not something limited and mundane but unlimited and supra-mundane while in the man it is found in the first form, in Cosmic Man it may be seen in the second meaning. Elucidating this meaning of Cosmic Man he writes "This personality which is the conscious principle of oneness, the centre of relationships, is the reality... therefore the ultimate object of attainment... this world exists only in its relation to a central personality. When that centre is taken away, it falls to pieces, because a heap of abstractions, matter and force, logical symbols, and even those thinnest semblance of reality, would vanish... if the logical person in the centre to whom they are related in some harmony of reason were nowhere". He is more for the 'saguna' form of reality rather than 'nirguna' form of reality which blinds human mind and soul by its sheer brilliance.

God is the perfect person. Man is a person in an imperfect sense: he is always in the process of becoming, moving toward the attainment of his true self. He is an individual whereas God is a person. He is a Cosmic Man. He is the super person who is seen in different forms which are virtually all-inclusive. He is anthropomorphic and is endowed with human attributes which make Him intelligible to man. It is in Him that human beings share their experiences. "The relational world is for me both individual and universal. My world is mine but it is also yours... it is not in my own individual personality that Reality is contained, but in an infinite personality.

Tagore avoids the solipsistic and mentalistic tendencies inherent in the philosophy of Berkeley, as well as the pitfalls of the philosophy of Nietzsche whose Super Man is the negation of both man and reality. Tagore's idea of Cosmic Man is human, is in and through the work and toil that spells human life, is responsive to human hopes and despair, in short, is one with man, is humane.

Status of Individual

Reality according to Tagore is one in which God, Nature and Man reside in a spirit of intimate relationship. The three are, infact, three dimensions of the same reality. Man is intimately related to God and Nature. Man and Nature are but two expressions of the same Divine. Divinity is panentheistic, it runs in and through the fabric of all creation; it permeates the cosmos. In his philosophy of education, Rabindranath considers the intimate relationship of man and nature as the basis of self-realisation. His system accepts both in a spirit of mutual dependence and harmony. Nature is propitious, is conducive toward man's attainment of his spiritual and material excellence. Nature and Man are mutually amenable. Tagore says "In the west the prevalent feeling is that nature consists exclusively of inanimate things and beasts, that there is sudden unaccountable break where human nature begins. According to it, everything that is low in the scale of beings is merely Nature, and whatever has the stamp of perfection in it, intellectual and moral, is human nature... the Indian mind never had any hesitation in acknowledging its kinship with nature, its unbroken relation with all".

The intimate relationship between man and nature is the hal-mark of Indian philosophy. This relation is conceived as companionship, a permanent source of inspiration, a state of communion. A life divorced from nature cannot be a complete life, according to Tagore, even in the liberated state our relationship with Nature continues. "The soul's birth in the spiritual world does not coincide with severance of relationship with what we call nature, but freedom of relationship".

It was this firm conviction of the intimate relationship between man and nature that made Tagore emphasise so much on the natural environment in schools. He wanted that "young mind should be saturated with the idea that it has been born in a human world which is in harmony with the world around it". Even the superiority of man lies in his ability to be in union with nature, an ability which is not quite possessed by other living beings.

Human Aspects

Derived from Latin 'Homo' meaning human being, Humanism is the philosophy in which man is the measure of everything. In historical retrospect whatever had been found to be useful for human welfare has been attached with the concept of humanism such as the ideas of social welfare, scientific attitude, progress of democratic institutions and other such concepts emerging out of the process of democratisation of man and society. As a philosophy, humanism has a definite notion regarding man, his problems and universe. Greatest good of the greatest number according to democratic means is the mainstay of this social and philosophical concept. Its major contributions have been:-

(a) Belief in life in harmony with the noblest ideas and the highest values.

(b) Affirms the dignity of man.

(c) Faith in the necessity of establishing a social order based on peace, progress and democracy.

(d) Commitment to peace and a meaningful concept must have far reaching influences on the social and educational aspects of a society. The impact, in brief, is as under:-

(i) Education is considered an important part of man and society.

(ii) Education has creative role in establishing an ideal society.

(iii) Education is an agency of freedom and responsibility.

(iv) Employment-oriented education.

To sum up, man is not only the centre, he is the measure and the sanction of all things. Humanism believes that the chief end of human life is to work for happiness of man upon this earth within the confines of nature which is his home.

Pointing out the human elements in Tagore's philosophy, Humayun Kabir wrote "Rabindranath Tagore was one of the greatest humanists that the world has known. The key-note of his life was resistance to tyranny in all forms. He struggled against economic exploitation, political subjugation, social inertia and injustice, and religious intolerance and insensitiveness". These words, however, do not convey the most important aspect of Tagore as a humanist. Undoubtedly he fought for human virtues but the more important point is that he presented a humanistic philosophy and a religion of man which again were the foundation stone of a gigantic system of humanistic education.

Tagore was essentially a poet, therefore, his Humanism is generally expressed in his literature. Pointing out this facet, he writes "Humanity is the very epitome of the wide and varied universe. To know it properly is to realise the highest manifestation of Brahma since all its world wide aspect of humanity is permeated with the spirit of God. This universal greatness of humanity has truly found its triumphant poetic expression in our age in the literature of Rabindranath".

Besides literature, Tagore's Humanism is expressed by his idea of religion of man. His works Dear testimony to his unstinted emphasis upon the uniqueness of the human individual, his greatness in the world of the living, and his intimate relationship with nature and God. It was due to his Humanism that while he opposed the British, he was not against the British people. It was again this Humanism which made him work relentlessly for the establishment of a cosmopolitan educational institution in the form of Shantiniketan. His educational system is as much the embodiment of his Humanism as his literature is its expression.

Educational Process

The most important means of education, according to Tagore, is the environment of the child. The importance of natural environment has been accepted by almost all contemporary educational psychologists. It is through the natural environment that the child trains his senses by his contact with plants and trees, flowers and leaves. Education, according to Tagore, should be imparted, "in an institution where the first great lesson is the perfect union of man and nature, not only through love but through active communication, can be had unobstructed". It is only in a natural environment that the child can realise the presence of a universal soul which is the root of his existence and also that of nature. The teaching of different subjects is made natural through the intelligent utilisation of the child's environment. His knowledge of science may be helped by his observation of insects and animals, plants and training is helped by his observation and appreciation of forms and colours and movement to the development of the child's sense organs and mind. His creative powers are expressed through his contact with natural objects. His co-curricular activities in natural environment result in the development of different virtues.

Tagore regretted that, "Ours is the only country in recent history where the educational institutions stopped at their boundary walls and were dissociated from the wide world outside". Pointing out to the gulf between bookish knowledge and the child's environment, Tagore lamented that the current education does not help in making the educand either an efficient worker or a good citizen. "It is not enough for a farmer boy only to grow into a good farmer, but he should also grow into a good citizen of the country".

Besides natural environment, social environment is no less important in the development of the child, in fact it is more valuable. The social environment makes the surroundings of the children in which they fulfil their needs and drives and develop their beliefs and ideas. It is the knowledge of this environment which creates the feeling of essential unity of mankind in the child. The impact of the social environment is more explicit in the relationship between the teacher and the taught on the one hand and the educand and his companions on the other. If this relationship is based upon love, sympathy and mutual understanding, the educand adequately develops moral virtues. Every educated person should learn to play a role according to his particular qualities in the human society. The cultural environ ment again is a part of the social environment. In educational institutions this is created through co-curricular activities and cultural programmes.

The most important means of education is the medium of instruction. Almost all contemporary Indian philosophers of education pleaded for the adoption of mother-tongue as the medium of child's education. Tagore was no exception. He said, "if education does not enter into the deeper strata of the society and does not attain permanence through mingling with the living streams of the mother-tongue, then it can only become an object of temporary beauty but can never become a lasting foundation of life". India needs education on a large scale particularly technical and vocational education. Tagore realised that this is possible only through the mother-tongue. The use of English language for this purpose had been the main cause of the poor state of education in India. Unless our educational institutions adopt regional languages and national language as medium of instruction and unless sufficient books are available in these languages, the aim of universal education in India will remain a distant dream.

Besides regular teaching in educational institutions through mother-tongue, Rabindranath discovered several other important means of education. He was very much in favour of reviving the old rural institutions in the villages. He attached much educational value to community entertainments, recitals of Ramayana and Mahabharata and religious education. Besides, the community fairs organised in villages from time to time are also useful means of education. The vocational education in the villages is very much helped by the fairs. To make education mass-oriented the means of education should also be indigenous and easily available in the rural areas.

His aim of education was the most comprehensive and included all aspects of human personality, different strata of Indian society, and the world community. Thus, his plan was developed on a very comprehensive perspective. His educational plan is activity-oriented. Its aim was to develop an all-round human personality by means of co-curricular activities besides bookish knowledge. He laid emphasis on physical, mental, oral, religious matters. The curriculum in his educational institutions was not fixed but would change according to the needs of the individual, of the rural masses, of the poor people, and that of man as a member of international community. He wanted to make student-life self-reliant. His aim was to develop a sort of communion between man and Nature. Freedom was the hallmark of his system of education.

Freedom Movement

Tagore believed in complete freedom of all types—intellect, decision-making, knowledge, action and worship—which could be achieved by the practice of equanimity, harmony, and balance. Through this practice the educand could learn to distinguish between true and false, natural and artificial, relevant and irrelevant, permanent and transient, liberal and narrow, universal and individual. Thus, the educand could achieve a harmony in the true and relevant elements. Once he acquired this ability he could progress by self-guidance. This, in fact, is the real meaning of self-education based on self-realisation. Education, according to Tagore, is a progress of self-realisation which lies in the attainment of freedom where intelligence, feeling and determination worked freely. It is not the absence of control but self-control. Once it is achieved there is no danger of straying away from right path because the senses, intelligence, emotions, feelings and mental powers of the educated person are guided by his own self.

Chosen System

The ideal educational system should aim at man's perfection which means the development of all the aspects of human personality. This is the sole aim of education which again should be realised on a universal scale because an individual can realise itself by acquiring an abiding faith in the universal soul. Thus, education should lead to the realisation of universal man. It should enfranchise human beings. An enfranchised human being has the following virtues: wisdom, steadfastness, emancipation, courage of conviction, sense of discrimination, attitude of friendship and cooperation.

Tagore tried to utilise the findings of modern western educational psychology as well as the wisdom of the ancient Indian sages, in his ideal educational system with activity as its basis. It required both the educand and the educator to be always active. He fully exploited the principles of active responding and learning by doing. Learning and exercise went together. He was against the orthodox or formal discipline and punishment, as he had ardent faith that "only through freedom can man attain his fulness of growth". In his ideal system of education discipline was intrinsic and self-imposed. The educands were allowed to commit mistakes and learn through them as mistakes provide depth to the process of learning as later advocated by Norman Crowder while constructing his Branching programme as a strategy of teaching-learning process.

Tagore was against the prevalent system of evaluation. In this field also he applied the principle of self-determination. Invigilation was absolutely unnecessary and the examinees themselves took their question papers and answered them. He tried to build up an ideal educational system and experimented in all its facets such as aims, medium, means, curriculum management and co-curricular activities. One may not agree with the details of his educational system and may not call it ideal, but nevertheless, the system bears the stamp of his genius and was a bold super-structure based on a comprehensive philosophy, with the best of intentions of developing perfect men and women as citizens of the world community.

Elementary Education

Tagore's ideas about the early childhood education may be traced in his plays such as Kabuliwallah, and Home Coming where Mini and Phatak respectively play the role of a growing child, as well as in the Child's Return and, the Crescent Moon. Tagore wanted the children to grow up into a free and open world. He was convinced that in early years the child should arrive at truth through natural process spontaneously by coming into contact with things and persons. Learning for a child, according to Tagore, is explorative, active and full of joy, where the learning programme is activity-centred. Education "in play and activity precedes all else, and... was followed by training through activity and play in order to develop hardy youth" (William Cenker). Tagore also stressed on the creative and artistic aspects of learning, crafts, work and play. "Art for Tagore, is the bridge between man and the world".

In conformity with Froebal and Montessori, Tagore emphasised on learning through movement and rhythm which establishes harmony between body and mind. "... Children must express themselves with their whole bodies and... education of the body must be in contact with air, water, earth and light. The body should sway with the inner movement of the thought.

Employing the whole body, movement must accompany thoughts and emotions". (William Cenker)

Rabindranath Tagore's philosophy of education aimed at developing a system of education for human regeneration through literature, poetry, social activities and educational programmes. He was a humanist in the real sense of the term. Though not a rationalist, he believed in something higher than reason in man. He did not think science alone to be capable of delivering the human goods and, therefore, wanted to synthesise it with Vedanta. He was a nationalist yet transcended the barriers of narrow nationalism: in him the line where the two meet is invisible. As a matter of fact, the concept of internationalism finds meaning and clarity if viewed with reference to nationalism: nationalism should be the springboard to internationalism, and the two should be mutually inclusive. Short of this there shall always be gaps and contradictions.

In fact, the author has a firm belief that it was Tagore's spirit of Internationalism, so much evident in his literary works, that enabled him edge past another great poet and visionary of his time, Mohammad Iqbal, for the race toward the Nobel Prize for literature. A cursory comparison of the poems 'Where the heart is fearless and the head is held high' and 'My country, the most beautiful land', may reveal the two facets of nationalism, but whereas Tagore rises above himself, Iqbal is confounded in the shackles of narrow and parochial nationalism. To Tagore the ultimate God was the Cosmic Man, and the only aim of all the man's efforts was the realisation of God. Human regeneration was his sole aim, and the virtues such as freedom, purity, sympathy, perfection and world brotherhood. He possessed a philosophy which possessed him: the end result was one of the biggest experiments ever conducted in the field of education in contemporary India.

Life Sketch

Rabindra Nath Tagore was one of the fifteen children of Maharishi Davendra Nath Tagore. founder of Brahmo Samaj movement in Bengal. Rabindra Nath Tagore was the fourteenth child. He had six brothers and was youngest amongst brothers. Rabindra Nath Tagore was born in Calcutta on 6th May 1861.

Rabindra Nath Tagore was allergic to formal system of education. He had most of his education in his home at Calcutta through private tutors and private readings. For higher education. Rabindra Nath was sent to Bengal Academy but he was soon fed up with the rigid and lifeless education imparted there. He developed aversion for it and he left Bengal Academy. In 1877, he was sent to England to get education in Law, but, there too he did not complete this education and returned to India without getting the degree.

At the age of 8, he started composing verses and very early in life, he started writing for the Bengali magazines. Gradually love of learning increased by leaps and bounds in him and he wrote many stories, novels and poems. This earned him world wide reputation. He came to be affectionately called as Gurudev.

Rabindra Nath Tagore was married and had children. One of his children died during his life time and this shook him.

In 1913, Rabindra Nath Tagore was the first Indian to have won Nobel prize for literature for his work "Gitanjali". The same year Calcutta University adored him with the degree of D. Litt. In 1915, the Indian government adored him with knighthood which he returned after the notorious Jallianwala Bagh incident in 1919.

Dr. Rabindra Nath Tagore attended M.A. English Classes at the University of Oxford. He travelled widely. He went to Japan, Europe and USA. He had his own philosophy of life and education. To put this into practice, in 1921 he established the famous Vishwa Bharti at Shantiniketan Railway Station. Bolpar, about 140 miles from Calcutta? Vishwa Bharti is now a famous university and is a seat of learning of Indian philosophy and arts. He remained associated with it for nearly 20 years till his death on May 9 (some say May 6) 1941.

Tagore was a philosopher, poet, novelist, dramatist, short story writer, actor, painter and prophet all rolled into one. He enriched Bengali and English languages. He loved humanity and man was divine for him. His works are read all over the world. He has given to us classics.

1. Rabindranath Tagore was married at the age of 18 years to Mrinalini.
2. Tagore had five children three daughters and two sons. Two of them (one son and one daughter) died before they were 13 years. Tagore remained in grief.
3. His wife died in 1902.
4. Tagore started his school in 1901 at Shantiniketan with five teachers and five students.

Educational Philosophy

Concept of Reality/God : Tagore says. "I have never looked at God, Man and Nature as problems which can be considered in isolation from each other. I could never conceive of their occupying watertight compartment."

Therefore his philosophy presents an integral picture of God, man and nature. He says, "My mind is used to look at reality as an integral whole is being understood of course, that I am referring to the wholeness of the spirit not to material unity."

God is a postulate. It is axiomatic reality. No proofs for the existence of God are needed.

Man is always incomplete. He feels completeness only when he comes in touch with nature. But still he does not get complete satisfaction. "Our satisfaction in Nature, though real, is still incomplete. It is a satisfaction of our empirical ego. But we have our higher self which finds contentment only in infinite."

There are moral grounds for the existence of God. There is no such thing as 'personality of God.' Relationship between God and man must be that of joy and affection.

Independent reality is also self or self is also regarded as independent reality. To him, the independence of self is necessary for Reality as a whole, to quote Dr. S.P. Chaube. In Gitanjali, Tagore describe 'God' and 'man' as two separate realities floating 'at will'. It is true that the human self derives its contents from its affinity with the infinite. But his affinity does not imply that it is not free to have its own individual experiences. Therefore, Tagore does not like to undermine the independence of the self by making it entirely subsequent to the still of God. He believes that self has power to work on its own initiative as well. Reality thus means two things:

(a) Existence of God.

(b) Independence of self.

Concept of Man : He had his own way of looking at man and life was well versed in the teachings of Vedas and Upanishads. For him, supreme is all blissful and the cosmos and the individual as manifestation of the blissful asked of supreme reality. Everything in this world is harmonious and beautiful. Man's life is a saga of discovering and establishing this harmony between his own personality and the universal person and the supreme person. Harmony, beauty and bliss or ananda are the bay votes of his philosophy and approach to life.

Tagore recognises absolute blisship between Man and Nature. And he says, "When a man does not realise his kinship with the world of nature, he lives in a prison house whose walls are alien to him." Man is indispensable element of Reality. Man and nature are independent. There is active communication between the two.

Man occupies a place of pride in universe. He gives high status to man. God himself may be considered in terms of humanity. "Reality is human." "Truth is human." We rank Tagore as humanist of first rank because he gives man the highest place within the phenomena of the world. Even ultimate Reality is depicted in human terms.

Concept of Mind : It is that of psychic mind. He believes in consciousness and he believes in raising it above the level of lower desires by austerity, but by healthy preoccupation with social or intellectual activity.

Theory of Knowledge : Opportunity for self-expression should be provided. This will develop creative faculties.

Values : His views on values are known from his views on ethics. To him, highest ethical ideal must satisfy the whole of human nature. Therefore he regards moral discrimination as an essential part of human nature. He says:

"The life of an animal is immoral, for it is aware only of immediate present, The life of a man can be immoral but it cannot be immoral, it must have a moral basis."

Moral ideas have influenced the course of civilization. Moral values are highest values. Morality makes us conscious of our personality as man.

Tagore also accepts humanistic values and attitude.

He criticises ego and the egoistic man.

Tagore does not reject pleasure but he does mean that it must be regulated by the higher or spiritual nature of man. Seeking of pleasure should never be the only value to cherished by man. Tagore accepts worldly values. Since he wants to live on amongst man, he believes in a life of action and to transcend himself beyond worldly wants. He also believes in freedom but not absolute freedom.

Different Aspects

Tagore is an individualist, idealist, humanist—all these rolled into one, we shall examine him from these angles.

Tagore as Individualist : Tagore was out and out an, individualist. He believed in the right and freedom of the individual to shape his life as the individual desired. Everyone knows that no two individuals are alike-so why bind all of them with the same rope? It was thus in the development of the individual that Tagore wanted the unity of the mankind. With the development of the individual that Tagore wanted the unity of the mankind. With the development of the individual the Creator will be realised by the individual. Some of us are likely to misunderstand Tagore. The development of individual is compatible with the growth of the social units! This is not to be forgotten.

Harmony with All Things : The basic principle of the philosophy of Tagore is "harmony with all things," harmony with nature, harmony with human surroundings and harmony in international relations. The highest education is that which does not merely give us information but our life in harmony with all existence. Education system should be in tune with the young growing life. He saw harmony between nature and man, man and man.

Tagore as Naturalist : Tagore's naturalism is based on the Indian belief in fundamental unity of creation and man's kinship with nature. The essential fact is that this world has a vital meaning for us and we have to know it, we cannot ignore it, we have to establish a contact with it. This way, we shall be happy. When a man does not realise his kinship with the world. Tagore says, "He lives in a prison house whose walls are alien to him." He loved nature immensely—the moon, the stars, the hills. Nature had deeply moved him-had stirred the poet in him. He stood inspired by the flowers, trees, fruits. And for its freshness, beauty of form and colour, nature attracts the child and develops his love of freedom. So know nature, realise your relationship with it.

Tagore's Humanism : According to Dr. R.L. Ahuja, the humanism of Tagore, has two aspects: the actuality of individual joy and suffering, and the reality of a world-culture of humanity as its background. He worked unwearingly, to relieve the distress due to flood and famine in his own villages of Bengal. Equally untiringly did he endeavour to spread to the four corners of the world the message of the coming together of the races of mankind of universal humanity.

Tagore as Spiritualist (Spiritualism of Tagore) : Tagore's naturalism as described above, paves the way for spiritualism. Music is an aid to the process, he started the Shantiniketan school to give spiritual culture to Indians. His belief was that every Indian should attain spiritual perfection.

(i) *Tagore's Conception of Universe is Purely Human.* All values have their origin in man. Truth is realised through man; Beauty is felt as such by man. He says, "Reality is human and even Truth is human."

(ii) *Tagore's Conception of God is also Human.* To quote him, "He is there where the tiller is tilling the hard ground and where the pathmaker is breaking stone. This is the high point in Tagore's philosophy."

Tagore and Cultural Cosmopolitanism or Internationalism : Rabindranath Tagore was an internationalist. He looked at the world as a whole. He was for unity of mankind and its brotherhood. He hated distinctions made on caste, creed, sex. He was for the unity of soul between East and West. Thus in conformity with his culture and philosophy, he advocated a synthesis between East and West, so that the East should give its best to the West and in return assimilate the best that Western civilization gives it. He faced the both-East and West. He was grateful to both—East and West. His University is "Vishwa Bharti". It is very much international.

Tagore Believe in Truth, Beauty, Peace and Non-violence : He was also a lover of art, painting and music.

Belief in Spontaneous Expression and Creativity : He never wanted to curb this. This again supports the first point in the philosophy—individualism. This forms the high mark of his educational philosophy which is now to follow:

The Backdrop

His educational philosophy sprang up from two sources:

(a) hatred towards school.

(b) love of nature.

To quote, "Tagore's philosophy of education is, therefore, a result of the memory of his school days, when the school resembled an educational factory, lifeless, colourless, dissociated from the context of universe, within base white walls staring like the eye balls of the dead.

His contributions revolve round the two above.

Concept of Education : Education to be real must be of the whole man of the emotions and the sense as much as of the intellect. Man in his fullness, said Tagore, is not limited by the individual but overflows in his community. And so in his school, along with training in individual initiative and self-reliance, equal emphasis was laid on community service.

Nor is education a plant that can be made to grow as an exotic variety in the hot house. If it does not strike roots in the soil and adapt itself to the natural environments, it has little value for the people as a whole.

In short, education according to Tagore meant development of the individual. It meant enrichment of personality and education should be Indian one and not borrowed from the West.

Aims of Education : The aims of education according to Tagore are:

(1) *Emancipation and Perfection of Man.* About this Tagore says, "The highest education is that which does not merely give us information but makes our life in harmony with all existence." He aims at the emancipation of man from all kinds of bondages. He aims at a perfection not only that of body or mind but also that of soul. It is the fullest growth and freedom of soul. In

order to achieve that aim in his endeavours he makes education as broad based as possible.

(2) *Unity of Truth.* Another object of education, according to Tagore, was that of giving man the unity of truth. He says that physical, intellectual and spiritual life are one and we must give this idea to the children. This way harmony will prevail and when we do not do this, there is break between the intellectual, physical and spiritual life.

(3) Moral Development of the child is the third aim of education according to Tagore. Tagore attached far more significance to moral values in education than for mere results of science which produced a system and physical power.

(4) Education should develop international outlook is another aim.

(5) *Education should be Creative.* Tagore does not want education to be mere informative but desires that it should be creative also. He says, "The great use of education is not merely to collect facts, but to know man and to make oneself known to man."

(6) *Physical Development.* Tagore always believed that a healthy mind lived in a healthy body. Therefore physical development of the child is a must. This is possible only through some physical activities like swimming, diving in ponds, climbing on trees, plucking fruits etc. A healthy diet was also prescribed.

The Curriculum : Tagore was a naturalist and also an idealist and he wants things of beauty and nice virtues to be taught in the curriculum. He lays stress on those subjects which make a child full and rich in knowledge. He also wants them to appreciate truth, beauty and goodness. This guides us towards the curriculum. Subjects recommended by him to be taught are: History, geography, nature study, language, science. Activities or finer subjects will include music, art, poetry, dancing, dramatics.

He was very particular about Music and Drama. Music is essence of life and drama releases the children's tensions and anxieties.

Vishwa Bharti is known the world over for its wide and varied studies, hobbies and cultural refinements.

Methodology : Rabindranath Tagore does not believe in routine methods of teaching. He broke new ground in the methodology of teaching. His belief is not in routine methods of teaching. Even at the outset, to quote Dr. R.S. Main, when he opened his new school, he declared that the ordinary routine methods of teaching were not to be expected in his institution. To quota Tagore, "Those who still require an artificial method of feeding in their lessons, who need constant watching and goading from their teachers will find themselves out of place in Vishwa Bharti." He rejected mechanical methods of teaching. These methods were uninspiring. Tagore wanted the boys to progress at their own rate without being goaded by others. Tagore points out, "When I was young I gave up learning and ran away from my lessons. That saved me and I owe all that I possess today to that courageous step taken when I was young. I fled the classes which gave the instructions, but which did not inspire. One thing I have gained, a sensitivity to the touch of life and of nature who speak to me."

What then is his method?

It is clear that his method of teaching is method of freedom in teaching as well as learning and, therefore, does not like the lessons being forced upon the children.

Secondly, it is activity method. He wants teaching-learning to be a joyous adventure, full of thrills, wonders, surprises. It could be Heuristic approach. Let the child find out through activity. It is also sense training through and through. It is also naturalness in teaching. School is not to be a factory and learning has got to be enjoyable.

His approach is Gestalt approach. He believes that children learn their lessons with the aid of their whole body and mind, with all the senses fully active and eager. He thus believes whole methods of teaching rather than part methods.

He also believes the child's mind is quite sensitive and it will pick up things of its own.

And to quote him, "Teaching while walking is the best method of education."

The Discipline : Tagore does not want that we should be harsh to children. They should be treated with all sympathy and consideration. Discipline was never, in fact, a serious problem for Tagore.

Tagore says that if the atmosphere is good, discipline problems will not arise. It is only control that breeds in scandals and indiscipline. So where there is freedom, no question of indiscipline. He also believes in self-discipline. He wants children to experiment but not in undisciplined manner.

Tagore recognizes that the boys are full of enthusiasm and when they find opportunities for self expression, they may be little uncontrollable. He could rather enjoy the children expressing themselves freely in their outbursts of playful spirit which may seem uncontrollable, but not tolerate the repression of the child with no freedom to expand. Therefore, after analysing the psychological cause of indiscipline, he gave the children unrestricted freedom to do whatever they liked. This way many psychological complexes are eliminated and "naughtiness" seldom occurs.

Tagore wants us to understand the natural inclinations of children. Then those are to be stimulated and encouraged because he believes that it is out of this encouragement that true freedom of man emerges.

He gave much freedom to children in his school. He tried to arouse their interest in the various aspects of universe in a natural manner and not only through class teaching.

Tagore is against the so—called traditional school discipline because it does not take into consideration the individual interests and abilities. About the traditional school, Tagore says,

"It is a manufactory designed for finding out uniform results. It follows an imaginary straight line of the average in digging its channel of education. But life's line is not straight line."

Social traditions should not be imposed on children. According to S.P. Chaube, they interfere with their national freedom.

Tagore believes in self-imposed discipline. In Shantiniketan, he made a provision for boys 'own' court of justice wherein all breaches of conduct were dealt with.

Role of Teacher : Role of teacher is important. He is the Guru. He is to guide the students. He is to keep them on the track. He is also to keep in contact with them. Teacher is also to remain learner throughout his life. He who fails as a learner, fails as a teacher.

Tagore says, "A teacher can never truly teach unless he is learning himself. A lamp can never light another lamp unless it continues to burn its own flame. The teacher who has come to the end of his subject, who has no living traffic with his knowledge, but merely repeats his lessons to his students can only load their minds, he cannot quicken them. Truth not only must inform but also inspire......."

Tagore wants that the teacher should try to understand the relationship between their subjects and the human life and the same should be brought home to the students as well.

Vishwa Bharti University

Vishwa Bharti University at Shantiniketan : To give his ideas and ideals a practical shape, Tagore founded what is now known as Vishwa Bharti University at Shantiniketan (Rly. Station Bolpar in West Bengal). It is an international university for Tagore believed in internationalism very much. Vishwa Bharti means a place where universal knowledge is given or gathered. Infact, Vishwa Bharti University has grown out of an ashram founded by father (Maharishi Dabendra Nath Tagore of the Brahmo Samaj Fame) of R.N. Tagore in 1863. Since 1921, it is recognised as a university. It is said that India needs more such type of universities.

Why of Shantiniketan? The Vishwa Bharti University at Shantiniketan was opened with the following aims:

(i) To bring learned people from East and West together.

(ii) To promote internationalism.

(iii) To help Indians create.

Tagore said that our knowledge was second-hand knowledge. There was nothing original in it. At Shantiniketan, all freedom will be given to create.

(iv) Lastly to provide for the fullest development of man.

According to Dr. S.P. Chaube, Tagore had three main purposes in establishing the Vishwa Bharati. He has described these as follows:

1. To teach the different cultures of the East, especially those that originated in India or found shelter within her stores.
2. To establish the Institute of 'Rural Reconstruction' in order to lay the foundation of a happy, contended and human life in villages and lastly.
3. To seek to establish a living relationship between East and West, to promote inter-cultural, inter-racial amity

and understanding and fulfil the highest mission of the present age—the unification of mankind.

Select Disciplines

1. Vidya Bhawan is school of research. Here research is carried on in all languages and in Indian Philosophy.
2. Patha Bhawan (Just ordinary school).
3. Teacher's College.
4. Music and Drawing School (Kala Bhawan).
5. Hindu Bhawan.
6. Industrial Training School.

Various Elements

1. It is located in natural surroundings.
2. Classes are held in the open under the trees.
3. More stress is laid on teaching and learning of music, art, drama, poetry.
4. Unlike Gandhiji, Tagore did not lay much stress on manual work. He stressed on something fine and delicate. He did not reject gradual work altogether.
5. Individual attention is paid to each and every student.
6. Students themselves make rules and run the university.
7. Atmosphere is homely, prayers are sung, and due stress and place is given to extracurricular activities:

In fact, what Tagore said is fully practised here. Students work hard here.

The Assessment

1. Religion and religious education were neglected by Tagore.
2. He was much influenced by Nature. According to him man and nature have original integration.
3. Love for nature does not make Tagore a Naturalist. He was basically an idealist and remained so.
4. He condemned British system of education and gave to us his own fresh system of education.
5. To quote H.B. Mukherjee, "Tagore was the greatest prophet of educational renaissance in modern India. He waged a careless battle to uphold the highest educational ideal before the country and conducted educational experiments at his own institution which made them living symbols of what an ideal should be."

Impact on Education

Tagore was the youngest son of Maharshi Devendranath and the grandson of Dwarikanath Tagore. He was born in 1861 in Calcutta. His family was famous for its progressive and enlightened views. He was taught Upnishads, Astronomy and Sanskrit by his father. In the school he was not able to adjust to the dead routine and its lifeless teaching. He, then, left the conventional studies and was sent to England in 1877 to study law. But, the study of law did not suit his taste and temperament. He developed interest in English Literature. He started writing for Bengali periodicals. After having stayed at London University for three months he returned to India and continued his writing work. His first collection of poems was published when he was only twenty. In 1901 he established a school at Bolpur which in 1921 became the famous Vishwabharati, an international university. In 1909 his. "Geetanjali" was published which in its English edition appeared in 1912. This was a turning point in his life as he was awarded the Nobel Prize for literature for this in

1913. He was on the side of the national leaders in the struggle for freedom from imperialist rule in India. He had renounced his title of "knighthood" in protest against the repression by the British government in India. Then, he devoted himself to the furtherance of the cause of education in India.

Tagore was a great humanist. He had a great faith in humanity. He believed and propagated that all men on this earth are alike in the eye of God who alone is the source of man and nature. He emphasized that there is unity between man and man, and also between man and nature. He said that every human being had the right to shape his life in his own way. Human dignity, his individuality and inner potentiality must be given due regard and full opportunity for development. In this way, he was an individualist.

Tagore was a Vedantist. He believed that all living beings are a manifestation of Brahama (God) though not in the perfect form. Human life, to him, was a continuous struggle for reaching nearer and nearer to perfection and realization of Brahama (God). All living beings having a common source of origin and a common ending in Brahma represent a grand unity, unity of origin and purpose. Superiority of any individual on the basis of caste, race, religion, country, etc, was denied by him. He said that the doctrine of special creation is out of date. No culture is superior or inferior to any other one. All are born equal. He believed that spiritual unity was reigning supreme over all human and non-human living beings.

New Trends

On account of the children having sensitive receptivity, sub-consciously they learn many things from nature. The lessons from nature influence the mind without strain and have a lasting impression on the mind. He was pained to find that in city schools, nature, the greatest of all teachers, is thwarted at every step by the human teacher. Nature, the unseen educator, should, therefore, be given a free hand in educating children according to her own principles; what she alone can do can never be done by anybody else. Education in nature is knowledge through direct experience. Such knowledge is not only first hand but is also accurate and vivid. The direct experience stimulates more observation, experimentation and reasoning, while knowledge from books is second hand, dull and is passively assimilated.

Besides the physical and intellectual development of children by education in nature, they have the education in sympathy. "The highest education is that which does not merely give us information but makes our life in harmony with existence. Thus harmony is possible through the realisation of our kinship with all the forces and phenomena of the universe".

For education, he said, there should be a place where men have gathered for the highest end of life in the peace of nature, where life is not merely mediative but full in its activities, where men aspire to realise man's world as God's kingdom; they must aspire to be the citizens of the world. It should be a place where the young and the old, the teacher and the students sit at the same table to partake of their daily food and the food of their eternal life. He founded a school, which was not imposed upon the children by autocratic authorities. It was impressed upon their minds that it was their own world, upon which their life should fully and freely react. Freedom of mind, heart and will are the governing features of Tagore's institution—"The Shantiniketan".

Tagore wanted an equilibrium of the 'Natural' and the civilized forces in man. The art of education, according to him, should consist in training the child, to inhibit all those impulses that are anti-social. "For our perfection we have to be vitally savage and mentally civilized, we should have the gift to be natural with nature and human with human society." It was why he suggested that besides communion with nature there should be communion of man with man. This would enable them to learn social behaviour and cooperation in educational activities.

Tagore also advocated freedom for children. He was convinced that "only through freedom can man attain his fulness of growth". Freedom and joy are the key words of his educational philosophy.

QUESTIONS

1. Tagore was the forerunner of humanism in India. Discuss.
2. Evaluate Tagore's philosophy of education.
3. Briefly discuss the aims of educational philosophy according to Tagore.
4. What is the status of teacher in Tagore's educational philosophy.
5. Tagore's contribution to education presents practical synthesis of individual and social ideals in education. Discuss.
6. Tagore based his philosophy of education on human regeneration. Discuss.
7. Discuss physical development aims as seen by Tagore.
8. Tagore and utilitarian aim. Discuss.
9. Discuss major concept of Tagore's humanism and its relevance to education.
10. Place of environment in child's education according to Tagore. Discuss.
11. Place of medium of instruction in Tagore's system of education.

11

Gandhiji

"There is no such thing as Gandhism and I do not want to leave any sect after me. I do not claim to have originated any new principle or doctrine. I have simply tried in my own way to apply the eternal truths to our daily life and problems. The opinions I have formed and the conclusions I have arrived at are not final. I have nothing to teach to the world. Truth and non-violence are as old as the hills. All I have done is to try my experiments in both on as vast a scale as I could do." Yet Gandhi insists that "there is no 'ism' about it."

A Great Life

Mohan Das Karam Chand Gandhi was born on October 2, 1869 at Porbandar, Kathiawar, Gujarat. His father was the Diwan of Rajkot. Gandhi's mother was a very courteous and kind hearted lady. Gandhiji was married with Kasturba at the age of 13 years. He passed the Matriculation Examination as an ordinary student. In the same year he was sent to England by sea voyage for studying Law where he spent three years and nine months as a student. On 10th June 1891, Gandhiji passed the Law Examination and returned to India as a Barrister. He practised law for some time, but did not do well here. In 1893, Gandhiji went to South Africa as a legal adviser where he resisted for twenty years the inhuman treatment of the British Government against the Indian subjects in a non-violent way. After his return from South Africa in 1915, he started a non-violent struggle against the British rule in India. In 1917 he established Sabarmati Ashram at Ahmedabad for propagating Harijan uplift, Village industries, other social reforms and launching creative programmes for national uplift. Not only this, in 1921, he launched his world famous non-violent civil disobedience movement against the British Government. Side by side, the Indian National Congress passed a resolution for complete independence. At this the English Government in India was forced to sign a pact known as 'Gandhi-Irwin Pact' to start negotiations for the independence of India. Accordingly Gandhiji went to England to participate in the Round Table Conference, but nothing came out of that and the British Government in India continued its reign of terror in India. In 1942 Gandhiji was arrested and sent to jail. On his release from jail, he gave a 'Quit India' call to the British Government. The struggle for independence flared up tremendously and the whole country rose in revolt against the alien rule. The British Government tried to crush the movement with cruelty and terror but later started negotiations for some agreement. Finally, on 15th August 1947 the British left India and declared its independence. Soon the country was enveloped into the fire of communal riots resulting in heavy loss of life and property. Gandhiji tried his best to pacify and stop this terrible carnage. He died on 30 January 1948.

The Ideology

Gandhi's philosophy is based on Idealism. He believes in God implicitly. The soul is the part of a bigger entity. Just as sunrays in the Sun which is absolute and one whole, so are the individual persons, innumerable, yet the same soul pervades in them. Reality for him is unity in diversity.

Significant Aspects

Truth: is the means to God realisation which is the ultimate aim of life. Reality for Gandhi is one and all encompassing. God is life, truth and light. He is Love. He is the supreme God. "God is Truth i.e. Satya, and 'Satya' cannot be destroyed. The ultimate aim of one's life should be the realisation of God".

Non-violence: According to Gandhi devotion to truth can only be practised through devotion and strict adherence to Ahimsa. To him Truth and Ahimsa are the two sides of the same coin. "Ahimsa is complete absence of ill-will against all that lives. In its dynamic condition, it means conscious suffering. Non-violence in its active form is goodwill toward all life. It is pure life. "Ahimsa is the means, Truth the end."

Fearlessness: "Fearlessness connotes freedom from all external fear—fear of disease, bodily injury and death, or dispossession, of losing ones nearest and dearest, of losing reputation or giving offence, and so on."

Satyagraha: Satyagraha is change of heart by self-suffering, by adherence to truth and non-violence. The "doctrine came to mean vindication of truth not by inflicting suffering on the opponent but on one's self."

Educational Philosophy

Gandhi's philosophy of education is a dynamic concept. It provides for the fulfilment of man's needs, biological, sociological and psychological. He believed that education should bring about the development of the whole man. Such a thing can happen only when a man has his basic needs fulfilled.

Green had remarked that Pestalozzi was the starting point of modern educational theory. This may be true as far as western education is concerned. An impartial study of Gandhi's educational teachings will reveal that he is the starting point of the modern educational theory and practice in the East.

The Perception

Education, according to Gandhi, is a means to draw out the best from the child and the man, physically, intellectually and spiritually, Education should not confine itself to the teaching of 3 Rs. According to Gandhiji, teaching of 3 Rs, is neither the beginning nor the end of education. He paid greater attention toward the personality of the educand. He, in fact, intended at the balanced development of the child, physically, psychologically and intellectually, to enable him to achieve the ultimate aim, i.e. Truth.

He has expressed his thoughts about education in the 'Harijan' of 31st July, 1937 in the following words:

"As a nation, we are so backward in education that we cannot hope to fulfil our obligation to the nation in this respect in a given time during this generation, if this programme is to depend on money. I have, therefore, made bold, even at the risk of losing reputation for constructive ability to suggest that education should be self-supporting. By education I mean an all-round drawing out of the best in child and man—body, mind and spirit. Literacy is not the end of education nor even the beginning. It is only one of the means whereby man and woman can be educated. Literacy in itself is no education. I would, therefore, begin the child's education by teaching it a useful handicraft and enabling it to produce from the moment it begins its training. Thus, every school can be made self-supporting, the condition being that the state take over the manufacture of those schools." Gandhi called it Basic Education.

The Fundamentals

(1) From seven to fourteen years of age, education of each child should be free, compulsory and universal.

(2) The medium of instruction should be mother-tongue.

(3) There should be no place for English in the education of a child.

(4) Mere literacy cannot be equated with education.

(5) Education should develop human values in the child.

(6) Education should develop all the powers of child according to the community of which he is an integral part.

(7) Education should achieve the harmonious development of child's body, mind, heart and soul.

(8) Education should employ some craft as a medium of education so that the child gains economic self-reliance for his life.

(9) All education should be imparted through some productive craft or industry and a useful correlation should be established with that industry.

(10) Education of all subjects should be imparted through some local crafts or productive work.

(11) The industry should be such that the child is able to achieve gainful work experience through practical work.

(12) Education should be made self-supporting through some productive work.

(13) Education should lead to economic independence and self-reliance for livelihood.

(14) School should be a place of activity where the child gets busy in various experiments and gains newer and newer experiences bringing forth new researches.

(15) Education should create useful, responsible and dynamic citizens.

The Definition

"Literacy is neither the beginning nor the end of education. This is only a means through which man or woman can be educated. By education I mean an all-round drawing out the best in child's and man's body, mind and spirit."

High Goals

Immediate Aims

Vocational Aim: Education for self-reliance, should be job-oriented to act as a safeguard against economic exploitation. Education should be self-supporting.

Cultural Aim: "I consider the cultural aspect of education as more essential than its academic aspect. Culture is the main foundation and an essential spirit of education. Hence, all types of human activities should bear the imprint of culture and refinement."

Perfect Development Aim: "The real education is that which fully develops the body, mind and soul of children."

Moral or Character Development Aim: "I have always given top position to culture, to heart and character development in the process of education. I consider character building as the main and essential basis of educational development."

Liberation Aim: Education should liberate body, mind and soul. By liberation he meant liberation from economic, social, political and natural slavery, as well as that of the soul from worldly pursuit and to devote itself to higher forms of spiritual living.

Ultimate Aim

Gandhi wished every child to grow into a divine human being by realising Godliness in his self. "Self-realisation is the summum bonum of life and education."

The Textbooks

The curriculum of Gandhi's system of education has been constructed with the definite view of achieving the aims and objectives laid down by him. His scheme of education is known as 'Basic Scheme of Education.' It aimed at the development of intellectual, physical and spiritual powers of a child in the best possible manner and make him grow into a whole man. With this point of view, he has suggested the teaching of the following subjects in his scheme of education:-

1. *Basic Craft:* Education should be craft-centred and, therefore, teaching of craft has a primary place in Gandhiji's system of education. This craft should be related to the local conditions of life and society.
2. *Mother-tongue:* Gandhiji has stressed on the teaching of the mother-tongue, because it is effective instrument for the expression and communication of ideas and acquisition of knowledge. The mother-tongue is to be used as the medium of instruction in these schools.
3. *Arithmetic:* This is very useful subject for the day-to-day life.
4. Social studies.
5. *General Sciences:* This branch of subject shall include teaching of Nature study, Botany, Zoology, Phraseology, Chemistry, Hygiene and Physical education.
6. Art and music.
7. Domestic science for girls.

Instructional Approach

Gandhiji lays stress on the following principles in his methods of teaching:-

(1) To achieve mental development, training of senses and parts of the body should be given.

(2) Reading should precede the teaching of writing.

(3) Before teaching of alphabets, art training should be given.

(4) More opportunities should be given to learning by doing.

(5) Encouragement should be given to learning by experience.

(6) Correlation should be established in the teaching methods and learning experiences.

In addition to the above, Gandhi emphasised the need of co-curricular activities, planning, realistic experiences, initiative and sense of individual responsibility to be associated with the craft-centred teaching methods.

The Discipline

1. Discipline should not be imposed.

2. Create conditions for self-discipline.

3. Stress on cooperation, hence craft-centred education. Craft should be related to local conditions.

4. *Social Discipline*. Education should build up ideal citizens capable of shouldering social responsibilities with success.

Distinct Features

1. Ideal of world citizenship.
2. Free and compulsory education.
3. Mother-tongue to be the medium of instruction.
4. Well equipped teachers.

Elementary Education

Gandhiji had appointed a committee under Dr. Zakir Hussian in 1937 to draw up a scheme of education for free India. Nai Taleem or Basic Education was the outcome of these deliberations. The committee observed that "we feel very strongly the necessity for some organisation of pre-school education for children between the ages of three to seven years... it will go a long way forward helping the pre-school child to get a better home training than he gets now." However, the scheme initially aimed only for those children in the given age group who were either disadvantaged or,/whose mothers went for work: more of a welfare measure. But the present day concept of pre-school, or early childhood education, goes far beyond that and covers all children of the said age group as a matter of necessity because the rate of intellectual development is at the highest acceleration during the child's early years, and education must capitalise on that. It was in 1944 when Gandhiji returned from jail, that he realised that the education of the child below seven, as earlier envisaged by Basic Education, cannot be neglected as it is an important stage in the period of human growth. It led to the emergence of Pre-Basic Education, which was experimented at Sevagram Ashram in 1945 under the supervision of Smt. Shanta Narulkar.

Stages of the Programme

(a) Stage 1: Conception to birth.

(b) Stage 2: Birth to two and a half years.

(c) Stage 3: 2½ years to 4 years.

(d) Stage 4: 4 years to 7 years.

Essentials of Pre-basic Education : According to Gandhiji, Pre-Basic education in its fullest sense is the education of children under seven for a development of all their faculties, conducted by the school teachers in cooperation with the parents and the community in school, in the home and in the village.

Essentials of Pre-Basic Education, therefore, be considered as under-

(a) The teacher and parents should cooperate in carrying out the education of young children.

(b) The home where the child is born and lives, influences him and that becomes the first centre of his education and learning.

(c) Pre-school education must not be expensive so that it can reach the millions in the villages.

(d) A child has to be active, creative and playful. He has to learn to do something through the medium of play.

(e) Though the child in pre-school cannot be self-sufficient or self-supporting, an attempt should be made to develop this quality. Self-sufficiency, according to Gandhiji, is an attitude of mind. One must not be a parasite.

Stages of Learning : As seen above, the Pre-Basic has four stages of learning spread over from conception to 7 years of age where basic education takes over. As a matter of fact, the first two stages are the real pre-school learning. In the first two stages, i.e., conception to 2½ years of age, it is all between the mother and the child where "opportunities are provided to the mothers to learn more about new and scientific trends and methods of child rearing, health, and hygiene, and mother craft. Children are given custodial

care and medical attention." The scheme still smacks of a welfare slant without showing any awareness of early interventions, environmental manipulation, and home stimulation, to enable a child to learn, as the stress is more on the care component rather than on education. Hence, a damp squib.

The next two stages, i.e., stages 3 and 4, from the age of 2½ to 7 years of age, cover an active period of learning where the children are left free so that an atmosphere is created toward doing something (how vague). They get full freedom to act, to move about, are free to choose their own activities, and a teacher only supervises so that a child handles the learning material correctly and effectively. Gandhiji's concept of early childhood education, therefore, upholds the principles of activity and freedom, manual work, and art and craft. It, however, lacks the sophistication and refinement of new learning techniques and procedures, as later envisaged by the missionary movement of early childhood care and education (ECCE).

Aims of Pre-Basic Education : The aim of the Pre-Basic education was "to cultivate good habits, character, cleanliness (personal and communal), discipline, good speech, self-expression, development of body and mind, and self-adaptation."

Programme Planning

(a) Community singing.

(b) Clean-up, personal and communal.

(c) Work play activity which included climbing the trees by using bamboo-made ladders; walking on a coconut tree trunk bridge and keep the body in balance; swinging with ropes; playing water games; playing with old tennis and rubber balls.

Free-Choice Activity Period: This included free choice, different types of play with educative apparatus-creative or constructive play, experimental play, imaginative and initiative play, picture making, clay modelling, picture book reading, cutting and pasting. Using apparatus bricks, blocks, cubes, sand, water, clay, tins and boxes of different sizes, funnel, bottles, wood hammer, saw and nails, dolls, toy cooking utensils, picture books, small boards, pieces of coloured chalks, paper paints, brush, scissors, old magazines, glue, beads, shells, toy measuring scale and some Montessori and Froebel apparatus.

The Evaluation

1. Psychologically, socially and biologically sound.
2. Emphasis on manual work.
3. Opportunities for self-expression.
4. Provision for affection and self-respect.
5. Pedagogically sound educational theory.
6. Combination of Naturalism, Pragmatism and Idealism.

Gandhiji's contribution to education is unique. He was the first Indian who advocated a scheme of education based upon the essential values of Indian culture and civilization. The methods and techniques advocated by him and the environment he prescribed revolutionised Indian thinking and way of living. At heart he was devoted to Idealism. He wanted to translate his ideals and values into practice. His philosophy of education is a harmonious blending of Idealism, Naturalism and Pragmatism. It may be noted that there is no inherent conflict between the three philosophies. They are contributory to one another. Idealism is the base of Gandhiji's philosophy whereas Naturalism and Pragmatism help translating that philosophy into practice. Gandhi advocated the ideals of truth, non-violence and moral values to achieve the ultimate truth of self-realisation. He is a devotee of Naturalism when he speaks about the development of the child according to his nature, and he becomes a Pragmatist when he advocates learning by doing and learning by experience. All these lead to an integration, so essential to effective education and development of the total personality. Dr. M.S. Patel remarked," The real greatness of Gandhiji as an educational philosopher consists in the fact that the dominant tendencies of Naturalism, Idealism and Pragmatism are not separate and independent in his philosophy, but they fuse into a unity, giving rise to a theory of education which would suit the needs of the day and satisfy the loftiest aspirations of the human soul."

Past Experiences

It was in January 1948 that M.K. Gandhi died. Much water has flown in Jhelum since then. More than 55 years have passed. Yet the ideas which he gave to us are still fresh and will continue to inspire us for the years to come because Gandhi was not a small man. Gandhi was a genius and had a multi-coloured and faceted personality.

Gandhiji, the Father for us or of the Indian Nation, the apostle of Truth and Non-violence was born at Porbander in Kathiawar. His full name was Mohandas Karam Chand Gandhi. Mohandas was indeed a Karamyogi and that was his plus point. What he said or preached, he did.

M.K. Gandhi did Law from U.K. He started practice in Bombay but cases took him to South Africa where he spent lot of time. He led many movements there. His experiences in England, South Africa and in India made him bitter against the British rule. What he did for the liberation of the country after his return to India in 1915 at the age of 45 plus is known to all of us. We cannot repay his debt.

Other than being a politician, he was an educationist also. He gave to us his own system of education which is popularly called as Basic Scheme or Basic Education. In this question, we are concerned with his educational philosophy and background of it.

There are three important elements in the background of his educational philosophy:

1. Gandhi's philosophy of life.
2. His dissatisfaction with British system of education.
3. His educational experiments at Tolstoy Farm, Sabarmati Ashram and at Sewagram Ashram at Wardha. We shall mention in brief these three points here:

Salient Features

(a) He had firm faith in God. God is the creator. God is the ultimate reality according to Gandhi.

(b) Lover of Truth. He had absolute faith in Truth. In fact God is Truth and Truth is God. He was a seeker of Truth. He wanted everyone to idealise truth.

(c) Non-violence. This is a new element in his personality and philosophy. Absolute non-violence. It was his creed and he lived upto it. Non-violence is a weapon of the strong and not of the weak.

(d) Satyagraha. If you want to achieve something, suffer for it. It is the application of Non-violence or Ahimsa. If you want to be a satyagrahi then you have to live in discipline.

(e) Love for all, for all humanity.

(f) Gandhi believed in the dignity of labour. He worked with his own hands and compelled people to do so. It purified the spirit.

Rejection of Western Pattern

Long before he came to India, Gandhi had come to realise that the British system of education did not suit Indians or the

Indian socio-economic conditions. Teeming millions of Indians were wrought in ignorance, superstition, inertia and illiteracy. The education which the British were providing was bookish and examination ridden. There was hardly any scope for originality. The education was in a nutshell related to life. It made Indians foreigners in one's own home.

New Experiments

Very few people know that Gandhi had four sons. He never educated his sons in the British system of education. He educated them in his own way. He started experiments in education while he was in Africa. His first farm is known as Tolstoy farm (Gandhi was influenced by Russian story writer Leo Tolstoy) near Johansburg in South Africa. That was the year 1905. And when he came to India, his educational experiments continued at Sabarmati Ashram (Gujarat) and at Wardha (Sewagram Ashram). In these Ashrams, the inmates, living and working together, adopted certain codes. All the inmates were to work with their hands. There was no servant. Every job was performed by the inmates. Gandhi found that manual work has great virtues in its trait. One can earn and learn and can also be self-sufficient.

These experiments encouraged him to put forward the important principle of the educational philosophy: Education through a craft and self-sufficient education. This is how his educational philosophy took shape.

Impact of Ideology

Concept of Education. Education is not literacy. This is a point which should be understood once for all.

Gandhiji defined education thus, "By education I mean an all round drawing out of the best in child and man-body, mind and spirit." Through education, Gandhiji wanted to develop the whole personality and he wanted to ensure all round development.

The British education was only intellect centered. Gandhi was concerned with body and spirit as well. And education should draw out the best. "True Education", says Gandhiji, "is that which draws out and stimulates the spiritual, intellectual and physical faculties of children."

Educational Objectives

Aims of education are implied in the very meanings of education. He has given two sets of aims-viz. immediate and ultimate aims of education.

Ultimate aim of education is identical with the goal of life, which is 'Self-realisation'. Self-realisation is the realisation of the self proper. True education should result not in the material gains but in spiritual uplift.

Gandhiji laid great stress on religious education which teaches fundamental virtues of truth, love, justice and non-violence. According to Gandhiji, "Life without religion is life without principles." Gandhiji is also of the opinion that God could be achieved not by returning into jungles but by living in a society and serving it. He preferred to call a student "Brahmchari", a searcher after God.

Self-realisation can take place through self-control, character and abstinence. Immediate aims, include 'bread and butter aims', the cultural aim, the harmonious development of all powers, the moral or character development aim, and sociological aim.

Bread and Butter Aims. This is also called utilitarian aim. It is due to this aim that he gave the principle of 'self-supporting education.' The educated should not only be made capable of earning his own livelihood in later life after school but also during the schooling. The child must be an earning unit who must be self-sufficient right from the beginning of his education. This aim is really an important aim of even modern education. No education can command the respect of the society if it does not enable its citizens to be economically efficient.

Cultural Aim. Cultural aim refers to the refinement of the personality. Mere knowledge is not enough. Education should lead to that quality of mind which may be reflected in daily conduct. Speech, behaviour and manner must be refined. Culture brings in humility and frankness. Education should not take Indian children away from its own culture. There is a need of synthesising cultures so that one could inherit world cultures. This aim enables the students to assimilate and appreciate other cultures.

Harmonious Development Aim. Harmonious development or perfection of nature is another aim that Gandhiji advocates. Harmoniously developed person is that who adjusts to his life and environment. He laid greater emphasis on the development of 3 H's i.e. Head, Heart and Hand than on 3R's i.e. reading, writing and arithmetic. Present system of education leads to unbalanced development.

Moral or Character Building Aim. It is the chief aim of education. The central purpose of education is to build character. If choice is to be made between character and other things in life, then everything else can be subordinate to the former.

Man must be a man of word. He must be ready to do something for the humanity at the first call to his conscience.

Sociological Aim or Training for Citizenship. Gandhiji reconciled the individual and social aim of education. In democracy the first slogan is 'Educate your Masters.' Thus Gandhiji advocated 'Universal education.' Every member of this Samaj should be educated so that he could uplift it. He must have qualities of a good citizen. Essential qualities are—spirit of courage, self-sacrifice and industry.

Gandhian curriculum includes following subjects:

1. Basic craft which may be agriculture or spinning and weaving or cardboard work and metal work.

2. Mother tongue both as a language and as medium of instruction.

3. Arithmetic/Mathematics: More emphasis is to be laid on numerical and geometrical problems connected with craft and commonly life.
4. Social Studies.
5. General Science.
6. Drawing, Painting and Music.
7. Domestic science for girls at higher stages. At lower stages same for boys and girls.

The Basic school curriculum is supposed to be a comprehensive one, covering all aspects of child's life.

In the Handbook for Teachers of Basic schools, K.G. Saiyidain wrote on Basic school curriculum.

The framers of basic scheme or education have tried to make the syllabus coherent. This was organised around three centres:

(i) The child's physical environment.

(ii) The child's social environment.

(iii) The child's craft work.

The Child's Physical Environment: The child must know his physical environment. This helps him to adjust. The curriculum of basic school concerns itself with the study of the physical environment and aims at giving the child not only knowledge but a proper orientation towards it.

As such Physical sciences, Biological sciences, Hygiene and Geography, Astronomy are to be included in the syllabus to cover the physical environment of the child.

The Child's Social Environment: This section of the curriculum has been broadly named as "Social Studies."

This way you understand the interaction of groups, socio-economic and cultural life is also understood.

Craft Work: Education round and through a craft is perhaps the outstanding feature of basic scheme of Gandhiji. All subjects of curriculum are integrally related to craft.

Basic education curriculum thus means three things:

(a) Craft

(b) General Science.

(c) Social Studies.

(d) Special emphasis on mother tongue. Mother tongue is to be used as medium of instruction at all levels of Basic Education.

(e) Drawing: It is a medium of expression. It helps in developing aesthetic sense. It has utilisation value.

(f) Knowledge of mathematics. It is a must in any curriculum.

Teaching Methods

Gandhiji favoured teaching through physical and mental activities. Activity is the starting point of his methods of teaching. Gandhiji advocated education through a basic craft. Correlated knowledge should be given through a craft. This way of teaching has a number of advantages. Craft suits the nature of the child and is also socially useful being productive and all education is to be in mother tongue of the child.

Perhaps the things have got jumbled up in the para given above. The main points about methods of teaching are:

(a) Activity method or learning by self-experience. This way learning is very effective.

(b) Education through a craft. This has been repeatedly stressed that all education is to be through a craft. All subjects are to be woven round it.

(c) Correlation principle or Cross-subject principle is to be followed. Knowledge is one and as much should be given as one. There should be correlation with craft and with environment. Correlation should be natural and spontaneous. It should not be forced. Only expert teachers can do it.

(d) Questioning method can be applied.

(e) All education is to be in mother-tongue. It is easier to learn.

Disciplining Oneself

Gandhian concept of discipline was that of discipline through self-control. It has to be Voluntary discipline. It has to be self-discipline. This is possible if you lead a life of self-restraint and self-sacrifice. This discipline is achieved through non-violent conduct of life. With Gandhi, non-violence was an article of faith.

Secondly, we have to work on a craft. That work is possible only when we have social discipline-otherwise not. He believed in social discipline also. That will make ideal citizens.

Teacher's Status

Gandhiji had given to us Basic Scheme of Education or "Nai Talim" as he was tempted to call it. An ordinary teacher just does not fit into his scheme of education. In order to implement Basic Education, a special brand of teachers was required. He defined the duties of a teacher:

"The teacher has to enable the students to understand the distinctions and qualities implied in various things. If the student does not learn to distinguish between things, there will be no difference between him and the machine. Man is a thinking animal. Therefore during the study period, we should be able to distinguish between truth and untruth, sweet and harsh language and clean and dirty things." The teacher must have those qualities which he wants to promote in children. Gandhiji believed that students learnt more from the personality of a teacher than from books and lectures.

Gandhiji wanted the teacher to be one with his students. Gandhiji did not mean that students should imitate their teacher blindly. He gave full freedom to students. He recommends that the teacher should urge the students to think and ponder over everything told before they decide to follow a course of action.

Teacher therefore has role to play in Gandhian Education. The teacher should be a virtuous person and should be able to establish a heart to heart contact with the students.

Ascertaining Nature

Mahatma Gandhi was a unique personality. He was an idealist, naturalist—and a pragmatist—all rolled into one. He was a rare human being. In brief, we describe all the three facets of his wonderful personality.

An Idealist: Gandhi was an idealist and this is evident from the following points:

1. Gandhi believed in God. To Gandhi, God is the ultimate reality.

2. Gandhi believed in absolute values. There is such a thing known as truth, beauty and goodness. Gandhi always spoke the truth.

3. Non-violence was a creed with Gandhi as an idealist. He was ready to die for this ideal. Non-violence was a weapon of the strong.

4. His was a life of sacrifice.
5. Gandhi believed in earning one's own living. He loved to work with his own hands.
6. He believed in morality. Idealist only think of moral and religious education. Morality should be practised.
7. Gandhi was broad-minded in religious views. He was tolerant of all other religions and views.
8. His life was his message. Whatever he preached he practised. He set example before others to emulate.

A Naturalist

1. Gandhi believed that the nature of the child was good. Gandhi was simply following Rousseau.
2. Gandhi wanted that education should be child centered. He gave due importance to the child. The nature of the child is that the child is active. The child cannot sit still. The interests of the child must also be taken into consideration. We should not bore the child with lectures.
3. The child be free. Gandhi believed in the freedom of the child.
4. Natural Surroundings: Gandhiji wanted children to be educated in natural surroundings. The atmosphere should not be restricted.
5. Gandhi had his ashrams in open places. This very fact is reflected in his education. Let village children be educated in villages. This gives them the first hand experience.

A Pragmatist : The word Pragmatism has been derived from Greek word 'Pragma' which means action. It is an American

School of Philosophy. Charles Pierce, William James and John Dewey are its founders. They believe in action and not in contemplation, and for them, reality is changing. There is no such thing as absolute values.

Let us now examine Gandhi and his philosophy in the light of the above para.

Gandhi comes out as a pragmatic thinker. Gandhi believed in action. This is reflected in his "Satyagrahas". That way Gandhi was a real Karamyogi.

Gandhi did not believe in verbal education. His scheme of education is based on activity. The craft centered education is pragmatic education. It is also self-supporting education.

Gandhi believed in learning by doing. It is activity all the way. Activity, expression and construction are the fundamental principles of their teaching methods. Gandhi was a democrat. He believed in the freedom of man.

Learning should be in co-operation with the society. It cannot take place in isolation.

So we can conclude that Gandhi was an idealist, naturalist and pragmatist-all rolled into one.

Basic Education

M.K. Gandhi was not a theoretical person. Whatever he propounded as an educational philosopher was reflected in his scheme of education known as Basic Education or Bunyadi Shiksha or Nai Talim. This shows that Gandhi was educationist in true sense. He was a practical man. We shall now make ourselves familiar with Gandhian System of Education known as Basic Education or as Wardha Scheme because it was 'born' at Wardha (Maharashtra).

In April 1935, Gandhiji founded what is called Sevagram Ashram, a village with an ideal 13 miles from Wardha towards the Nagpur side. It was here that Basic Education was born in October 1937 at a Conference convened by the Mahatma which was attended by the then leading educationist of the country. The following four resolutions were passed and these in themselves comprise Basic Education or Bunyadi Shiksha or Nai Talim. Those are:

1. That education be free and compulsory for all children between age group 7-14, i.e., for eight years.
2. That the medium of instruction be the mother tongue.
3. That the process of education throughout this period should centre round some form of manual work, and that all other abilities to be developed or training to be given should, as far as possible, be integrally related to the central handicraft chosen with due regard to the environment of the child.
4. That this system of education will be gradually able to cover the remuneration of teachers i.e., a self-sufficient scheme. Gandhiji was not bothered about the school building.

Later Zakir Hussain Committee drafted the syllabus for said scheme and submitted it on December 2, 1937.

To sum up, Mahatma Gandhi's educational theory was determined by the following factors:

(a) His educational experiments.

(b) His philosophy of life.

(c) His dissatisfaction with the prevailing system of education.

(d) Gandhiji's conviction that salvation of India lay in educated Indians.

Basic system of education is a national system of education in extent, scope and administration. It possesses the following distinguishing features:

Free and Compulsory Education : This resolution meant that education must be free and compulsory for all boys and girls between the age of 7-14 irrespective of caste or creed. As a concession, however, girls, if their guardians so desired, could be withdrawn from the school after their twelfth year. In all, a child will spend 8 years at school and during these eight years, the child will come up to the level of traditional matriculation minus English. Mahatma Gandhi was convinced that what a child learnt in traditional schools in ten years will learn in eight years except English, which according to him was not required. This will also effect a saving of two years and the knowledge which the child will get in Basic schools will be solid one and related to the life of the child. It was the duty of the state to provide free and compulsory education to children.

Medium of Instruction : Mahatma Gandhi emphasised the mother tongue of the child both as a subject of study and as medium of instruction. In his own words, "It has been my conviction that Indian parents who train their children to think and talk in English from their infancy betray their children and country." He was of the opinion that the greatest defect in the existing system of education was the foreign medium of instruction. Learning through mother tongue has several advantages:

(i) Language is an essential tool of thought. We can think best in our own language. It is difficult to think critically and clearly in a foreign language.

(ii) Teaching through mother tongue meant saving of time also.

(iii) Having mother tongue as medium of instruction will make the child national minded and patriotic.

(iv) If education is carried out in mother tongue, parents also can help their children a lot in studies.

(v) It is economical. We do not have to employ English language teachers in our schools.

(vi) By having mother tongue as medium, tendency to learn things by rote learning is curbed. It is an obvious psychological advantage. There is no undue strain on the minds of little children.

(vii) It leads to quickness in conservation.

(viii) Children can appreciate things including others' views, better in their own language.

The Craft Centredness : As per the original resolution, education is to be provided through a craft or some purposeful activity. This craft or activity is to serve as the nucleus of all education or all other types of instruction. In fact, this clause i.e. education through a craft gave a special status to basic education. The development of body and mind which Gandhiji aimed at was possible only through a craft and not otherwise. There are numerous advantages of this or it has been found out that craft centred education is (i) psychologically, (ii) sociologically, and (iii) physically sound.

As a result of exercise one becomes physically sound. A healthy mind exists in a healthy body. We get able citizens. Craft is in agreement with child's psychology. The child is active. When he works on a craft, he feels satisfied. Further it gives concrete shape to abstract knowledge.

Sociologically, craft is useful in teaching live and let one live. It teaches one co-operation.

Let us see in detail how craft is Physically, Psychologically and Sociologically sound.

Physical Aspect of Craft : It is good to develop children physically. These days we are having intellectual giants but very weak people on the physical side. In fact the healthy mind will exist only in healthy bodies and not otherwise. Physically healthy inhabitants are an asset. Able bodies citizens are all the more needed in a country which is threatened by the enemies. During these years after freedom, we have become so lethargic or have kept ourselves busy with intellectual pursuits that the very thought of enemy attacking us sends a chill down our spine. We get nervous breakdown and the business community especially runs for their lives. Education through activity or work or craft, thus, has numerous advantages. It will strengthen the muscles and build resistance power and stamina of the child and will keep numerous diseases away. Good physique also means less temptation to commit a crime as the power of resistance is much more.

Psychological Aspects : The introduction of craft in education is psychologically sound because of the following reasons:

(i) It is in agreement with child's psychology. The child is active. He likes to do things and roam about. It is simply criminal on our part to make him sit at a place or in a corner for hours together and bore him with what we call teaching in an attempt to put into his little brain alt which is bookish and dry. Education through craft is based on the psychological principle of learning by doing.

(ii) Education through craft makes education interesting. Children get added pleasure if they can produce something of their own as a result of their own efforts.

(iii) Abstract thoughts are hard to learn. Learning by doing and through a craft, gives those ideas concrete shape and children learn quickly.

(iv) Craft suits children of all levels of intelligence. It appeals particularly to children of low intelligence. They will be enable to do something worthwhile in school instead of sitting like dump driven cattle and going home blank.

(v) Craft gives confidence to children in the sense of the success which they achieve while doing a work.

(vi) Craft work releases the children from the tyranny of hooks. They feel happy and refreshed while working. Being a book-worm sometimes affects one's health badly.

(vii) Through craft, children will also be sublimating their instincts and it will keep them mentally healthy and alert.

(viii) Lastly, one more principle which makes the introduction of craft in education psychologically sound is the principle of transfer of training. While educating through a craft we are going to instill many habits like cleanliness, orderliness, honesty, truthfulness etc. in our students. They are bound to transfer these habits picked up during their school age into the other spheres of life later when they grow up.

Sociological Aspects

(i) We shall teach them the principle of live and let live. One for all and all for one.

(ii) Through craft, we shall teach them the dignity of labour. Self help is the best help. That babu type mentality must disappear and this way it can go. Teaching through craft be all the more stressed during the year 11-14 because it is here that children feel enchanted by the white collared professions and shirk manual work.

(iii) When all work together, barriers of caste, creed and religion amongst different human beings disappear. It will bring in kinship and solidarity. We shall not grow in isolation and be ready to help one another in time of need. It diminishes social prejudices.

(iv) It will teach us cooperation.

That is why craft is to form vehicle of all education. It is not present system of education plus a craft but education through craft. The former approach means that we want to give training in a special trade. It has not to be understood like that. Mahatma Gandhi suggested two crafts i.e. Agriculture and Spinning and Weaving for education.

Self-sufficiency : To Gandhiji, self-sufficiency was the acid test of basic education. It may be noted that the traditional system of education being costly did not appeal to Gandhiji and that was why he laid stress on the fact that his system of education should be self-sufficient i.e., the students do not have to pay anything for their education. The salaries of the teachers would be met by selling the produce which we get as a result of work on the craft. Every student will also get something i.e., mid-day meal and two uniforms of khadi in a year. Naturally everybody would run for such type of education. By working on craft, children can pay in kind and that could be the only fees for their education. Gandhiji was never worried about the building of the school. He considered it a responsibility of the society to provide shelter for its children. By working for one another and for their benefit, children will learn the importance of money. It will also teach them to be economical and will also tell them that it is sin to exploit the poor ones. This type of approach will also prepare the individual for life. Further, it will also help us in realising Gandhiji's objective of educating each and every Indian.

Correlated Teaching : Mahatma Gandhi wanted all education to be imparted through craft. He had suggested two crafts for the purpose i.e. agriculture and spinning and weaving. He wanted to present knowledge as a whole, as an integrated whole. He never wanted to pigeon hole it or give it in the shape of air-tight compartments. He wanted to relate knowledge to life and also correlated teaching to craft as the centre of education and the only means of doing so. Other advantages of correlated teaching are:

(i) It makes education easier.

(ii) It raises the standard of education.

(iii) It makes the subject interesting.

(iv) It checks and reduces note learning, and

(v) It increases love of environment in the child and makes him a good citizen.

A.B. Solanki has tried hand to tell us about the concept etc of correlation in his book, "This Technique of Correlation in Basic Education." He has given us various types of correlation i.e. Unilaterai, Bilateral and Multilateral type of correlation. There is another classification and which is more realistic and comprehensible viz. natural and forced correlation. About this we shall talk more when we come to criticism part of this aspect.

Creed of Non-violence : Mahatma Gandhi was sick of the communal and international strife. He wanted to create a generation who knew to live in harmony and was based on mutual love, regard and admiration for members of different communities. He wanted to create a generation who should believe in non-violence and that was possible only when we taught that to little children from the very beginning. He saw that it could be realised through basic education.

Ideal of Citizenship : Gandhiji (as a corollary to the above feature) wanted to make children ideal citizens of the country. After all, a child of today is a potential citizen or citizen of tomorrow. He must know his duties and rights, responsibilities and privileges. In the set up of pre-partition days, education in this direction was not given i.e. education to develop civic sense was completely ignored. Through basic education, he wanted to make children right type of citizens.

Basic Education and Teacher : In the traditional system of education, the teacher has got hardly anything to do at his own initiative except to follow and finish the rigid syllabus laid own for him by somebody else, sometimes not connected with education at all. There is little that the teacher can do on his own. His schedule is tight and his hands are full. In basic education, the things are the other way round. There is ample scope for experimentation. This system will keep the teacher active and will compel him to do something. Other than this, Gandhiji assigned to the teacher position of great responsibility and importance. The chief concern of the teacher is moral training or character building of the child and that only could make us a strong nation. The teacher is expected to be a selfless worker and ready to suffer consciously to any extent for truth and non-violence.

Bright Prospects

1. There is more of elasticity and variety in it.
2. It is child centred education.
3. Basic Education is not text-book ridden. To be precise, Gandhiji was dead against the use of text-books in basic education.
4. There is no importance of formal examinations. Day-to-day work of the child is to be assessed. It has radically changed the concept of evaluation in modern education.

This system was accepted as the National System of Education immediately after independence. And Shri G. Ramachandran has rightly called it the most dynamic educational concept in Indian educational history.

What Makes Basic Education Basic? It is indeed a very relevant question which needs an answer. Gandhiji's system of education is basic because of the following reasons:

(i) The word 'Basic' is derived from the word 'Base' which means the foundation of a thing on which the entire superstructure rests.

(ii) Gandhiji's system is basic because this much education is mere fundamental to individual's survival in the world. It is the minimum education which every Indian is expected to have or receive without any consideration whatsoever.

(iii) The system of Basic Education is closely reacted to the basic needs and interests of the child.

(iv) It is basic became it comes first in time i.e. when it is the primary period of the education of the individual.

(v) It is basic because it takes into consideration Indian culture, basic potentialities of the person and professions of the community.

The Analysis

Free and Compulsory Education : Gandhiji told us that education for all children would be free in the age group of 7-14. Later on the Committee headed by Mr. B. G. Kher recommended that it should be so for all children between 6-14. The Punjab Government Passed an act in this direction. It also went further and made education upto the higher secondary level free. This created a lot of fuss for there was a mad-rush on the part of children who sought admission in government schools. The private management's felt strongly about this also as these schools too were badly hit by large scale migrations to the state-run schools. After a while, the Govt. also felt the economic strains of this step and it withdrew its order of making education upto the higher secondary level free. These days in Punjab, education is free for all children between the age group 6-11. The reasons as to why we have not been able to expand and make primary education free in the entire country have been discussed in the chapter on primary education.

Mother-Tongue as Medium of Instruction : In principle, it is an ideal thing to educate children in their own language which they comprehend and follow. But in practice, this is not possible as it has generated much heat in political quarters and we have with us what is known as language problem. Further, in a country like India by educating children through mother-tongue (in many cases the provincial-language) are we not creating unbreakable barriers on the basis of language? A Tamilian will not be understood in Punjab and a Punjabi will not be followed at all in Assam. Is not it a step towards national disintegration? This criticism, though valid has been met. Mother-tongue is good, say excellent, as far as early education of the child is concerned but for higher education, we have to think of a medium which is understood all over the country. Further, in mother-tongue we may not have enough books for the child in a subject and sometimes suitable vocabulary for technical terms be not available in the mother-tongue. That is why we advocate the study of two languages or three languages. Unfortunately, we have not been able to ban English because of sentimental or other seasons. So mother-tongue be used as, medium of instruction for the early education of the child and then we shift to either English or Hindi unless the child has a mind to specialise in that language (his mother-tongue). (See also Language Problem).

Craft Centredness : Craft centredness is the only unique and distinguishing feature of basic education and befittingly, maximum criticism has been directed against this aspect of basic education. This aspect has been least understood and appreciated. Let us examine briefly the points of criticism and how those have been met with:

(a) Education through craft is nothing but child labour as through his handwork, we are going to pay off the teachers. This is true when the concept of self-sufficiency is understood in old context (pre-independence days) or stretched too far. Now-a-days we are not so rigid about self-sufficiency and there is no harm if the child works a little on it.

(b) Working on a craft for sometimes or some hours in day may exhaust children. They may not be able to concentrate on their studies in the class later when they assemble for the purpose. They may get tired or fatigued early. This criticism is met by the saying that man is but a creature of habit. Soon, children will adjust to the routine and habit of working will be formed.

(c) By talking of craft and by making it a centre of all education, are we not going back to the cow dung age? Are we not putting the clock back when this is an atomic age and a century of rapid industrialisation? This point too stands contradicted. Well 'by installing the industry', what do we do? The answer is production. We are interested in production (other than 'population' of course) and through the craft, if we can produce something other than educating the children, well and good. It certainly goes to our advantage and our economy stands strengthened.

(d) Introduction of craft will make education all the more costly. After all to run the show successfully, we need tools and implements and also a room to store those and a chowkidar to take care of them. We have to spend money on their maintenance also in the years to come. Further, we need craft teachers also. All this adds to the cost of education. But then the question is which system of education is cheap system? In all systems of education, initial investment has to be made and what is the harm if we invest a little more in basic education when we know that this is a better system of education and the results are going to be splendid. You be the judge and decide.

(e) Introduction of craft leads to a compressed sort of atmosphere. There is no freedom. It is wrong allegation. We have to learn discipline and work as team to produce something useful.

(f) Craft makes basic system a rural system of education. Well, we can make some changes in its content to have its universal appeal.

(g) Teachers are lazy. They misuse (or 'use') craft to the maximum and have a lot of free time. Their attitude is bad attitude. They assign some task to children i.e. to dig up a field and themselves enjoy the leisure thus afforded in idle gossip. It is indeed sad and I, being a teacher myself, hang my head in shame for all teaching community. It will be good if right attitude is inculcated in them towards craft work.

(h) Education through work does not appeal to intelligent and brilliant children. We can tell them the importance of work and the obvious advantages of physical labour and convert them to our side rather than force them. Further, there will be few such cases and they can be ignored also if no other way is available or let them do that work which is intellectual and is related to craft such as maintaining stock store register and accounts.

How to Select a Craft ? We have to apply certain criteria while selecting a craft. The criteria suggested are:

(i) Select only that craft which has got educational potentialities, which has horizontal and vertical dimensions or deep enough so that all education could be provided through it.

(ii) It must be in accordance with the geographical conditions of the locality.

(iii) It must suit the needs of the people. It must be also interesting.

(iv) It must have productive aspect otherwise, the self-sufficiency aspect is bound to suffer.

(v) There must be availability of raw material-otherwise the students may sit idle and waste their time and energy.

(vi) It must suit the age of children so that they are able to handle it suitably and with confidence.

(vii) It must provide children with good experiences.

(viii) Tools must be available.

Urban Schools and Craft : Another problem is craft for urban schools. Gandhiji has suggested only two crafts viz. agriculture and spinning and weaving. But these are suitable for rural schools or for those urban schools with which sufficient land is available. But what about craft for those schools which are located in congested localities or in big cities e.g. for schools in Bombay where children have not even seen real cows or buffaloes? To talk of agriculture to them will be like casting pearls before swine. So it was quite a lot of problem to think of a craft suited for urban cities. Answer is that we should not be rigid in having only in those two crafts as suggested by the Father of the Nation. Let us choose one in the light of the geographical conditions and educational potentialities. We can have wood-work or utensil making as craft in the city schools. Those can serve us well for the concept of teaching solely though craft has undergone a change as discussed in the next pages.

Self-sufficiency Aspect : Just like craft, this aspect of basic education has also been vehemently-criticised and naturally we had to change the concept. In fact the failure of basic education has been due to over-stress on this aspect. The chief points of criticism are:

(a) A basic school will be self-sufficient only when 15 acres of land is attached to it. It is thus next to impossible to have 15 acres of land attached to each and every school. Will it not thus check the opening of new schools and spread of education which we aim to provide to each and everyone?

(b) Tools and implements are required. Children cannot work with bare hands. It is said that sufficient number of tools are not available and in a number of places, those are not well maintained, or are out of order. In many teacher training colleges, for 100 students only 30 'Kahis' are available and during the agriculture period, 30 students are busy while the rest i.e. 70 loaf about. The same is true at the school level. When workers are idle, how can you expect basic education to be self-sufficient?

(c) Self-sufficiency is possible only if we have all eight classes in the school and in every class there are thirty students. After all, we need workers to work and we are not going to employ outsider to work for us. This i.e. to have eight classes and each having thirty students is next to impossible. It may be noted that we must have thirty students in the last two classes because it is the grown up children who are going to be of tremendous help in realising the target of their school being self-sufficient. This again is not possible, populated as our country is. In many of the modern high/higher secondary schools, the number of students in the last two classes is three sometimes. So, under these circumstances we cannot achieve self-sufficiency.

(d) The quality of the goods that we are going to produce in school be much better or should be favourably in comparison to the same produced in the factories or elsewhere only then people are going to buy it and we are going to earn something from it. We do not bother for quality and as such we suffer. The product manufactured in the school thus has to be thrown in the gutter. We may take the case of ink or chalk or soap which we make in our schools (even in colleges in the hobby classes). The quality is horribly inferior. This amounts to waste. Thus the self-sufficiency target cannot be realised.

(e) Further, if we remain obsessed by the aim or realising self-sufficiency in our schools, the quality of education stands lowered down. We achieve this at the cost of education. Our school then ceases to be a school, it becomes a factory and the students become factory workers. Is it not child labour? It is not exploitation?

Because of all this and because of changed circumstances (In 1937, Gandhiji never realised that we shall be free so soon), the concept of self-sufficiency has undergone a change. We have a national government—our own government, and education is its responsibility. It will pay the teachers. Children do not have to bother now. Further, we cannot do away at the same time with self-sufficiency. It will rob much of the charm of craft centredness of education. The only thing is now that we are not rigid about our schools being self-sufficient. These days, the concept of self-sufficiency is that if we can provide a child with one uniform in a year and mid-day meals, the school be taken as self-sufficient. Let us see how far we shall achieve this target though in many cases it stands practically abandoned.

Correlation and Basic Education : Correlation was indeed a unique feature of this scheme but correlated teaching somehow or other has not been possible. Gandhiji suggested craft as a centre or the only centre of correlation. This was not possible. All knowledge could not be correlated with the one centre i.e. craft which was suggested. In later days two more centres viz. Physical and Social Environments of correlation were added. In all, there are now three centres of correlation-(i) Craft, (ii) Physical environment, and (iii) Social environment. But the tragedy is that we do not have those teachers who are experts in correlated teaching. If at all, there is any correlation, it is all forced, unnatural and foul. Ultimately, we had to make concessions in this direction also. Further correlation is possible only in lower stages but at higher stages say in post-graduate classes, this cannot be done. The 1963-version of correlation in basic education is, "Correlate what you can, where you cannot, do not bother." What it amounts to actually is basic education with all the changes highlighted earlier minus correlation. Other points of Criticism against Basic education are:

Confusion in the Understanding : The great master M.K. Gandhi, now being dead, there is hardly anyone left now who could clarify our doubts from time to time. There is a wild charge in some quarters that the founder himself, M.K. Gandhi, was not clear about his contribution. This is not so. He in fact, was so busy in other activities, that he could not devote much time in this direction in his life time.

More of Sentiment : Gandhi was a great man and we revered him, therefore all that he said or did was equally great and needs all attention from us all. It may be true as sentimentality makes one coward and he closes his eyes towards the defects of the scheme. But it is again our fault. Gandhiji never wanted us to be sentimental.

Attitude of Teachers : It is all the more painful when we come specially to teacher education because their attitude is picked up by those who are going to teach in basic schools. In a study conducted by the author in 1964, it was found out that most of the teacher educators teaching in Basic training colleges in erstwhile Punjab in 1963-64, were neutral or had no attitude towards Basic education. It is better to have negative attitude than to have no attitude towards thing. The conclusion is that they have many doubts in their minds and those very-doubts are being passed on to posterity and thus incalculable harm stands done to Basic education. It is a question of lack of faith and availability of right type of teachers.

Apathy of Parents : As the case with teachers, so is true of parents. By Basic education, parents understand work. This is how it has been interpreted to them. A parent sends a child to school to learn something and when on return from school, the child tells his parents that he did this much digging and that much spinning, the parent is flabbergasted. He prays that sooner the Basic scheme fails, the better.

Suitable Text Books not Available : But it has been found out that we cannot do without these. Text-books have to be used as an aid towards education. Those have to supplement the scheme. It will be unwise to outrightly reject the text-books. After all, the labour of man over the past so many centuries lies stored up in books and text-books. So we accept the use of text-books in basic education. Suitable text-books are not available.

Lack of Funds : It is better to keep quiet on this aspect. Much has already been said elsewhere.

Opposed by Certain Traditionalists : They do not want any change in the existing system of education. In the traditionalists, we may have some administrators also. They have crippled it. It is a vicious circle of blaming one another perhaps. Educationists and teachers blame the administrators and stand blamed in return. The thing stands where it was.

Lopsidedness of Reform : It only touches one aspect of Indian education and does not bother for other stages.

All said and done, Basic education in itself was something unique and good. We have given it a different colouring and instead of implementing it by making suitable changes in the scheme as originality conceived in order to achieve something positive we have played with it. It is tragic that we have given it our colouring and by making it a point of controversy we have rung its death knell. It as a topic, occupied an important place in postgraduate courses of many universities and now it has been reduced to the status of a mere educational problem which hardly merits anybody's attention. That was why because of the poor quality of basic schools, Dr. Zakir Hussain, one of the founders of Basic education scheme was led to remark that the system of Basic education as it was practised recently was a fraud. Other epithets which are associated with Basic education are FARCE, FAD, FAULTY. The sooner thus we correct our mistakes the better it would be but we must remember that the main contribution of Basic education has been to make us realise the fact that a system of book-centred education which the traditional schools have been providing so far is no good for the country. We are not going back to purely bookish learning at least in the primary stages, even if we have to abandon Basic education. We are to have work in our curriculum and that itself is the biggest success of Basic education. It has convinced us that for some more years to come, if we do not learn to work with our own hands and stick to white-collar attitude, we are going to perish.

Basic education exists as a fad at some places in the country. In reality, it has vanished from India especially after 1969-Gandhi Birth Centenary Year! Strange! No funds were allocated for Basic education in 4th Five Year Plan ending in 1974. The National Institute of Basic Education at New Delhi was also wound up in 1969.

Over all, the future holds no promise for Basic scheme unless we reaffirm our faith in the ideals of Basic scheme and rededicate ourselves to it. What is now important is to have Basic education attitude.

Gandhiji meant by education, "an all round drawing out of the best in child and man—body, mind and spirit". Harmonious development of all power-innate and acquired, was the chief goal of Gandhian education. "True education", he said, "must stimulate the spiritual, intellectual and physical faculties of the children." This all round education, he believed could be given through craft. His emphasis on it is composed, advancing, and conversely, no individual can advance without the nation of which it is a part, also advancing." Gandhiji held, "that the individual must work out his perfection in a spiritual society."

He did not agree with Rousseau that the individual can develop in a social vacuum. Self-realisation and social service must go hand in hand. An individual, according to him "can make the best of himself in a State and the State can achieve its highest development only on the condition that each of its citizens gives the best that is in him." The individual develops in a social atmosphere. It is there that it can have common interest and can engage himself in common activities. Like John Dewey, Gandhiji wanted to transform the schools into communities where individuals get abundant opportunities of social contact and co-operation.

Gandhiji synthesised the individual and the social aims of education. He proved it by example and precept that 'self-realisation' and 'social service' were not contradictory. A fusion of the two in a man made him complete.

QUESTIONS

1. There are three sources of education according to Rousseau. Discuss with special reference to education by Nature.
2. Briefly discuss maxims of Rousseau's educational philosophy. Discuss in detail the twin meaning of 'nature'.
3. What are Rousseau's views on curriculum? Discuss the curriculum suggested by him for childhood period.
4. What are the salient features of Rousseau's methods of teaching? How would you consider him the forerunner of some of the most promising methods of teaching?
5. "The educational ideals of Pestalozzi rest upon his social philosophy". Discuss and compare with Rousseau.
6. What do you understand by Pestalozzi's Utopian tendencies? Discuss.
7. What are the aims of education according to Dewey? Discuss and elaborate his aim of moral education.

8. How does the Project method reflect Dewey's approach to education? What are the essential steps of a good method of teaching?

9. What are the principles of curriculum construction according to Dewey? What do you understand by flexibility of curriculum?

10. What are the three principles of Tagore's educational philosophy? What is the place of 'freedom' in his system of education?

11. How does Tagore combine Naturalism, Humanism and Internationalism? Discuss his objective of education through Nature.

12. What are the salient features of Gandhi's educational philosophy? Why should education be self-supporting?

13. What is the bearing of Russel's philosophy on various aspects of education? Discuss.

12

Vivekanand

"Rooted in the past and full pride in India's prestige, Vivekanand was yet modern in his approach to life's problems and was a kind of a bridge between the past of India and her present. His mission was the service of mankind through social service, mass education, religious revival and social awakening through education." (Jawahar Lal Nehru). His call to the youth was "Arise, Awake, Rest not till the goal is achieved". Such was the dynamic impact of Vivekanand's personality and views, especially educational.

Life Sketch

Swami Vivekanand was born in 1883 in a Kshatriya family in Calcutta. His real name was Narendra Nath Dutta. His father Shri Vishnu Nath Dutta was an advocate at Calcutta High Court. The atmosphere in his family was religious. Hence, from early childhood he was initiated into religious ceremonies with the result that he developed a keen eagerness for the study of religious scriptures. He possessed a keen intelligence. When he was five years of age, he was sent to a school. There he studied History and Literature as well as Indian philosophical traditions, and after becoming well-versed in these he studied in detail the Western Literature and Philosophy. Herbert Spencer and John Stuart Mill were his favourite philosophers and Wordsworth was his favourite poet. In this way, from early childhood Narendra Nath developed a sound and handsome physique and being endowed with a keen and penetrating intellect and pleasing art of conversation, he gained popularity very soon. Once his Headmaster Heasty said about him. "I have travelled far and wide, but I have not met such an intelligent, gifted and scholarly student even in German Universities". One day Heasty introduced him to Ram Krishna Paramhansa. Swami Rama Krishna had a profound impact upon Narendra Nath. Narendra Nath remained in close contact with Swami Ram Krishan Paramhans for more than six years and after satisfying Swamiji with his erudite scholarship and intense devotion to spiritual values, he got initiated into the saintly order and came to be known as Swami Vivekanand. In 1896 Rama Krishna Paramhans died. Swami Vivekanand established Ram Krishna mission in the sacred memory of his Guru and preached throughout his life in Asia, Europe, England and America the teachings of Vedanta as delivered by his Guru, Paramhans. He also toured extensively and by his untiring efforts established branches of Ram Krishan Mission throughout the world. By his organisational abilities and far-sight he could translate into practice the teachings of ancient Vedantic philosophy as interpreted and preached by his Guru. He showed the way that the ancient philosophy of Vedanta could successfully meet the various problems which the national life of India was facing in modern times. In short, Swami Vivekanand, by synthesising the idealistic philosophy of the west and creative philosophy of the ancient Hindu Dharma, brought glory and greatness to the Hindu thought and way of living. He died in 1902.

The Ideology

1. Only study of books is not education.
2. Knowledge lies hidden in the mind of man. He uncovers and develops it by his own efforts.
3. Concentration is the key to all knowledge. For this, Brahmacharya is very essential.
4. Purity of thought, speech and deed is self-discipline.
5. Education should develop a child physically, mentally and spiritually.
6. Education should foster spiritual faith, devotion and self-surrender in the individual and should cause full development through service and sacrifice.
7. Education should develop character, mental power, intelligence and self-confidence coupled with self-reliance.
8. Religious education should be imparted by example.
9. No sex differences in the content of education.
10. Women should specially be imparted religious education.
11. Mass education schemes should be formulated and launched.
12. Provision for technical education.
13. Teacher to be a friend, philosopher and guide.
14. Closer relationship between teacher and students.
15. All subjects which promise the physical and spiritual advancement of a child, should be included in the curriculum.

Meaning of Education : "Education is the manifestation of perfection already in man".

Aims and Objectives

The Aim of Reaching Perfection: The prime aim of education is to achieve fulness of perfection already present in a child. According to Swamiji, all material and spiritual knowledge is already present in man covered by a curtain of ignorance. Education should tear off that veil so that the knowledge shines forth as an illuminating torch to enliven all the corners by and by. This is meant by achieving fulness of the latent perfection.

Physical and Mental Development Aim: The second aim of education is the physical and mental development of the child so that the child of today, after studying Geeta, is able to promote national growth and advancement as a fearless and physically well-developed citizen of tomorrow. Stressing the mental development of the child, Swamiji wished education to enable the child to stand on his own feet economically rather than becoming a parasite on others.

Moral and Spiritual Development: According to Vivekanand, a nation's greatness is not only measured by its parliamentary institutions and activities, but also by the greatness of its citizens. But the greatness of citizens is possible only through their moral and spiritual development which education should foster.

Character Development Aim: According to him character development is a very important aim of any education. For this, he emphasised the practice of Brahmacharya which fosters development of mental, moral and spiritual powers leading to purity of thoughts, words and deeds.

The Aim of Development: Faith in one's own self, Shradha and a Spirit of Renunciation-All through his life Swamiji exhorted the individuals to keep full confidence on their powers. They should inculcate a spirit of self-surrender, sacrifice and renunciation of material pleasures for the good of others. Education should foster all these qualities in the individual. He gave this call to his countrymen-"Arise, awake and stop not till the goal is achieved".

The Aim of searching Unity in Diversity: The true aim of education is to develop insight into the individuals so that they are able to search out and realise unity in diversity. Vivekanand has further asserted that physical and spiritual worlds are one, their distinctness is an illusion. (Maya). Education should develop this sense which finds unity in diversity.

Religious Development Aim: To Swamiji, religious development is an essential aim of education. To him, each individual should be able to search out and develop the religious seed embedded in him and thus find the absolute truth or reality. Hence, he advocated the training of feelings and emotions so that the whole life is purified and sublimated. Then alone the capacities of obedience, social service and submission to the teachings and preachings of great saints and saviours will develop in the individual. Education should foster this development.

The Textbooks

According to Vivekanand, the prime aim of education is spiritual growth and development. But this does not mean that he did not advocate material prosperity and physical well-being. He advocated the inclusion of all those subjects and activities in the curriculum which foster material welfare with spiritual advancement. For spiritual perfection he prescribed Religion, Philosophy, Puranic lore, Upanishads, company of saints and their preachings, and for material advancement and prosperity he recommended Languages, Geography, Science, Political Science, Economics, Psychology, Art, Agriculture, Industrial and Technical subjects together with Games, Sports and other Physical exercises.

Teaching Approaches

Swamiji prescribed the same ancient spiritual methods of teaching wherein the Guru and his disciples lived in close association as in a family. The essential characteristics of those religious and spiritual methods were as under-

(1) To control fleeting mental faculties by the practice of Yoga.

(2) To develop the mind by concentration and deep meditation.

(3) To gain knowledge through lectures, discussions, self-experience and creative activities.

(4) To imitate the qualities and character of teacher by intelligent and clear understanding.

(5) To lead the child on the right path by means of individual guidance by the teacher.

Place of Child : Like Froebel, Vivekanand emphasised the education to be child-centred. According to him, the child is the store and repositor of all learning-material and spiritual pursuit.

Education of Masses : "I consider that the greatest national sin is the neglect of the masses, and that is one of the causes of our downfall. No amount of politics would be of any avail until the masses of India are once more well-educated, well-fed and well-cared for."

Women's Education : A strong advocate of women's education, he emphasised that they should have the same curriculum as the boys.

The Assessment

Though an idealist to the core, Vivekanand's philosophy of education contains traces of Naturalism and Pragmatism. He insisted that the chief aim of education is to develop to the full the moral and spiritual nature of the child, the essence of which is already present in him. He ceaselessly strove that education should develop nationalism as well as international brotherhood. His educational philosophy is a mixture of the ancient Vedantic philosophy and the modern western philosophy, omitting the pitfalls of both."

According to Dr. R.S. Mani, "Vivekanand's life mission was to advocate that people should be possessed of Shradha (Faith), of Virya (Courage) to attain the knowledge of Atma, and to sacrifice their lives for the good of others."

The Stature

Some call him (Swami Vivekananda) the Militant Hindu, others call him a great reformer and crusader and yet many others remember him with various other epithets. The fact remains that he was one of the great Indians who refused to be placed second to any one in any sphere. He shook the world with his discourses on philosophy and religion. He wanted to establish the supremacy of Hinduism and he wanted to set and reset the glorious traditions of our great motherland. Swami Vivekananda was a great teacher. He wanted to strike a balance between the spiritualism of the east on one hand and materialism of the west on the other. Unfortunately, his life was short but he did his days' work.

Swami Vivekananda (a name he took in 1893 while sailing to U.S.A.) was born as Narendra Nath Dutt in a family at Calcutta in 1863. During his student days (he was an ardent student of philosophy and poetry), he came in contact with another great teacher-Swami Ram Krishna Paramhansa who made him incharge of his seminary with the words, "Take care of these boys." Narendra Nath resolutely undertook the conduct of young seminary and did not permit it to indulge in the idleness of God. He kept its members ever on the alert, he harried their minds without pity; he read them the great books of human thought.......he led them indefatigably towards the wide horizons of boundless truth.......Narendra Nath became a monk and preached the Gospel of Vedanta throughout the world. He participated in the Parliament of Religions held in U.S.A. in 1893. He toured India—its length and breadth. He even went to Ceylon. On Dec. 25, 1896, he swam the Indian Ocean and meditated on the rock at Kanyakumari. Swami Vivekananda died in 1902.

Staunch Individualist. In Swamiji we had a staunch individualist. "Individuality is my motto," he wrote to Abhayananda. "I have no ambition beyond training individuals."

He said again:

"If I succeed in my life to help one single man to attain freedom, my labours will not have been in vain."

That he was an individualist can be known from one more fact. The subjects of his interviews were 'Liberty', 'Courage', 'Charity', humane treatment of delinquents and so on.

Dignity of Humanity/Faith in Man. From the above point, it can be easily concluded that Swamiji had immense faith in man and in the dignity of humanity. About it he said, "No religion on earth preaches the dignity of humanity in such a lofty strain as Hinduism." He regretted that it is again Hinduism which treads upon the necks of poor and the low but then the fault is not of Hinduism but of Pharisees, and Sadducees. And about the faith in man, the quotation given in the beginning is an indicator enough. He says, "The only God to worship is the human soul, in the human body. Of course, all animals are temples too but human is the highest—The Taj Mahal of temples. If I can not worship in that, no other temple will be of any advantage. The moment 1 have realised God sitting in the temple of every human body, the moment I stand in reverence before every human being and see God in him-that moment I am free from bondage, everything that binds vanishes, and I am free". Know the man, he says. That is also the message of Vedanata.

Doctrine of Divinity/Concept of God. Like Swami Dayananda, Swami Vivekananda believed in the immortality of soul. That is also the message of Vedas, Swamiji says, "Each soul is a star, Man is potentially divine." And then God is omni present. He is Supreme. He creates man in His own image. The manifestation of God is in man. According to Swamiji, the worship of man is the worship of God.

And all religions are equal. No religion is inferior to the other. To quote him, "If God exists it must be possible to reach him. Religion is neither word nor doctrine. It is realisation. It is not hearing and accepting. It is being and becoming. It begins with the exercise of the faculty of religious realisations."

The Four Great Paths. In order to achieve salvation (freedom and liberation) Swami showed four paths: Paths of work, worship, contemplation and knowledge. It could be Karma, Bhakti and Jnana and the Propylacum. The motive force of all three is the science of inner forces, consciously controlled and mastered: the Science of Raja Yoga. Of these four Gospels of Vivekananda, his four Yogas, the most deep and moving is the Gospel of Work-Karma Yoga although to many others, it is the lowest of the three ways to achieve salvation but there is no 'high road' or a 'low road' for this purpose. Karma Yoga says, "Work incessantly but give up all attachment to work......Hold your mind free. Do not project into it the tentacle of selfishness......'I' and 'mine'.

We learn from Karma Yoga the secret of work, the organising power of work.....work is inevitable.....but we should work to the highest purpose......All duties are His! Doctrine of service is the essential part of Vivekananda's teaching and practice.

Swami Vivekananda also made masterly analysis of three other paths leading to freedom and liberty. He dwelt in detail on Bhakti Yoga, Raja Yoga, and Jnana Yoga.

Swami Vivekananda was patriot of the first order. He wanted every resident of this land to be first and last an Indian, He sang the Glory of the motherland. He wanted all of us to sink our differences-religious, linguistic, cultural and to lead a life as citizens of this great land. India has rich cultural traditions and these be cherished by us all. India is also spiritual leader of the world. He states it emphatically.

Universalism and Science-Religion. He believed in religion which is of universal acceptance and which is science based. He says, "All narrow, limited, fighting ideas of religion must be given up.......The religious ideals of future must embrace all that exists in the world and is good and great, and at the same time have infinite scope for future development. Religion is synonymous with universalism. And it is not until "religious" conceptions have attained to this universalism that religion is fully realised. He advocated rationalistic religion.

On Women. He was all for them. He preached for equal rights between men and women. He made no distinction between man and woman. He asks, "Is there any sex distinction in Atman?" Again he said, "the best thermometer to the progress of a nation is treatment of its women."

Pioneering Status

The personal philosophy of Swami Vivekananda lies reflected in his educational philosophy and practice of education. Some points.

Theory and Ideas

(a) Knowledge comes from within: (Rejection of Behaviourism which believes in everything external). Vivekananda says, "All knowledge that the world has ever received comes from mind: infinite library of universe is in your mind. The external world is only a suggestion, the occasion which sets you to study your mind. The falling of apple gave suggestion to Newton. He rearranged all the precious limits of thought in his mind and discovered a new link among them which, we call the Law of Gravitation. This is just an example to prove that knowledge resides within the individual."

(b) Education for all was creed with Swamiji. It hardly needs any elaboration.

(c) Swamiji was a Yogi. He believed in Brahmacharya. It was a must for concentration of mind which helped in education of the individual.

(d) Education must suit the needs of the child—psychological education. He says, "Their needs should be determined in terms of tendencies inherent in children and not according to what the parents of the children think". The point is that parents are not to determine the needs of children.

(e) Swamiji was in favour of women education. Their uplift, welfare was a part and parcel of his basic philosophy.

(f) Concept of Education: Swami Vivekananda defined education as: Education is the manifestation of the perfection already in the man. Swamiji believed in the development of inner powers. He did not believe in book learning. To him, book learning was not education.

What is education? Is it book learning? No. Is it diverse knowledge? Not even that. The training by which the current and expression of will are brought under control and become beautiful is called education.

Aims and Objectives

In some books, you will find that about ten aim education according to Swami Vivekananda have been listed and Swamiji was not an educational theorist. That listing is mere irrational. From the philosophy of Swamiji and his teaching, the following aims of education can be deduced:

(a) Strong moral character should be developed through education. The main aim of education is this character building and not merely feeding information to the brain.

(b) *Self-realization:* The education should enable one to realize one's self is the second aim of education. And before that it should create self-confidence. Only a self-confident man can realize oneself. Education should take man to freedom, to liberty, to salvation.

(c) Education should enable man to meet his needs. The economic aspect or the practical aspect of life can not be ignored. The education which does not help the common mass to equip themselves for the struggle for life, which does not bring out strength of character, a spirit of philanthrophy and the courage of a lion, is it worth the name? Real education is that which enables one to stand on his own legs.

(d) To promote universal brotherhood is another aim of education. He said, "Through education, we should gradually reach the idea of universal brotherhood by flinging down the walls of separation and inequality. In everyman, in every animal, however weak or miserable, great or small, resides the same omnipresent and omniscient soul. The difference is not in the soul but in the manifestation.

Content of Education. It cannot be purely western. Swamiji at the same time was born in modern times. Sciences could not be neglected. He did not specify any subjects to form the content of education-it was a broad approach-a sort of synthesis between Science and Vedanta. He also wanted Indian students to learn their own languages—particularly Sanskrit. He also wanted the students to learn Religion. Theology on one hand, English and technology on the other to keep with the current times, as already pointed out.

In the words of Swamiji, "My idea of education is personal contact with the teacher-gurugrha-vasa. Without the personal life of a teacher, there could be no education."

Process of Working

Swamiji was a monk. He also believed in inner knowledge. His methods of education would be determined by these two facts. You can at once say that the methods will be along the following lines:

(a) Meditation—for the concentration is a must.

(b) Faith or Shraddha

(c) Discourse and Discussion

(d) Self-study.

In Swami Vivekananda's own words, "To me the very essence of education is concentration of mind not the collection of facts. If I had to do my education once again I would not study facts at all, I would develop the power of concentration and detachment and then with a perfect instrument, I would collect facts at will." That speaks of his methodology.

Teacher's Status

According to Swamiji, only few can become teachers. The personal life of a teacher is of much more importance than the knowledge a teacher possesses. He says that only a Tyagi can become a good teacher. A teacher must first be pure at heart and then a dedicated one.

Great Services

Swami Vivekananda, original name Narendra Nath Dutta son of an eminent lawyer of Calcutta High Court was born in 1863 in Calcutta. He graduated with honours from Calcutta

University. In the beginning he was a teacher for some time. But, his interest in philosophy and religion drove him to adopt the life of a monk. His contact with Sri Ram Krishna Param Hans in 1888 transformed his life. He left home and became a wandering monk. He travelled all over India preaching the vedantic scriptures and philosophy. In 1893 he was invited to participate in the deliberations of the world's Parliament of Religions at Chicago, America. He gave a soul-stirring address there. He was, then, invited to lecture on vedanta at several universities of the U.S.A. In 1896, three years after, he was invited to lecture at Oxford University of England. He established Belur Math in 1899. The same year he was invited to lecture at California University and founded the Vedanta Society at San Francisco. He died in 1902 when he was only 39 years old.

Belief in Vedas

Swami Vivekananda was a Vedantist. Hence, he was a teacher of spirituality preaching that every soul is destined to be perfect and that every being in the end will attain to that state. He also preached that whatever we are now, is the result of whatever we have been in the past; and whatever we will be in the future depends on whatever we do or think now. Spiritual perfection of man was the aim of life according to him for which one has to struggle. He believed in God, in the Vedas and in the birth-death-rebirth cycle. His belief was that this whole universe is one, that it is one Being manifesting itself in all the various forms. The human being has a divine nature. God is the material cause of this universe. It is only by name and form that one thing is differentiated from another. In reality they are one and the same. In the lowest worm as well as in the highest human being the same divine nature is present. When a person has realized his own nature, the whole world has vanished for him. His philosophy represents the highest spiritual and ethical values of mankind. His teachings having their roots in the upanishadas were believed by him to be helpful in solving social and political problems.

He advocated that spiritual knowledge is the only thing that can destroy our miseries for ever; helping man spiritually is the highest that can be given to him, because spirituality is the true basis of all our activities in life.

High Morality

Swami Vivekananda had an unflinching faith in eternal values. He said that these alone can ensure stability; they provide the driving power for progress. About education he said "There is no problem of modern India that can not be solved by that magic word *Education.*" He emphatically said that education is a man-making and nation-making process. It is the process which awakens the sleeping soul to self-conscious activity. It is the fundamental basis of human development, a means of human enlightenment and purification of human heart. He strongly pleaded for providing a spiritual orientation to education.

Vivekananda's concept of education was that "it is the manifestation of the perfection already in man" *(Education* by Vivekananda, chapter-I). He further said that education is not the amount of information that is put into the brain undigested all the life. We must have education which is life-building, man-making, character building, assimilation of ideas. True education is that which helps the common mass of people to equip themselves for the struggle of life, which brings out strength of character, a spirit of philanthropy and the courage of a lion. He said, "We want that education by which character is formed, strength of mind is increased, intellect is expanded, and by which one can stand on one's own feet.... the end of all education, all training should be man-making. The end and aim of all training is to make the man grow.....The training by which the current expression of will are brought under control, and become fruitful is called education" (Ranganathananda, p. 148). This is education that may be said to 'be true education, education which makes for growth and expansion of personality.'

Education, as stressed by Swami Vivekananda, must develop in man a sense of honour and dignity and also a sense of social responsibility, a respect for man as man and a respect for the dignity of man in their own persons. Character, efficiency and humanism should be the aim of all education. Vivekananda strongly pleaded that development of character through the service of his fellow men, the utilization of his talents for ensuring the happiness and welfare of the millions of his less fortunate fellow-citizens should be the aim of the education (Ranganathananda, p. 163). Education for total human development was the vision of Vivekananda. He stressed the need to educate the millions of our common people as the national development depended on the "goodness and greatness of men to be achieved through education".

His approach to education was humanistic. He was highly spiritual and intensely human. His humanism in education centered around man emphasizing that man was the measure of all things. He held a belief that through education it was possible to develop in human beings qualities of 'heart and mind which make them tremendously powerful, full of hope, endowed with a firm mind and will, strength of muscle and nerves. It is these men and women who build a strong nation. Through education, he asserted, nations can unfold the humanistic and divine possibilities lying hidden within their people. To him, in fact, education ,was the basic means for achieving human excellence and solving national problems.

Vivekananda stressed education for democracy, and national development. The strength of democracy was, to him, hidden in the young men and women who are free, responsible, politically aware, full of deep patriotic feelings and sensitive to human welfare. Education was thought to be a powerful instrument to achieve these developmental qualities in the people. He was a nationalist through and through and wanted that education should produce such enlightened democratic citizens who can build a strong and prosperous nation. "A nation is advanced in proportion as education and intelligence spread among the masses" said Swamiji.

Women education was considered by Vivekananda an essential component of India's national system of education. He said "daughters should be supported and educated with as much care as the sons". He further, held that it is only in the homes of educated and pious mothers that great men are born. He said that women should be taught History and Puranas, house-keeping and the art, the duties of home life and principles that make for the development of character. Sewing, culinary art, rules of domestic work and upbringing of children, Japa, worship, meditation, development of the spirit of valour and heroism should form the content of women education.

National integration through education was one of the prominent objectives of Swamiji. He had a great faith in the youth of the country for national regeneration. For that reason he emphasized that they should get the right type of education which enables them to be endowed with an alert mind and full of hope. strong in mind and firm in purpose and physically strong. Nation building through man-making was his precious dream. Swamiji said, "keep the motto before you: elevation of the masses without injuring their religion". He further said, "Teach yourselves, teach everyone his real nature; call upon the sleeping soul and see how it awakes. Power will come, glory will come, and everything that is excellent will come when this sleeping soul (of man) is roused to self-conscious activity".

On the basis of the foregoing discussion following aims of education may be inferred from Vivekananda's philosophy :

Individual Aims

(1) Physical development of the students

(2) Character development of students

(3) Spiritual development of students

(4) Development of total personality-i.e., developing self-confidence, self-reliance. self-discipline and self-sufficiency.

Social Aims

(1) Education for serving humanity

(2) Education for developing feelings of brotherhood, acquisition of the spirit of renunciation, i.e., giving up of worldly pleasures as well as a life of arrogance, pomp and show.

(3) Education for enlightened citizenship and responsibility.

Choice of Teacher

Vivekananda said that every soul is destined to be perfect and every being, in the end, will attain to that state. But, this does not preclude our receiving help from outside. The quickening influence comes from another soul, called the guru (Collected Works, p. 45). He, then. stressed that the soul from which this influence comes must possess the power of transmitting it. He must be a real teacher knowing the secret of the scriptures. Knowing is not so important as to grasp the spirit of the scriptures. Again, Swamiji said that the real teacher is one who is sinless because it is impossible that there can be any spiritual light in that soul which is impure. A vision of God, glimpse of the Beyond never comes until the soul is pure. Hence, in the teacher, purity is the one thing indispensable.

Another important quality that a teacher should have is that he should not teach with any ulterior motive, for name or for fame or anything else, but simply for love, pure love. When spiritual forces are transmitted from the teacher to the taught, they can only be conveyed through the medium of love. In other words the teacher must have a high level of morality and spirituality..

The teacher, according to Vivekananda, has a great role to play in the task of educating the child. The relationship between the teacher and the student has to be that of the father and the son. *Guru grahavas* is recommended by Swamiji saying that this is one of the best ways a teacher can help the pupil. In this *Grahavas* the student has to live in the house of the teacher, under 24-hour guidance and supervision of the guru. The teacher during this period imparts knowledge and inspires his intellectual and spiritual development through his personality. The teacher has to be an enlightened person himself apart fiom being knowledgeable. He should have a great love of humanity.

Swami Vivekananda did not make any recommendation about any specific subject to be taught in the schools and colleges. He, however. stressed that children should be taught about their cultural heritage expressed in history, poetry, literature, grammar, languages and lives of the great men. It was also emphasized that the study of vedantic literature. *Ramayana* and *Mahabharata* should also be taught along with the story of India's past.

Swami Vivekananda was not against the teaching of science and technical subjects. He was aware of the advances in the field of science and technology. He said that scientific knowledge through a study of the various branches of modern science must find a place in the curriculum of schools. The same he recommended about technology and engineering subjects.

Vivekananda being a nationalist was very keen to see that India was economically prosperous and well-developed. So he stressed teaching of science and technology. He also said that the schools should produce self-reliant individuals who can earn their living after finishing their education. In a way he suggested that vocational courses should also form a part of the curriculum. The curriculum for girls, he said, should incorporate training in needle-craft, cookery, child-rearing. and other useful subjects.

It was emphasized by Vivekananda that understanding and meaning are more important than just knowing. For that discussion, analysis. arguments and reaching the truth were considered essential. That was the way how students were made to learn at Guru's ashrama. The student would ask the question and the guru will answer. This interaction between the teacher and the student would involve illustrations, analogies, reasoning, examples and sometimes further readings by the student till he was convinced of the teacher's answers. Self-learning was very much emphasized. Experience based learning was considered more valuable.

Aspects of Contribution : Vivekananda emphasized the importance of the following and contributed significant ideas as follows

(i) He stressed humanism in education

(ii) Advocated free and compulsory mass education.

(iii) Emphasized formulation of a national system of education.

(iv) Emphasized importance of women education.

(v) Emphasized national unity and national integration.

QUESTIONS

1. "Fear is wrong life." Discuss.
2. "Real education prepares a man for social service, develops character and imbues courage." Discuss.
3. What are the basic principles of Vivekanand's concept of Education?
4. "Education is the manifestation of perfection already in man." In the light of the above statement discuss Vivekanand's aims of education.
5. Briefly discuss Vivekanand's aims of education.

13

Dayanand Saraswati

The Stature

Mulshankar who came to be later known as Swami Dayanand was born at Tankara (Gujarat) in 1824. He was born of very devout Brahmin parents. He was brought up on strict orthodox lines. When he was fourteen years of age, his father asked him to keep a complete fast on the Shivratri day and to observe an all night vigil in honour of Lord Shiva. As Mulshankar sat through the night, in front of the idol (of Siva), making many efforts to keep himself awake, a serious doubt crept into his mind. Could the stone image before him really be the great God of Kailash? The immediate cause was the sight of mice running freely on the idol and taking away the offerings placed before it. He sought explanations for this but the explanations failed to satisfy him and he vowed not to visit a temple again for worship. These events also aroused in him a keen desire in his mind to devote himself to search the solution of great mysteries of life. He studied Sanskrit to know the Vedas. The parents were worried about him. They tried to marry Mulshankar. He ran away from home. The year was 1845.

Dayanand wandered for fifteen years all over India, visited all places of religious interest. He gave himself to the study of Vedanta philosophy and the practice of Yoga under very able teachers. He became adept in Yoga.

After wandering for fifteen years from place to place, during which he acquired a deep insight into the various aspects of Hinduism, he came to Mathura where he became the disciple of Swami Virjanand, a profound scholar of Sanskrit language and a severe critic of the popular Hinduism of the day. It was under the guidance of Swami Virjanand that the future programme of Dayanand took definite shape.

He founded Arya Samaj in 1875—a movement to reform dogmatic Hinduism. He denounced idolatry as having no sanction in the Vedas and preached the worship of one God.

It was on 30th October (Diwali) 1883 that he died at Ajmer. He had been poisoned (glass in milk) by his trusted cook whom he pardoned and even gave money to escape to a place where the police should not catch him. Dayanand gave to us Satyarth Prakash.

We shall examine the philosophy of Dayanand in detail:

The Ideology

Faith in Vedic Truth and Righteousness. The philosophy of Swami Dayanand stands on Vedas. According to him, time-old wisdom contained in Vedas holds key to all our social and religious problems. To him, the Vedas are the source of all knowledge and this knowledge is final. And it is these Vedas which teach one one's character or righteous living.

Concept of Religion. Swami Dayanand regarded religion as the true conduct of life. Equitable dealings, the acceptance of truth and the rejection of untruth constitute the true conduct of life, or religion, and the reverse of this is irreligion. The religion of Dayanand was a simple affair. It was not idol worship but meditation.

Also Swami Dayanand believed that reason and faith are not hostile to each other. Of course, in many ways faith goes beyond reason, but no belief is to be accepted if it contradicts the findings of the reason. He wanted that religion should be free from irrational beliefs and superstitions. The repudiation of superstition in all its forms found the negative aspect of his teaching on religion. Many sensitive people criticise him for having exposed the superstitions inherent in all religions and thereby wounding the religious susceptibilities of his followers.

To Dayanand, all men were equal. He made no distinction between the followers of Hinduism. Christianity and Islam and other religions. But he wanted all irrational beliefs in religions to go so that the people realise the priceless gem of religion.

Prayer and meditation are best means of worship. Swami Dayanand prepared a Sandhya or a collection of Vedic verses for daily worship for he laid a great emphasis on the daily need of worship. He was against idol worship, to repeat.

Concept of God. The Swami held that the ancient Aryans accepted the oneness of God, and that the worship of numerous Gods and Goddesses were introduced in later time. There are many verses in the Vedas, which clearly teach the oneness of God. "They call him Indra, Mitra, Varuna, Agni and He is the heavenly, noble winged Gurutman (i.e. the Sun). He is one, sages call him by various names."

"He watches over creatures, those that breathe and those that breathe not. He is the sole, the one alone. In Him all gods become one," (Atharva Veda, XIII, 4. 14-21).

Dr. Radhakrishnan and Sri Aurobindo fully support the teachings of Dayanand.

Thus Dayanand believed in the oneness of God. God is pure universal spirit. God has no form. Swami Dayanand holds that God permits the whole universe. He creates, sustains, and dissolves the universe.

Belief in Yoga. Dayanand believed that Yogic exercises were a must for life. These exercises are of great help in the process of mind transformation and are a part and parcel of religious Sadhana. These exercises should be invariably accompanied by disinterested performance of one's daily duties, of the cultivation of a pure, loving and compassionate heart.......

Transmigration of Soul. According to Swami Dayanand attainment of moksha (or salvation)—which is the ultimate desire of all mortals is not an easy process and one may have to have pass through a number of births before one reaches the final goal of life. Thus Swamiji believed in the doctrine of transmigration of soul. It is a common belief with Hindus. The death of body does not mean the end of the soul and this is a belief which is also held by followers of Christianity and Islam but in a different sense. While Hindus believe that each soul passes through a succession of births till it qualifies for emancipation, the Christians or Muslims believe that each soul appears only once in the world and after death it remains in a state of quiescence till it is revived on the day of judgement. To Hindus this view does not appeal much.

The doctrine of transmigration goes along with the law of Karma which is an application of the universal law of causation in the domain of mind and consciousness.....

The doctrine of transmigration explains, in more or less satisfactory manner, the existence of inequalities amongst living beings. Each one gets in the next birth what he deserves, as a result of his karma or action in the present life Soul thus is immortal and migrates.

Equal Rights for All. (Social and Political Philosophy):

Salient Features

(i) While an individual should make every effort to make himself perfect physically, economically and spiritually, he should at the same time bend his energies to bring out the development of other members of the society. It is highly essential to develop social sense of human beings. Swami Dayanand says, "A person should not remain satisfied. He should seek good in the good of all others."

(ii) Swami Dayanand wants individuals to carry out their duties.

(iii) Swami Dayanand denounces caste system.

(iv) Dayanand believed in the equality of man. In the sight of the God, all persons are equal, and colour, community or sex makes no difference. And he gave equality to woman also. Educational opportunities were open to both boys and girls. Swami Dayanand advocated equal rights for men and women in all matters, in education and in marriage and in the holding of property. He was in favour of inter-caste, international marriages. Widow remarriage is also advocated by him. All respect must be given to women.

(v) State should maintain law and order. It should also look after the economic welfare of the individual.

(vi) He wanted men and women to observe Brahmacharya. He fixed age limits. For men; it was 25 years and for women, it was 16 years. The advantages of brahmacharya are known to us all.

Arya Samaj. He wanted to establish Arya Samaj with aims, firstly to protect Hinduism from the attacks of Islam and Christianity, and secondly, to reform the perverted Hinduism of Puranic age by reviving the original Hinduism as propounded in the Veda. Creation of Arya Samaj was a landmark in the socio-cultural history of India.

Concept and Theory

Swamiji attached great value to the education of the people. The D.A.V. movement was his personal initiation. Certain basic ideas in his educational thought and practice can be referred as under:

Education as a Continuous Process. Dayanand holds that education begins in the mother's womb. During the whole period of pregnancy the mother has to be on her guard against all sorts of distractions and evil effects. It continues even in the later life. Dayanand has given details how education has to be imparted in accordance with each period of the child's physical and mental growth.

Compulsory Education. Being an Idealist, Dayanand believed in the compulsory education for all. Gandhi seems to have borrowed this principle from Dayanand. State and society should make it compulsory for all (both boys and girls). There should be no discrimination in educational institutions. All should be treated on equal footing. Social regeneration is only possible through universal and compulsory education.

Aims of Education. Development of Character or moral development. Dayanand advocated righteous life as the sole aim of life. Thus the main aim of education was moral aim. He advocated the fostering of ethical and moral virtues among the students. He believed that a true and sound system of education should have character formation as its main objective. Children should always speak the truth. In the matter of dress and diet also they should so conduct themselves as to gain in health, strength, general behaviour and knowledge.

The Curriculum. Dayanand emphasises the study of Vedas and allied Sanskrit literature. He says "..........those who read the Vedas do righteous deeds, practise Yoga and thereby know God, stabilize themselves in God and attain the highest happiness of salvation."

Educational Programme

1. Panini's Phonetics—to be taught for correct pronunciation.

2. Science of knowledge and Grammar—to be taught for 3 years.
3. Nighantu and Nikarata (Study of Vedic Vocabulary and Philosophy) duration 6 to 8 months.
4. Prosody (Rules governing poetry) duration 4 months.
5. Manusmriti, Vidurniti, and Mahabharata for one year.
6. Six Shastras (Philosophy) for 2 years.
7. Four Upvedas—for two years.
8. Jyotish-Shastra (Astronomy)—for two years.

Besides, he prescribed practical religious training, Sandhyopasana Yajna and Homa (Havana) etc.

Dayanand also favoured science and technology. He, however, prescribed a separate curriculum for women.

Dayanand did not make mention of any special method of teaching. But on the basis of his philosophy and educational principles, he seems to be in favour of discussion and lecture methods. Discipline is an essential element in the educational programme of Dayanand.

Teacher. Dayanand gave an important place to teachers. There should be male teachers for boys' school and female teachers for women institutions. Teachers must be men of high character and sound ideals. There should be close relationship between the teacher and the taught. The most important influence in the school should be the personality of the teacher—Guru. He must be dedicated to his profession.

Views about Women Education. As Dayanand advocated equal rights for women, he was strongly in favour of women education. He quoted the Vedas where women enjoyed equal right with men and were qualified for higher learning. Dayanand recommended for girls Grammar, Dharma, Medical Sciences and practical arts. The main sphere of duty of women is home. Thus he is the first Indian reformer who vehmently pleaded for their education.

The Assessment

Primarily Dayanand was a socio-political reformer. He was a Sanyasi, a Brahmachari, a scholar and an educationist. In his quest to regenerate the society, he established the Arya Samaj, and advocated certain principles of education which became the guidelines for various institutions.

It can be said that Dayanand was not an educationist to be compared with Froebel, and Dewey as he did not give us any special system of education. He was an idealist and as an idealist, his educational principles were unpracticable like all other idealists. His emphasis on moral values, character development and democratic approach to education are the chief contributions to education.

QUESTIONS

1. Write a profile of Swami Dayanand as an Educationist.
2. Explain the key points of Swami's philosophy of education.
3. What was his scheme of studies ?

14

Muhammad Iqbal

Life Sketch

Muhammad Iqbal, one of the greatest Urdu Poets was born in Sialkot on November, 7, 1877. He was the youngest child of a tailor Shaikh Nur Muhammad and his wife Imam Bibi. Originally the family had been Kashmiri Brahmin, and became converts to Islam some generations previously. The young Iqbal learnt Urdu, Persian and English, and was brought up as an Orthodox Muslim. In his early life he learnt the Koran and studied commentaries on the text. He was a lover of sports and bird-watching was also his hobby. He completed High School in 1892 and won a Merit scholarship for College education. His parents got him married at the age of fifteen.

In 1895 when Iqbal was eighteen, and had passed his Intermediate from the Suthsh Mission College in Sialkot, he was admitted to the Government College Lahore, where he studied Arabic, English and Philosophy. He graduated in 1899, and was awarded a Gold Medal for his outstanding scholastic performance.

Iqbal used to compose poetry when he was at school. However, it was in Lahore that the young college student gained fame by his recitations at various poet symposia and mushairas. His friend Shaikh Abdul Kadir (Later Sir) encouraged him to write more poems and persuaded him to get them published in an Urdu Magazine Mukhzan. He became well known in Urdu literary circles, and Professor Thomas Arnold (Later Sir) composer of The Light of Asia took note of Iqbal's poetic ability, while he was studying for the Masters degree. Iqbal was appointed Reader in Arabic in the Islamia and Government Colleges, while studying law at the same time. He appeared for the Provincial Civil Service Examination, but due to medical reasons, he did not qualify.

Iqbal went to Europe in 1905, and took the Master's degree in Philosophy from the Cambridge University. Later he succeeded in learning German and obtained a Ph.D. from the University of Munich. At the same time, he was composing prose and poetry pries in Persian, and was held in high esteems by classical scholars. The three years that Iqbal spent in Europe, influenced Iqbal's ideas greatly. The impact of western ideology upon his Islamic background, brought about a change in his outlook. While he admired the philosophy of the Sufi Mystics, he now refused to consider life transitory or unreal. He detested the materialism of the West, and was upset by the decadence of Islamic values. Western ideology made him realize the importance of Will Power (KHUDI) and the development of the self. This self is to be merciful but assertive. Power and wealth are desirable but only if obtained by hard work and determination and not by inheritance on by chance or exploitation.

His education in Europe, made Iqbal believe strongly that intellectual and poetic endeavours are not in any way superior to a life of action. He even considered giving up writing, but was persuaded by his friends not to do so.

He was a member of the Punjab Legislative Council and was made a delegate to the First Round Table Conference in London in 1931.

He died in Lahore in 1938, after achieving great honour as a distinguished scholar and Urdu poet.

Educational Ideology

Although not an educator, in the professional sense of the word, Iqbal as a poet and a philosopher, has left a legacy of thoughts and ideas, that are useful to educators, and can give inspiration to young people.

It requires a proper knowledge of the Muslim heritage, to appreciate many of his ideas.

Just as Swami Dayanand, and Swami Vivekananda, gave a new understanding and appreciation of the thoughts and ideals embedded in Hinduism:

(i) Iqbal the poet gave new understanding and interpretation to the teachings of Islam. Iqbal was attracted to the teachings of the prophet, because of two fundamental beliefs :-

(a) The Oneness of God.

(b) The Brotherhood of Man.

He fervently believed that no religion other than Islam preached or practised these two ideas effectively.

(ii) Iqbal loved Hindustan and considered it the best country in the world, yet he denounced narrow nationalism. He believed that only nationalism, without an understanding of other nations, leads to conflicts and wars. He believed that "there is only one unity— the brotherhood of man which is above race, nationality, colour or language." He detested discrimination.

(iii) Iqbal had faith in the individual, and in the individual's ability to attain the highest level of development. He held that man's faith, his culture, his historical traditions are the things in life, for which one may sacrifice any thing.

(iv) According to Iqbal direct knowledge comes through the affective and not the cognitive process. Although Iqbal disliked Plato's idealism, yet his own view of art is platonic. Instead of dreaming, however, he is inclined to theorize. He does not discover or uncover the meanings of things, he assumes that he already knows them.

(v) A devout Muslim, Iqbal, criticised the Mullahs, and exhorted Hindus and Muslims to come together. He wanted them to build new shrines where they could worship together, and regarded every corner of India as sacred.

(vi) The world is real, life has a purpose to serve. Within every man is a superman, who can ceaselessly strive to make a better world. This aspect of Iqbal's philosophy appeared after his education in Europe and is termed the philosophy of KHUDI or self-hood. From Khud Ego to Khudi Super-Ego, Khudi, refers to an assertive will power which is charged with moral values.

(vii) Human beings should strive for perfection or Fakhr—a pride in what comes from the highest endeavour. They should constantly work for the good of humanity without an eye on material gains. The poor man who works for the betterment of humanity, is a truly wealthy man.

(viii) A ceaselessly agitated mind, and a state of tension within the individual are needed in man, if he is to achieve anything. Meditation and relaxation cannot lead to achievement. One of his Persian poems reads thus:

> "May God bring or storm in your life
>
> The sea of your life is placed, its waves
>
> Devoid of humult"

In one of his Persian works Secrets of the Self—he says "Personality is a state of tension and can continue only if the state is maintained." He advocates that the state of tension is one of the most important attributes of man, and he should not fall into a state of relaxation.

Role in Education

From the ideas derived from a reading of the poetry of Iqbal, both in Urdu, and in Persian, we can see that he is indeed a very great poet, philosopher, and in a sense a revolutionary. He has many new ideas to offer, and these may be incorporated in education.

1. *Patriotic Fervour*—Iqbal loved Hindustan—and considered every part of it as sacred. He exhorted Hindus and Muslims to come together.

2. *Internationalism*—He decried narrow nationalism and urged equality between races, creeds and nations—He detested war and conflict.

3. He was not a Conventional Muslim but provided a new insight into the teachings of Islam. His faith in the Prophet-Muhammad was the mainspring of his thought. He believed in the Oneness of God and the Brotherhood of man.

4. He gave us the idea of KHUDI and Fakhr (Super Ego and Pride), which combination are very similar to the Hindu ideal of Nishikarma, or striving for perfection without hope of a reward. He urged mankind to have a pride in striving ceaslessly towards the goal of perfection.

5. Iqbal condemned the strong who exploited the weak. He advocated a better life for the poor people. His ideas may be regarded as Marxist revolutionary in a sense, because he urged the peasants to rise against their oppressors, to destroy the crops and the monsoons

of the rich. Yet he was a supporter of the highest Muslim values and a pan-Islamist. He denounced Capitalism because he considered it cruel and heartless.

6. Iqbal had full faith in the individual and in his ability to rise to the highest pinnacle of development. He urgest ceaseless striving for perfection by the individual.

7. Iqbal urged universal, social reconstruction—He despised discrimination of groups, individuals and communities amongst themselves. All should be one, and no different treatment should be meted out to any one. "It is in the temple of love and compassion", he writes in his poems, that we can create a new world with new dawns and sunsets because there are new worlds beyond the stars we see". He was a humanist to the core.

8. Iqbal's perfect man is one who is truthful compassionate and fearless. He can face death with courage and without any fear whatsoever.

Status as Educationist

Iqbal has given us many valuable ideas, on the dignity of man, based on the ideals of Islam, as well as those of a humanist. He has stressed the importance of the Super Ego and Pride in the process of attaining fulfilment of one's goals as a human being.

Iqbal the nationalist with patriotic fervour, was yet an internationalist. People may question why he supported the idea of Pakistan. Iqbal wanted a Pakistan or Muslim homeland within India, he wanted a homeland based on humanitarian ideals within India, he wanted a homeland based on humanitarian ideals, which was not confined to any one region or territory.

According to one of his poems

"God-possessed dervish is neither of the

East nor of the West.

My home is neither Delhi, nor Isfahan nor Samarkand".

Again, in another poem he wrote—

"You are on the highway, How can you be confined to any particular place?

Pass through Egypt and Hijaz. Leave behind

Persia and Syria".

A few months before he died in Lahore he said "Only one unity is to be depended upon—that unity is the brotherhood of man."

Iqbal has left us many of the highest ideals of humanity through his beautiful poetry, and these may be incorporated in education.

Past Experience

India is rightly proud of Dr. Mohammad Iqbal because he occupies a unique position in contemporary Indian thought. He applied academic philosophical standards to Islamic thought. Iqbal carries the Islamic tradition with him whereas Indian philosophers thought in the background of Hindu tradition.

Sir Mohammad Iqbal was born in 1876 at Sialkot. Others say that he was born in 1873. Ariyway, Iqbal got his early education at Sialkot and Lahore. His academic career was excellent. He obtained his M.A. in Philosophy from Govt. College, Lahore. He did his Ph.D. from Cambridge. He taught philosophy. He also practised law but primarily Iqbal was a poet and a philosopher. Poetry was his first love. While Tagore wrote in Bengali in East India, Iqbal wrote in Urdu in Western India. Both wrote and rose to great heights. Iqbal's books are well known. Iqbal wrote for children, for the youth, for the romantics and for the old. His "Saare Jehan Sey Achha" or "Tarana-i-Hindi" is well known. It was written in 1904 and published in a Kanpur paper for the first time.

In old age, Iqbal accepted a pension from the ruler of Bhopal which he enjoyed till his death. Iqbal died in 1938 at Lahore. Iqbal stands honoured all over the world.

The Awareness

Iqbal feels that the intimate truths are not known in an ordinary way which is the way of experience. Iqbal does not deny of experience but this only represents a normal level of knowledge. Reality can not be known directly. Experience approaches reality in a very indirect manner. Reality can be approached directly and Quran has spoken about such a process.

The Quran describes the source of knowledge—the one that can be known directly as Faud or Qalb-heart. To quote Iqbal, "The heart is a kind of inner intuition or insight which, in beautiful words of Rumi, feeds on the rays of the sun and brings us into contact with aspects of Reality other than those open to sense perception." It is according to Quran, something which "sees", and its reports if properly interpreted are never false. The "heart" thus is the seat of intuition.

(i) Immediacy-i.e. It is immediate knowledge of Reality or God because it knows it without the help of any medium. Iqbal says that intuition has the directions of sense-experience.

(ii) Intuitive experience is always as a whole. It is an unassailable unity.

(iii) Relation with Supreme. This experience, according to Iqbal, is a moment of very intimate relation with the supreme. It is an awareness of God, a feeling of the presence of the Divine.

(iv) There is an objectivity about Intuition. It transcends the individual and causes an awareness in which the individual feels that the object—the supreme self is there.

(v) According to Mr. Basant Kumar Lal, Iqbal asserts that this experience is incommunicable. It is sometimes, taken as a defect of intuition.

Concept of God : Islam believes in Monotheism. It conceives God as one omnipotent all, knowing and supremely good creator of the world. It believes that God is a personal God. In Islam we do not make any distinction between God and the Absolute.

Iqbal has conceived same attributes of God. His attributes are intellectual in nature like-

(i) Creativeness

(ii) Knowledge

(iii) Omnipotence

(iv) Eternity

(v) Immanence

(vi) Transcendence.

Creativeness : This attribute appears to be a necessary attribute of God on account of the fact that God has been conceived as an Ego. An Ego-life is always a creative life. The Supreme Ego is also creative in the ways in which Ego is creative.

Knowledge : "In Him thought and deed, the act of knowing and the act of creating are identical." Divine knowledge is creational, and as there outside God. He himself is the object of His knowledge. He knows as He creates and creates as He knows.

Omnipotence : Omnipotence is not to be conceived as a whimsical or arbitrary concept capable of doing everything and anything. It must appear to be "a reasonable" concept. It must be emotionally and intellectualy satisfying.

Eternity : Eternity has to conceived by Iqbal as a time concept, it is not an idea of endlessness in time. Real time is duration which leaves nothing behind and which potentially everything

that is to happen. God is eternal because He is the possibility of all expressions. Basant Kumar Lal says of time-process is one of the expressions of the infinite possibilities contained in God. It is in this sense that God is eternal.

Power of Prayer : Iqbal believes in prayer. He believes in patience. Prayer and patience are related. Patience hardens the self against every kind of ills, and enables him to cultivate the capacity of applying concentrated energy to every situation that confronts an individual. The purest example of concentration of patience is prayer.

Prayer intensifies life. It is the way in which ego is able to affirm itself even in the midst of adversity.

Man's Ego : Iqbal believes in Ego. Ego is two fold—

(i) Efficient Ego, and

(ii) Appreciative Ego.

Efficient ego means the worldly life or material life whereas appreciative ego is spiritual existence which is experienced when the efficient ego is in abeyance.

Concept of Man : Man is the apex and crown of all creations of God. Iqbal believes in freedom and liberty of man. Man is vice-regent of God. He believes in high destiny of man. Man on his part must strive towards perfection. If Man has bad habits and performs bad deeds, he must be able to justify these.

Man must develop all his powers. Man must exalt himself.

Good Man : Let us know Iqbal's concept of good man. A good man according to Sir Mohammad Iqbal must have the following characteristics:

(i) *Creative Life:* Man must lead creative life so that he is able to transform this crude world into beautiful world.

(ii) A good man is he who applies his intelligence.

(iii) *Subordination:* Man is subordinate to God. He must lead a humble life.

(iv) Good man refuses to compromise with evil.

(v) A good man is courageous.

(vi) *Active Contact.* A good man is in active contact with material and cultural environment.

Faith in Mankind : Man is the representative of God on earth. Iqbal has faith in man's high destiny. Man is to strive towards perfection only. And you can have perfection only when you develop all your powers.

Views on Religion : To quote Iqbal, "Religion in its higher manifestation is neither dogma nor priesthood nor ritual. It can alone ethically prepare the modern man for the burden of great responsibility which the advancement of natural science necessarily involves and restores to him that which makes him capable, of winning a personality here and retaining it hereafter?" It was the practical approach to religion.

Educational Philosophy : We have seen Iqbal's philosophy of life. From it, it can be easy to deduce his educational philosophy.

Iqbal was not an educationist in the strict sense but was a teacher throughout his life. He had the feel of education. Thus we can know about his educational philosophy from his personal or general philosophy and his experiences as a teacher.

Educational Aims

The aims of education according to Iqbal are:

Development of Self-hood or Individuality or Khudi : This is the chief aim of education according to Iqbal. As individuality develops, the power and capacities of man become sharpened and well defined. This growth of individuality is in no way isolated from the rest of the mankind. Iqbal quotes Quran,

"Blessed is he who hath made it grow and undone is he who has corrupted it."

Development of Creativity : Every individual has creative powers in him. These are to be developed. The process of education is to ignite these creative powers. Creativity is to be developed.

Morality and Character to be Developed : This is the next important aim of education. Morality is to be developed. Character is to be developed. He wanted the moral code which "arises out of willing cooperation of free egos." For him 'goodness is not a matter of compulsion.' True morality develops only when there is a choice, freedom and experiences acquired through social interaction.

Education Must Develop Patriotism and Nationalism in the Students : This is another aim of education according to Iqbal.

Social Development. Education should also develop a child socially. It means that one should be well adjusted with the society.

Cultural Values should also be Developed : The cultural values of community should be appreciated. To quote Iqbal, "Education enables a child to adhere to the highest on its cultural values enables and traditions. Any form of education which ignores this fundamental task is utterly superficial and sterile."

The Textbooks

Dr. Iqbal suggested that curriculum should be broad based. It is only this that will develop national self-respect and understanding.

He also suggested that the curriculum should be life centred and realistic. It should be related to the needs and aspirations of the students. Accordingly, Dr. Mohammad Iqbal wanted the teaching of:

(i) Sciences—Physics and Chemistry must be taught. They help in saving life.

(ii) Morality and Religion are equally must. To quote him, "Religion has always elevated the individuals and transformed whole societies." The religion advocated by him was, "living nobly and adventurously in the name of God."

(iii) History should be taught. It helps in understanding the present.

(iv) Political Science and Economics are equally important.

(v) Languages like Urdu and Persian are a must. These help in understanding religious teachings.

(vi) Cultural heritage is equally a must.

(vii) Creative education and guidance should also be taught.

Approach to Teaching

Freedom : The process of education should be free. We have already said in the main part that Iqbal valued freedom like anything. Freedom is an essential condition for the growth of man. There should be no dogmatic teaching. Freedom is the watch-word of Dr. Iqbal in the learning process. He rejects all external restraints. He believes in intellectual freedom. Intellectual freedom assures of unlimited advances in knowledge. And he also believes in Moral freedom. Moral freedom is a freedom of choice between good and evil. Goodness is not a matter of compulsion-you are good because there is no way out. No! you are to be willingly good.

Principle of Experience : Like pragmatists, Iqbal values experience as a method of teaching. Experience is a great teacher. Man learns through first hand experience. Let there be errors. Never mind these errors. Error is indispensable factor in the building up of experience.

Principle of Activity : This means that education should be action-oriented. Action has great value in life. It helps in formation of character and personality.

Principle of Variety : Variety is the spice of life. Yon can't give the same activity to the child everyday. The child wants new activity, only then he will attend to it for long, otherwise the child will lose interest.

Memory should be encouraged. Let them remember verses.

Teacher to be a good model in teaching learning. These are some of the points highlighted by Iqbal in his Techniques of Teaching.

Education for Females

Equal opportunities should be provided to women for their education. He was all for the education of females. He wanted that moral, spiritual and religious education should be imparted to women as they inculcate and develop higher values of life in children. He was critical of the domination of women by men. He wanted equal place for women in society.

Action-oriented Education : Action has a place in life. He wanted education to be action-oriented. Action makes ideas valid. His doctrine was "the call to act, throw off lethargy and emerge, as supermen." He did not believe in defeatism. He did not believe in, "Those also serve who stand and wait"—a statement given by an English poet. Action and struggle form the keystone of the whole structure of life. Action, thus is all the more important in life.

Well Integrated Education : Iqbal believed in giving well integrated education. Integrated education helps in achieving balance between different aims—intellectual and spiritual activity and contemplation.

Humane Outlook : Education must promote humane outlook. Iqbal was a humanist to the core and he wanted education to be humane.

Educational Programme

Dr. Iqbal thought and believed that education was a part of our life. You cannot run away from it. We are alive that is a chance otherwise what is life? It is a passage of thoughts, a series of deaths. Education has to be sensitive and oriented to this dynamic character of inner life of man. Education thus is a process of adjustment. It is to be properly conceived and properly directed.

Value of Prayer : We have already highlighted this. Iqbal had great faith in prayer. It has been elaborated by K.G. Saiyidain when he says, "Within the educative process room must be found for that silent, reverent communion with the self and with the nature in all her beauty and majesty which is often a prelude to communion with God."

On the basis of philosophy of Iqbal, we can say that the system of education advocated by Sir Mohammad Iqbal was comprehensive and well integrated. Through it he wanted to strike a balance between the material and spiritual activity and contemplation. Iqbal was indeed a great poet, philosopher and original thinker. India is rightly proud of him.

QUESTIONS

1. Trace the early life and career of the Poet Muhammad Iqbal.
2. What are the main ideas underlying the philosophy of Iqbal?
3. In what ways may some of the ideas put forward by the poet Mohammad Iqbal be incorporated into education?
4. Comment on Iqbal's concept of internationalism.

15

Zakir Hussain

Life Sketch

Zakir Hussain belonged to the family of Afridi Pathans who had migrated to India in 1719 A.D. and settled at Qaimganj town in Farrukhabad District of Uttar Pradesh where other migratory Afghans had settled down.

We begin with the grandfather of Zakir Husain. Ghulam Husain Khan had two sons—Ata Husain Khan and Fida Husain Khan. Ata Husain Khan joined the army. Fida Husain Khan was a scholarly person. He was adventurous also. From Qaimganj in U.P., he migrated to Hyderabad and opened a shop of Moradabad Brassware there. But his scholarly nature surfaced. He studied law and started practice in Hyderabad. He was married at the age of 23 and fathered seven sons. Zakir Husain was third in order.

Zakir Husain was born on 8th February, 1897 in Hyderabad. He was brought up as any upper class Muslim would have been. He was nicely dressed and was put to puritanical discipline.

In 1905, when Zakir Hussain was nine years old and a student of Sultan Bazar Govt. High School in Hyderabad, his father Fida Husain died of tuberculosis at the young age of 39. The family had to shift to their ancestral home at Qaimganj. His mother Naznin Begum was worried about the education of her children as they could not get proper education at home.

In 1908 Zakir Husain was in a residential school at Etawah, the Islamic, started by Moulvi Bashiruddin, who hoped to impart English education as well as the Islamic way of life. The school was headed by a dedicated nationalist, Muslim Altaf Husain. Altaf Husain advised him to sacrifice the pleasures of life.

Zakir Hussain was studious. He religiously walked to the Etawah Railway Station daily to buy a copy of The Pioneer and on return would discuss contents with friends. Bright as well as respectful, Zakir Hussain won the confidence of his teachers and students alike, a peak of his Islamic phase was reached when at his persuasion, the management abandoned its practice of depriving a student of a meal for missing a prayer.

After having passed his matriculation examination in 1913 with distinction, he joined the MAO College at Aligarh from where he passed the Intermediate examination in Science with Biology. He could not become a doctor because he fell ill.

When still an undergraduate student, Zakir Hussain was married to Begum Sahjahan Bano. He was a loving father too.

Passed his B.A. in 1918 and won Iqbal Medal. At Aligarh he was popularly known as "Murshid" (Mentor). He wrote articles and was given junior lecturership.

The steel of his character was tempered when the non-cooperation call came from Gandhi in 1920. Zakir Hussain responded to the call with about 300 students, took the first 'conscious' decision of his life and left the MAO College. This strengthened the hands of Mohammad Ali who bounded Jamia Millia Islamia (National Muslim University) in 1920. Zakir Husain joined this institution as lecturer in economics but after a Ph. D. from Germany in 1926, he came back and joined Jamia Millia

Islamia as its Vice-Chancellor @ Rs. 80/-per month-Rs. 40 cash and Rs. 40 in credit. He worked selflessly for about 20 years in this institution.

In 1957, Pandit Jawaharlal Nehru offered him the governorship of Bihar.

Earlier he had contributed in the field of Basic Education.

In 1962, Zakir Hussain was elected the Vice-President of India. He attributed his success to his close involvement in education work and to the significance of education in the life of the people. From 1962 to 1967 he was chairman of Rajya Sabha in his capacity as Vice President of India.

He was elected President of India in 1967. He died in office in May 1969.

He had remarkable qualities of head and heart and personality of heart. He was a true and devout Muslim. He was a sufi. He had many hobbies also. He was a passionate lover of plants, flowers a connoisseur of art, music and culture. "It was rare to find so integrated a personality as Zakir Hussain's".

Philosophy of Education

Concept of Reality : This universe is real. There is reality of two worlds-material world or materialism and spiritual world or spiritualism.

(i) Material world is world of senses, and it deals with things or substances solids.

(ii) The spiritual world is soul. It is the soul which moves universe. Mind only apprehends it. Pleasures of the world are secondary. The spiritual world is to be realised by mind. Mind also catches ideas. Spiritualism is realised by ideas.

Concept of Man : An element of faith in "man" is clearly visible in Dr. Zakir Hussain's philosophy and educational ideas.

He attaches the highest value to man in his educational philosophy and seeks to evolve man to the best of his potentialities.

In this sense Dr. Zakir Hussain is also a humanist. He recognizes man's capacity to conquer nature. He did not consider man just a part of Nature. He deemed man not as a Progressive animal, in the words of K.R.P. Singh, but also a social impulse. Social impulse means that all members of a cosmic society, they are all brothers, children of the same father and therefore man must place universal welfare above other interests so much so that narrow national interests ought to be sacrificed at the altar of human weal. Dr. Zakir Hussain did not believe in caste, creed, colour, race and religion. He wanted a cultured man, rather than authentic man. No barriers anywhere in the interpretation of relations between human beings. He preached understanding and reconciliation. His ideas were to unite rather than to divide humanity. Truths must be applied for the good of mankind.

Dr. Zakir Hussain believed that man's destiny does not comprise of mere control over nature nor does it mean improvement in his productive efficiency just to satisfy his natural wants. Man must respect the source from which all creation springs and expands in order to deeper the meaning of man's life on earth. Therefore, Dr. Zakir Hussain exhorted the education to appreciate total human legacy—science, art, crafts, music, literature, philosophy etc. Man has, no doubt, come to be what he is as a result of biological evolution which is an endless product. The cultural volution centres round man's creative mind and own making. He writes, "Man is a part and product of the process but a very peculiar part, capable of effecting its further course on earth and perhaps elsewhere."

Concept of Mind : Mind is source of everything. If we want peace and culture, it is mind which has got to be cultivated. Cultivated mind will bring a balance between material and spiritual world. It should have peace. Its energy should be properly utilized.

The Values : Education must cultivate-values. He wanted best values for Indians and he commended values like selfless service, secularising democracy. He stressed truths, beauty and goodness.

Education indeed refers to a set of values or ideals embodied and expressed in the purpose, for which knowledge, skills and attitudes are imparted and so directing the amounts and types of training what is given. "Almost the same view is expressed by Dr. Zakir Hussain when he writes that implies an individually organised sense of values."

Value can be defined in different ways. Ordinarily, a "value is that which satisfies human desire. All things that satisfy human desire have value or are good." In subtler form we can say "that alone is ultimately and intrinsically valuable that leads to development of self or to self-realization." True to his conception of values Dr. Zakir Hussain laid due emphasis on self-realization as an integral part of his value systems.

Values can be classified into eight categories-bodily, economic, creation, association, character, aesthetic, intellectual and religious. An analysis of Dr. Zakir Hussain value matrix presents almost a similar set of categories which can be classified as follows:

(a) Material.

(b) Individual-Things necessary for the development of self.

(c) Social.

(d) Cultural.

(e) Religious.

(f) Moral.

It is evident that the question of values was uppermost in the thought process of Dr. Zakir Hussain.

Awareness Theory

Two types of knowledge were stressed upon by Dr. Zakir Hussain:

(i) Knowledge of substance.

(ii) Knowledge of essence.

Science gives knowledge of substance. Science has changed the face of the world and is doing so. Science is helping us.

Culture gives knowledge of essence. Knowledge of essence means,

"Knowledge of the qualities, of the purpose, the origin, the end of the object, it involves a knowledge of its totality of the context which it makes the structural context, its 'what' and 'how'. It also talks of relational context-its 'whence' and 'whither' and 'who'. Dr. Zakir Hussain was an idealist.

Education : Perceptions

According to Dr. Zakir Hussain, "Education is the work of whole life. It begins from the time of birth and continues till the last moment of death."

This means that according to Dr. Hussain, Education is a continuous process. Every stage has its importance and significance. Education is life long activity.

Education is not merely giving information. It is leading to the maximum possible development of the mind.

Value of Learning

To quote K.R.P. Singh, a truly educated man is one who has the following five essential qualities:

Breadth of Intellectual Horizon : The educated man has a certain breadth of intellectual horizon with reference to value attached to things and persons. He has no thinker.

Open Minded : He possesses a certain degree of lively open mindedness and accessibility of new value and new ideas.

Moral Growth and Perfection : He has an inner urge towards moral growth and constantly presses towards perfection in his own person or world around him. He is not conceited and never imagines he has reached the destination.

Flexible : He has a flexible and versatile relation to value relationships amongst things as against the rigorous sufferers of the zealot or the bureaucrat.

Absolute Objective Value : His value estimations having been organized around an absolute objective value, he gives clear evidence of a central psychic focus which irritates all his action, thought and feeling. He is no internally dissipated busy body.

Aims and Objectives

The aims of education for Dr. Zakir Hussain are neither completely unearthly nor merely mundane. They are rather a fruitful blending of the two. The aims of education should, therefore, constitute a kind of strong link between material ends and spiritual upliftment, between individual and social growth, between national and international perspective, and between man and man in every respect.

The aims of education according to Dr. Zakir Hussain are—

Fullest Development of Man : The purpose of education is to help man reach the fullest status as man. Educational programme must aim at man's creative and national values, besides inculcating in him a kind of religious faith. It is the fullest development that is important and all round development.

Stress on Creative Development : That we have already mentioned above. That leads to development of individuality.

To Enable One to Earn Livelihood. Vocational aims of education is so vital an aspect of education that no system of education would be complete unless it includes it. It is directly addressed to the breadwinning without which each man's existence would be jeopardised. Education must solve the problem of livelihood in a socially approved way. This is Zakir's vocational aim of education.

Ethical Aim. Moral development and ethical protection are most important aims of education. A truly educated man, according to Zakir Sahib is one who has a wiser urge towards moral growth and constantly presses towards perfection.

Spiritual development is yet another aim of education.

Preservation, conservation and transmission of culture is considered one of the most significant aims of education.

Preparation of Texts

Regarding curriculum, Dr. Zakir Hussain observed that it must not aim at meeting individual educational needs, aspirations and attainments only but also reflect the national ethos and expectations. They, like Dewey, he was not satisfied with any cut and dry item of curriculum. He firmly believed that curriculum should not only be organic but it should also be closely related to the real life of the educands.

He agreed with Pestalozzi also and believed that, man is much more truly educated through that which he does, than through which he reads. It is with this conviction that he wanted a child to develop some reasonable skill in a basic craft. In his thought on syllabus, he laid emphasis on pupils activities rather than on teacher's activities. For him experiences constituted the heart of the knowing process. He wanted to exploit activities and crafts for pedagogical purposes and for integrating theory with practice. By curricular content he also wanted to bridge the gap between real life and schooling. Dr. Zakir Hussain wanted a happy blending of knowledge provided by mathematics, physical and natural sciences and humanities. Thus, the curricular content, as recommended by Dr. Zakir Hussain, must cater to the multi-dimensional growth of the educand.

In short, the curriculum comes down to :

1. Languages.
2. Science and technology.
3. Social sciences.
4. Art and music.

Instructional Process

Dr. Zakir Hussain contributed a lot in the field of Basic Education and his method of teaching, thus cannot be different. It is:

(a) Learning by doing, it is manual work and useful productive work. Working with one's own hands—that the method of teaching.

(b) Principle of social orientation. Education should be socially useful.

Role of Teachers

He also gave full attention to the teacher, his role and qualities, his preparation, and his professional ethics. He did not conceptualize the teacher as one who was always original or a genius but rather one who in his words and actions, repeated common-place truths not once or twice but so often and in so many ways that the educands took them for granted and they become their convictions. His main role was to transform the individual's achievement into social and moral values. The qualities which he valued most in teachers were love for humanity in general and love for children in particular and a never diminishing 'faith' in their future. His training should also attune to his role and in order to perform his professional work satisfactorily, he himself should be a morally autonomous personality. The teacher, according to Dr. Zakir Hussain, was the 'custodian' of the highest human and social values. As such, he should be ethically alive to his over-all responsibilities to his students.

The Freedom : Dr. Zakir Hussain gave due consideration to this question: He created school to be true democratic society in which individuality is respected and human personality is considered as an end and not merely a means. He did not consider freedom and authority as contrary to each other. All educational theories value inner freedom and the authority is recognized voluntarily. Therefore the question of authority and freedom in schooling is resolved thus. The authority of values, freely experienced and freely accepted in the real life constitutes the test of real education. Dr. Zakir Hussain expected schools and colleges to develop students into useful citizens possessing free moral conscience personality. In a way he sought a happy blending of freedom and authority in the process of schooling at all levels and grades.

You can say that some sort of authority is required at the beginning of education for guidance.

Development of an Institution

Muslim National University is at New Delhi (near Okhla). For more than 20 years, Dr. Zakir Hussain was its Vice-Chancellor. It is a full-fledged University. Here the wisdom of East and West is pooled.

The educational views of Dr. Zakir Husain echo in a big way what other educational philosophers have said from time to time. His thought presents a synthesis of various different philosophies of education. His ideas present an essential unity between man and man, between man and nature and between man and God.

16

Sri Aurobindo

Education has been defined as a consciously controlled process whereby changes in behaviour are produced in a person, and through him in a group. It is a gradual adjustment of the individual to the spiritual possessions of the race. Hence, education is considered to be normative in that it explores various aspects of human personality so as to prescribe a generally suitable and acceptable programme of learning which should be conducive for the attainment of its objectives and goals. However, there has been a continuous change in the nature, extent and import of these objectives which are inversely related to the meaning and reality ascribed to human nature and to the environment in which education takes place. Hence, education is in dire need of some sort of a philosophy which may provide it with direction and roots, stability and purpose. Aurobindo, suggested a kind of education in conformity with the Indian needs, ethos and culture, thus providing it necessary depth and relevance.

Life Sketch

Aurobindo Ghosh was born in 1872 in Calcutta. His father sent him to England at the early age of six so that he grows up into an artificial Englishman. In England he not only mastered Greek and Latin languages to study the masterpiece creations of ancient philosophers, social thinkers and poets, but also became well-versed in many European languages namely, French, German, Italian etc. Upto the age of fourteen he received purely Western education. In 1890, Aurobindo passed the Indian Civil Service Examination but could not appear in the test of horse riding. As such, he found himself not qualified and returned to India in 1893 and served for thirteen years in the Baroda state under the Gaekwad ruler. Here he studied Sanskrit language and literature and prepared himself for his future mission. After the Bengal partition disturbances, he resigned from his job and jumped into the political struggle which was hotting up by leaps and bounds. Gradually, through his papers namely 'Bandematram', 'Karmyogin', 'Dharm' and fiery speeches, he roused the intense feeling of nationalism in the people of India and finally declared complete independence as the goal of struggle of independence. He suffered imprisonment many a time because of his active involvement in the struggle of freedom. Once, while lodged in Alipur jail, he realised the presence of God in a dream. He was so much influenced by the Divine Vision that in 1915, after his release from prison, he quitted all political activities and retired to the French territory Pondicherry for penance and spiritual advancement. There he built an Ashram which is famous all over the world as Aurobindo Ashram. He spent the rest of his life in this Ashram doing Yoga Sadhna, meditation for spiritual growth and development. In this way, Aurobindo was transformed from a politician to a philosopher and preached to the world his philosophy of Dharm, spiritual growth, Brahmacharya Yoga and Educational ideology. He died in 1950.

The Ideology

Aurobindo Ghosh was an Idealist to the core. His Idealistic philosophy of life was based upon Vedantic philosophy of

Upnishads. He laid great stress on the spiritual penance, Yoga practice and Brahmacharya as necessary for the development of human soul. He exhorted that the sole aim of growth should be to achieve the all pervading Divine Power. According to him this principle of growth continues to operate always in all conditions and in all times and places. During this cultural growth, a stage arrives where by virtue of his supreme development of mental powers, a man attains the status of Superman himself. After this, he grows from knowledge to more knowledge and from light and enlightment to more enlightenment progressively where he experiences the supreme happiness and divine bliss and gains the insight into all creation.

Aurobindo Ghosh was not only a great philosopher but an eminent educationist as well. He showed to mankind the way to the highest spiritual growth. As such, he is acclaimed as a great solace giver to the people. Shri Aurobindo expressed his thoughts in his weekly newspaper 'Karam Yogin' in which he stressed that the main aid of a teacher is his conscience. This conscience has four stages namely—(1) Consciousness, (2) Mind, (3) Intelligence and (4) Knowledge. Education should develop all these four stages as much as possible. As an Idealist, Aurobindo's philosophy of education is based on spiritual penance, yoga and brahmacharya. He held the view that education involving these three factors will definitely develop man to the fullest extent. According to Aurobindo a man does not possess a physical extent. According to Aurobindo a man does not possess a physical spirit only as he is endowed with higher mental, godly intelligency and a very high spiritual soul element. Not only this, he has a capacity to recognise and realise God by training his powers of thinking, concentration and deep meditation together with other divine faculties to the fullest. According to Aurobindo, real education provides a free and creative environment to the child developing his interests, creativity, mental, moral and aesthetic senses leads to the development of his spiritual powers. Shri Aurobindo himself writes—"That alone would be true and living education which helps to bring out to full advantage all that is in an individual man."

The Fundamentals

The basic principles of Shri Aurobindo's educational philosophy are given below:

1. Education should be imparted through the medium of mother-tongue.
2. Education should be child-centred.
3. Education should be according to the mental aptitudes and psychological needs of the child.
4. Education should develop to the full the latent powers of the child.
5. Education should achieve the physical purification of a child.
6. Education should develop consciousness.
7. Education should train the senses.
8. Education should develop the soul substance of an individual.
9. Brahmacharya should be the basic foundation of education.
10. Subjects of education should be interesting.
11. Education should develop all the facilities of child to make him a complete man.
12. There should be religious tinge in education otherwise it will spread corruption.

The Perception

Aurobindo Ghosh was against the prevalent education of his times. He admitted that changes have occurred in our system of education after the attainment of independence but these are not in conformity with the mental and spiritual needs of children and demands of the nation. According to him, our education should be in accordance with the needs of our real modern life. In other words, education should create dynamic citizens so that they are able to meet the real needs of modern complex life. Shri Aurobindo thus writes—"Education to be true must not be a machine made fabric, but a true building or living evocation of the powers of the mind and spirit of human being".

Aims and Goals

According to Aurobindo Ghosh, the aims of education are as under:

1. *Physical Development and Purity*—The first aim of education is to achieve complete physical and pure development of a child. According to Aurobindo, it is the body which performs all religious obligations. As such, he not only emphasised mere physical development but physical purity also without which no spiritual development is possible. In this sense physical development and purification are the two bases on which the edifice of spiritual developments is built.

2. *Development of Senses*—The second aim of education is to train all the senses namely, hearing, speaking, listening, touching, smelling and tasting. According to Aurobindo these senses can be fully trained when nerve, chitta and manas (mind) are pure. Hence, through education purity of senses is to be achieved before any other development is possible.

3. *Mental Development*—The third aim of education is to achieve mental development of the child. Mental development means the development of all mental faculties, namely, memory, thinking, reasoning, imagination and discrimination etc. Education should develop them fully and harmoniously.

4. *Development of Morality*—Another essential aim of education is to develop the child morally. Shri Aurobindo emphasised that without moral and emotional development mental development becomes harmful to human progress. Emotions, impressions or habits and nature or temperament are the three essential factors for the moral development of a child. He yearned to educate man in the true sense of the term by the purification and sublimation of these essential factors. According to him; hearts of children should be so developed as to show extreme love, sympathy and consideration for all living beings. This is real moral development. Thus, the ideals of a teacher should be so high that the child, by mere imitation, is able to reach higher and higher stages of development by accepting the teacher as a role model.

5. *Development of Conscience*—Another important aim of education is to develop the conscience. According to him, it has four levels namely—(1) Chitta, (2) Manas, (3) Intelligence and (4) Knowledge which teacher should develop harmoniously. This will promote the development of conscience.

6. *Spiritual Development*—Aurobindo emphasised that the main aim of education is to promote spiritual development. According to him every human being has some element of divinity in him. Education should find it out and develop it to the fullest. In his own words—"The chief aim of education should be to help the growing soul to draw out of itself which is best and make it perfect for a noble use".

The Textbooks

Aurobindo Ghosh prescribed free environment for the child to develop all his latent faculties to the full and suggested all those subjects and activities of child's interest to be included in the curriculum. Such subjects and activities should possess elements of creativity and educational expression. He wished to infuse a new life and spirit into each subject and activity through which the development of super human being could become possible. For this, he laid down the following principles for curriculum construction:—

1. Curriculum should be interesting
2. It should include all those subjects which promote mental and spiritual development.
3. Subjects of curriculum should be able to motivate children.
4. Curriculum items should involve creativity of life and constructive capacities.
5. Curriculum should motivate children toward the attainment of knowledge of the whole world.

On the basis of the above principles Aurobindo has prescribed the following subjects in the curriculum for the different stages of education:

1. *Primary Stage*—Mother-tongue, English, French, Literature, National History, Art, Painting, General Science, Social Studies and Arithmetic.
2. *Secondary Stage*—Mother-tongue, English, French, Arithmetic, Art, Chemistry, Physics, Botany, Physiology, Health education, Social Studies.
3. *University Stage*—Indian and Western Philosophy, History of Civilization, English literature, French Literature, Sociology, Psychology, History of Science, Chemistry, Physics, Botany, International relations and integration.
4. *Vocational Education*—Arts, Painting, Photography, Sewing, Sculptural drawing, Typing, Shorthand,

Cottage industries, Carpentry, Mechanical and Electrical Engineering, Nursing, Indian and European Music, Dramatisation and Dancing.

Approaches to Teaching

Aurobindo Ghosh has laid stress upon the following principles of methods of teaching:—

1. *Freedom of Child*—Children should be provided with a free environment so that they are able to gain more and more knowledge by their own efforts. According to Aurobindo any restrained and imposed environment stunts growth and natural development.

2. *Love and Sympathy for the Child*—Children should be treated with utmost love, sympathy and consideration. This promotes their normal and natural development to the full.

3. *Education through Mother-Tongue*—Aurobindo emphasised that education should be imparted to the child through his mother tongue. Thus, he will be able to grasp and understand even the most difficult subjects easily.

4. *Education According to Interests of the Child*—The teacher should first study the interests of the child and then provide education accordingly so that he feels really motivated to learn and develop.

5. *Education through Self-experience*—Aurobindo asserted that a child should be free to learn by his own efforts and experiences. This leads to permanent learning and will prove useful for his future life.

6. *Emphasis on Learning by Doing*—Aurobindo Ghosh gave much importance to the activities of a child. According to him the best method of learning is learning by doing.

Hence, Aurobindo has emphasised Montessori method for infant classes and the practice of art and drawing in primary and secondary classes.

7. *Education through Co-operation*—According to Aurobindo. teaching and learning is a co-operative process. Hence, he laid great stress on such activities in the educational process.

8. *Education According to the Nature of Child*—Each child has an element of divinity as well as his own latent gifts of mind and spirit. Education should develop the child spiritually to the fullest extent by developing these elements of divinity and inherent mental capacity.

Child's Role

According to Aurobindo, each child had his own inherent capacities and special abilities. To fully develop these divine gifts is the chief purpose of education. In his opinion, to develop the latent faculties, capacities and abilities of the child according to some predetermined plan or scheme by force of compulsion, is to stunt the growth and do great injustice to him. Hence, according to him, education should satisfy the needs and interests of a child and develop his personality according to these powers to achieve full and complete development. In this connection Aurobindo writes—" The idea of hammering the child into shape desired by the parent or teacher is a barbarous and ignorant superstition. There can be no great error than for the parent to arrange before that his son shall develop particular qualities and capacities. To force the nature to abandon its own Dharam is to do permanent harm, mutilate its growth and deface its perfection".

Status of Teacher

About the teacher Aurobindo upholds, that "The teacher is not an instruct or task master, he is a helper and guide. His business is to suggest and not to impose. He does not actually train the pupil's mind, he only shows him how to perfect his instruments of knowledge and helps him and encourages him in the process. He does not impart knowledge to him, he shows him how to acquire knowledge that is within, he only shows him where it lies and how it can be habituated to rise to the surface".

The Assessment

Like the Naturalists and the Pragmatists, Aurobindo Ghosh laid stress upon child-centred education. He accepted the teacher as a helper, guide and instructor only and formulated those principles of education according to which, under a free and conducive environment, the child should be made to develop in accordance with his inherent interests, aptitudes and latent capacities by receiving a loving and sympathetic behaviour from those who are engaged in developing him.

His aims of education were based upon the philosophy of Idealism. As a matter of fact, Aurobindo was an Idealist to the core. His philosophy of education was based on spiritual faith, brahmacharya and yoga. It showed the way to spiritual growth and fulfilment of a man to the fullest extent. Though he was sufficiently influenced by Western philosophy, yet he remained basically all through his life an Indian and an Idealist devoted to spiritual advancement to the optimum. He imbibed the qualities and merits of the Western thought to enrich and consolidate the Indian beliefs and culture. His philosophy is a transition from materialism to spiritualism.

Aurobindo Ghosh realised that Indians were gradually drifting from Idealism toward materialism with the result that the inherent divine light in them was gradually on the wane. He vehemently condemned the Western materialistic education as it could not sustain and develop Indian ideals, values and culture. According to Aurobindo we need an education which develops the powers of our mind and soul and achieves our fullest growth. With these ends in view, he opened an Ashram at Pondicherry and established an International University providing education suited to the ideals and values of the Indian culture and based upon Brahmacharya, Yoga, concentration and meditation through which an individual could harmoniously develop to the full his body, mind and soul. "Aurobindo's philosophy of education is based on the principle of evocation of potentialities of the individual in all its entirety and full development of as many sides as possible. His views on education reveal that Shri Aurobindo was one of the most eminent and distinguished educationists of our country." (R.S. Mani)

To sum up, the whole purpose of his teachings was "that man can achieve an extension of consciousness beyond the mental principle he will continue to be trapped by the dilemmas which beset him." Education, to him, must prepare the individual for this transformation. Integral Yoga was suggested by him to be the most practical and effective way of child's education for this purpose. It is only in Yoga that the psychological knowledge essential for attaining extension of consciousness and divine life exists.

Past Experience

Aurobindo hailed from Ghosh family which had come from Punjab and settled in Bengal. The name of his father was Dr. Krishna Dhan Ghosh and the name of his mother was Swaranlata Devi. Dr. Ghosh was a great admirer of English education and English way of life and hence he wanted his children to be educated in the British tradition. But the British attrocities in India turned him against them and made him a patriot. The mother of Aurobindo Ghosh was religious by nature, according to R. N. Pani. It was from such parentage that Aurobindo came.

Sri Aurobindo was born in 1872 in Calcutta. It was Janamashtami, the birthday of Lord Krishna,

As already stated, the father of Aurobindo was fond of English education. As such at the age of 7 years, Aurobindo was sent to England for education. He remained there for fourteen years in order to complete his education both at London and Cambridge. In England, Aurobindo's life of fourteen years falls into four distinct periods-Manchester-from 1879 to September 1884, London-from September 1884 to October 1890. Cambridge from October 1890 to October 1892 and London-from October 1892 to January 1893.

Some notable events of the period were:-

1. He acquired mastery in Greek, Latin and French languages which gave him direct access to the original classics and literature in these languages.
2. He developed abiding interest in English literature, mostly poetry and this continued till the end of his life. He spent much time in writing poetry.
3. He concentrated on the study of the classics, history and politics (but not philosophy) ancient and modern.
4. He also attempted learning Italian, something German and little.
5. The school and college studies engaged very little of his time but in one year he won all the prizes in King's College for Greek and Latin verses.

Sri Aurobindo passed the I.C.S. examination but as he did not present himself for horse riding test, he was disqualified. This happened in 1890. Sri Aurobindo left for India in 1893.

Aurobindo met Gaikwar of Baroda while in England. So on return, Aurobindo joined as a Professor of English and French in Maharaja's College at Baroda and remained in the service of Gaikwar of Baroda for 13 years from 1893 to 1906. During this period he distinguished himself as a teacher. During this period in the true spirit of a teacher, he learnt Bengali, Sanskrit, Gujarati, Marathi. He studied the Indian classics like Mahabharata. In a way during this period of 13 years, he prepared himself for future work.

Marriage: During his stay at Baroda, Aurobindo married Mrinalini Bose, eldest daughter of Bhimpal Chandra Boss at Calcutta. Aurobindo's married life was not of traditional life because he was more engaged during the period in the freedom movement of which he was one of pioneers. The married life of Sri Aurobindo did not last long and ended with Mrinalini's death in 1918. This did not have much impact on Aurobindo. The marriage was nearly a ritual.

Aurobindo resigned from Baroda in 1905 and came to Calcutta. He was Principal of Bengal National College, Calcutta which was the first of its kind. His teaching was unique. His students testified this. His political activities soon intervened in his teachership when he became an undertrial prisoner in connection unit Alipore Bomb Case.

Patriotic View

Aurobindo was out and out a nationalist. And practical life of Aurobindo goes back to his days in England when he at the age of 11 had the experience that he was bound to make his motherland free. He was born with patriotism, it began manifesting in his outward life first in England by joining the Indian majors and the formation of the Lotus and Dagger Society, the members of which had taken an oath, such to work in his own way to make India free. Aurobindo lived upto his oath.

As a teacher at Baroda, during vacations, he used to visit Bengal and organise revolutionary groups with a view to rising in revolt against the alien government. The partition of Bengal in 1905 shocked him and gave Aurobindo an opportunity to inspire the people and revolutionists come out in the open revolt against the British.

The political activities of Sri Aurobindo came to a sudden stop with his arrest and detection as an under trial prisoner in Alipore Central Jail for a year from May 1908 to 1909 in connection with the murder of Kingsford. After that, the Britishers were always after him. He had to quit the scene and he left for Pondicherry where he lived till the end of his life. He died therein 1950.

Literary Stature

Of the many heights that Sri Aurobindo reached, the poet in him was most significant and interesting. He always claimed himself to be a poet, first and poet last.

Among the poems he wrote lyrics, sonnets, blank verse, heroic poems, experimental pieces. His most important poetic work is Savitri, the theme of which is the mystery of life and death and love. Sri Aurobindo translated parts of Veda, the Ramayana and the Mahabharata.

In the field of literary criticism, the future poetry is his major work. His theory of poetry is developed in this book. His writings are expressed in thirty volumes.

Love for Humanity

Sri Aurobindo was a great lover of humanity. Though he loved motherland intently and wanted to see her great and free, it was not a narrow patriotism. Nation was a part of universal brotherhood. He granted India to be free but he never hated the British. He envisaged a world union where the entire humanity could exist in peace.

Spiritual Angle

Sri Aurobindo was a yogi. He was a born yogi. He had many spiritual experiences when he was a child of seven.

His practice of yogi was in the beginning confined to Pranayamma, six or more hours at a stretch in a day. He achieved many siddhis and one was in Alipore jail. He had no Guru as such but was influenced by Gita.

Reality : Perceptions

There are four theories of existence or reality:

(1) We affirm absolute as the origin and support secret reality of all things. The Absolute Reality is indefinable and ineffable by mental thought and mental language.

The absolute manifests itself in two terms-a Being and a Becoming-the Being is fundamental reality, the Becoming is an effectual reality; it is a dynamic power and result of a creative energy and working out of Being, a constantly persistent yet suitable form, process, outcome of its immunitable formless essence.

(2) The second concept of the fundamental reality of the Absolute is to our spiritual perception a divine existence, consciousness and delight of being which is supercosmic reality, self-existent but also the secret truth underlying the whole manifestation. All is a manifestation of That the one is the All it is not only an essential existence but an AP existence.

(3) *Maya*. The third concept of existence considers the manifested world as an illusion or 'maya' and views it as purely temporal and transitory constantly suitable. It believes in a supraterrestrial existence a heaven beyond the one in which man lives and where he hopes to enjoy all the delight of existence after the cessation of life on earth.

(4) The fourth is synthesis of these three views. These three views are partial is nature. They express only one aspect of truth and as such the synthesis to give us fourth aspect or concept of reality. There is material world, there is non-material world. There is sensual world. There is attraction to earth, to heaven and the supreme reality. A synthesis and integration of the three views is not only permissible but the possibility of which has been attempted by the ancient Indian culture through

the different ashramas-the Brahmacharya, Garhyastha, Vanaprastha the and Sanyasa.

Status of Individual

Sri Aurobindo's concept of man and his evolution was based on the Indian tradition of Vedas and Upanishads as his own yogic views and spiritual realisation of the concept as contained in them.

The Individual: What is man? Sri Aurobindo has answered the question man is a transitional being. He has absolved from matter. Matter is the first stage in evolution. It proceeds through the plant and animal and it has reached the stage of man. When matter reached the stage of plant, life was gained but not wholly possessed. Life was rooted to the ground. There was no movement. When the animal appeared body, life was possessed and the first form of mind was gained but mind as such could not be possessed. This mind was confined to body and energising its movements combined with instincts and memory, according to Dr. Pant. It is only in man that mind with its reasoning found its full expression.

What is man? Sri Aurobindo answers again.

"Man himself is little more than an ambitious nothing. He is a littleness that reaches to a wideness and a grandeur that are beyond him, a dwarf enamoured of the heights. His mind is a dark ray in the splendours of the universal Mind. His life is a striving, exaulting, suffering, an eager passion-tossed and sorrow-striken or a blindly and dumbly longing, petty moment of the universal life. His body is a labouring perishable speck in the material universe."

He is baulked of his luminous possibilities and shut off to his own divine powers. He is important to change his life beyond certain narrow and precarious limits.

Why is it so? Because man is nothing but a mind encased in a living body. He is only the third stage in the upward movement above matter and life and there are four more stages to be ascended to reach the ultimate Reality (these stages being Supermind, Bliss, Conscious-Force, and Existence). Though man is the highest of the created beings, he is not the last word in the evolutionary process. Mind is not the highest possible power of creation, for mind is not in possession of Truth, but only its ignorant seeker. It is only an ignorant, clouded and struggling power. Even when most luminous, it is possessed only of a thin, reflected and pallid light. This cannot be the end of the mysterious upward surge of Nature.

A great possibility awaits man. There is something beyond, something that mankind shall be. An immortal soul is somewhere within him and gives out some sparks of its presence, but the inner luminous soul is wrapped, stifled, oppressed in dense outer coatings. Above an eternal spirit overshadows him and upholds the soul continuity of his nature and this greater spirit is obstructed from descent by the hard lid of his constructed personality. Man's fulfilment lies in discovering his soul-consciousness, the emergence of the soul on the one hand and rising to the higher levels of consciousness with the pressure and help of the higher spirit that forebodes his destiny.

Therefore, Sri Aurobindo writes:

"Man's greatness is not in what he is, but in what he makes it possible. His glory is that he is the closed place and secret worship of a living labour in which supermanhood is being made ready by a value Craftsman. But he is admitted to yet a greater greatness and it is this that, allowed to be unlike the lower creation, he is partly an artisan of this divine change."

In other words, this would mean that till the stage of man evolution proceeded in a blind way. Matter did not have to consent to evolve into life nor the consent of life was needed to evolve into Mind. But after the evolution of man his conscious consent and collaboration has become a necessary condition for his evolution into the higher stages, his consecrated will and participation are needed that into his body may descend the glory that will replace him. Thus he is at once the created and the creator, though his role as the creator is nothing but the work of the Supermind to which he rises.

"Our humanity is the Conscious meeting place of the finite and the infinite and to grow more and more towards the infinite even in this physical birth is our privilege," says Sri Aurobindo.

Elucidating the concept of man Sri Aurobindo continues,

"This Man is the Manu, the thinker, the Manomaya Purusha, mental person or soul in mind of the ancient sages. No more superior mammal is he, but a conceptive soul basing itself on the animal body in Matter. He is conscious name or Numen accepting the utilising form as a medium through which Person can deal with substance. The animal life emerging out of Matter is only the inferior term of his existence. The life of thought, feeling, will, conscious impulsion, that which we name in its totality Mind, that which strives to seize upon Matter and its vital energies and subject them to the law of its own progressive transformation, is the middle term in which he takes his effectual station. But equally there is a supreme term which Mind in man searches after so that having found he may affirm it in his mental and bodily existence. This practical affirmation of something essentially superior to his present self is the basis of the divine life in the human being."

Thus it can be seen that to fulfil God in life is man's manhood, that is his destiny:

"The appearance of a human possibility in a material and animal world was the first glint of some coming divine Light, the first far off promise of a good head to be born out of Matter. The appearance of the superman in the human world will be the fulfilment of this divine promise."

Sri Aurobindo, therefore, affirms:

"The animal is a living laboratory in which Nature has, it is said, worked out man. Man himself may well be a thinking and living laboratory in whom and with whose conscious co-operation she wills to work out the superman, the god. Or shall we not say, rather, to manifest God?"

Thus according to Sri Aurobindo:

"If it is true that Spirit is involved in Matter and apparent Nature it secret God, then the manifestation of the divine in himself and the realisation of God within and without are the highest and the most legitimate aim possible to man upon earth."

Explaining the concept of Superman Sri Aurobindo writes:

"Supermanhood is not man climbed to his own natural zenith, not a superior degree of human greatness, knowledge, power, intelligence, will, character, genius, dynamic force, saintliveness, love, purity or perfection. It is a greater consciousness than the highest consciousness proper to human nature."

In other words this means that supermanhood is not an enlarged or inflated human consciousness. Not the greatest of our poets, philosophers, scientists or artists can ever be deemed to be Superman. Supermanhood is only a possibility yet to manifest in the terrestrial nature.

In this connection Sri Aurobindo brings in the concept of the Gnostic being who is man transformed into superman. Explaining the concept Dr. Ayangar says:

"The final or culminating assault or heave of the ascending ocean of consciousness is on supramental citadel itself. Man must now grow into complete Superman, the supramental being, or the Gnostic being. The introduction of the supramental principle and power into the human being must also mean the gradual supramentalisation of man's environment, in other words the transformation of nature into supernature. The 'gnostic being' should be the consummation of the climb of the spiritual man."

Indicating the nature of the spiritual man Sri Aurobindo says:

"His whole way of being, thinking, living acting would be governed by the power of a vast universal spirituality. All the trinities of the spirit would be real to his self-awareness and realised in his inner life.......all his action would originate from and obey the supreme Self and spirit's divine governance of Nature."

But supramentalisation or gnosticisation would not mean a sudden or wholesale annulment of lower order and formations of consciousness. The hierarchy from matter to overmind would continue but progressively emptied of the incursions of the ignorance. "The supplemental transformation", says Sri Aurobindo:

"The supplemental evolution must carry with it a lifting of mind, life and body out of themselves into a greater way of being in which yet their own ways and power would be, not suppressed or abolished, but perfected and fulfilled by the self-exceeding."

Finally Sri Aurobindo points out that all the developments and change that the individual has to effect are not outside, they are within himself. He says:

"What has to be developed is there in our being and not something outside it. What evolutionary Nature presses far is an awakening to the knowledge of self, the discovery of self, the manifestation of self and spirit within us and the release of self-knowledge, its self-power, its active self-instrumentation. It must lead inevitably towards an evolution in the knowledge, a self-finding and self-unfolding of the Spirit, a self-revelation of the Divinity in things in that true power of itself in Nature which is to us still a Supernatural."

In short the individual, according, to Sri Aurobindo, is a self ensheathed in body, life and mind and this self not different from universal self or the Transcendental Self. The individual shrouded in ignorance is not conscious of his triple selves. To discover his own self, the universal self and Transcendental Self and realise identity with them which are one and indivisible and manifest. It in life is the sole purpose and meaning of his existence upon earth.

Man in the Universe : Sri Aurobindo rightly prefer to think man as a part of universe and as a universal being rather than as a social being, for the universe far exceeds the society and a man, whether he identifies himself with society or not, he is always in the universe of which, the individual, the community and humanity are only diverse expressions of the one Reality.

Man the Divine Being : Aurobindo always considered man as a divine being, a self or soul with body, life and mind as its sheaths and instruments of evolutionary growth. This is the Upanishad view-point. Aurobindo writes. "India has always seen in man the individual a soul, a portion of the Divinity enumerated in mind and body, a conscious manifestation in nature of the universal self and spirit." Elsewhere he writes, "There is a soul, a self, a God in the world and in man who works concealed and all his self-concealing and gradual self-unfolding."

In other words the soul in man is the source of all light and love, his delight of existence and conscious of his unity with All Existence. It is due to this divine presence in man that he seeks delight in everything. The soul or pyschic entity which is different from life, mind and body and holds in itself the opening and flowering of essence of all to their own peculiar delight of self, to light, to love, to joy and beauty and to a refusal priority of being."

Sri Aurobindo speaks of a double soul in man-the surface or the desire soul and the subliminal or true soul. In fact man has double principles in respect of all parts of being body, life and mind and so with soul.

Describing man essentially as a soul or a psychic being. Sri Aurobindo proceeds to point out that man can attain his divinity by transforming his human nature into divine nature through the process of triple transformation-psychic, spiritual and supra-mental.

Mental Perceptions

In man, mind is the primary means of manifestation. It is important that we have a clear concept of mind in different ways:

The scriptures expound the concept in different ways:

"He discovered that Mind was Brahman"-Taittiriya Upanishad

"The mind is indeed endless," says Brihadranyaba.

In the first place, it has to be pointed out that mind is not a thing nor is it to be confused with the brain, it is a function or a process.

Hence we speak of 'Mental Process' rather than mind. The function express itself in higher mental processes-in feelings, emotions attention, memory etc. This is the ordinary concept of mind.

Sri Aurobindo's concept of mind is different. He was brought it out in his writings wherein he points out the different planes of mind, namely:

The Ordinary Mind

The Higher Mind

The Illumined Mind

The Intuitive Mind

The Overmind

The Supermind.

Sri Aurobindo points out that ordinarily the world mind is used to cover the whole consciousness, for man is a mental being and mentalises everything and it is concerned with higher mental functions. Mind is not to be confused with spirit. These are two different things, "The mind is an instrumental entity or instrumental consciousness", writes Sri Aurobindo.

Ordinary mind is divided into three different parts—thinking mind, dynamic mind, externalising mind-former concerned with ideas and knowledge in their own right, the second with the putting out of mental forces for realisation of the idea, the third with the expression of them in life.

Aurobindo also writes about thinking mind and vital mind. These could be the functions of mind. Thus the action of the thinking mind is to doubt, to question, to argue and to reason, to conclude and to be certain to reject it is uncertain and respect the process again and again. We shall discuss the concept of supermind.

Man's mind is an imperfect instrument so it cannot catch the full integral truth. Sri Aurobindo believes that the errors of conceptual mind must be corrected by the supermind which is intermediary link between Sachchidananda and universe, knowledge and ignorance.

Supermind is the divine gnosis (having special knowledge) which creates, governs and uphold's the world. It is the creator. It is omnipotent, omniscient and omnipresent. It is all inclusive. It is the Lord within. In it there is no distinction of knowledge, known or known.

According to Sri Aurobindo supermind is a state of consciousness. One can acquire it gradually. After acquiring it, one must use it for transforming his entire being, his body, mind and soul. When the man attains the supermind he becomes a superman, a jnani or gnostic individual in communication with our own plane of being.

Sri Aurobindo points out in the following manner the contrast between the working of the mind and that of the supermind.

"The mind acts by intellectual rule or device or by reasoned choice of will or by mental impulse or in obedience to life impulse: but supramental nature does not act by mental idea or rules or in subjection to any inferior impulse: each of its traps is dictated by an innate spiritual vision, a comprehensive exact penetration into truth of all and the truth of each thing; it acts always according to inherent reality, not by the mental idea, not according to an imposed law of conduct or a constructive thought or perceptive contrivance. Its movement is calm, self-possessed, spontaneous, plastic; it arises naturally and inevitably and, out of harmonic identity of the truth which is, felt in the very substance of the conscious being, a spiritual substance which is universal and therefore intimately one with all that is included in its cognition of existence"

Thus Sri Aurobindo finds a wide gulf between the ordinary mind and the supermind. He suggests that this gulf should be bridged by Yoga. We shall now understand his conception of Yoga.

The Awareness

It is through senses that one receives knowledge. Sri Aurobindo recognises six senses which help one to receive knowledge—sight, hearing, smell, touch, taste and mind. Except mind all the other five senses are dependent for their activity on the organs—eye, ear, nose, skin and palate. Sri Aurobindo attaches great importance to the training of these senses and advises that their training should be the first care of the teacher. Our senses must be accurate and sensitive and if there is any hindrance in making them so that hindrance must be rendered in order to make the senses perfect first of all the cause of their imperfection should be understood.

Sri Aurobindo believes that if the defects in the senses are not due to physical injury, these can be removed by the purification of nerve system i.e. by breathing.

The mind as a sense organ receives throughout impression from outside and from within. The impressions are perfectly correct but they may reach intellect in a distorted manner. The full development of the sensitiveness mind is called Sukhamdristhi or subtle reception of images in Yogic discipline. Sri Aurobindo deplores that the development of the sixth sense has never been included in the system of education of man. He advises that mind should be so trained as to give a correct report to the intellect in order to enable us to start our thinking correctly. Senses, mental faculties are the gateways of knowledge.

The Values : Aurobindo believes in physical and moral values. It is a tragedy that only recently we have corrected our defect in education

Educational Philosophy

Sri Aurobindo was a spiritualist. His political philosophy is based on spiritualism and as such his educational philosophy is also based on spiritualism. His educational philosophy is more spiritual and less political.

His Concept : Education thus becomes a product of his integral philosophy. The truc basis of education is the study of human mind, infant, adolescent and adult. Any system of education founded on theories of academic perfection which ignore the instrument of study, is more likely to hamper, and impair intellectual growth than to produce a perfect and perfectly equipped mind. For the educationist has to do, "not with the dead material like the artist or the sculptor, but with an infinitely subtle and sensitive organism. He cannot master a piece out of human wood or stone he has to work in the elusive substance of mind and respect human body.

His Aim : The aims of education are given below:

Physical Development : Physical development of the child is the first aim of education and it should be the pure development of child. It is the body that performs all religious functions. It should be strong. Physical development is a value with Aurobindo. It is wrong to say that those who are physically strong are mentally weak. Without physical development no other development is possible. And it should be pure.

Development of Latent Powers : To Sri Aurobindo, education must develop one's latent powers and enable him to enter into right relation with life, mind and soul of his nation as well with the total life, super mind and soul of humanity. Education should aim at building the power of mind and spirit of human being, this is the central aim of education.

Development of Morality: Moral development is a must. Without moral development, the development of child's emotions is not proper. And mental development would just not be very desirable. Education must develop the intellect and moral capacities of the child to the highest limit. As such education must be based on the psychology of the child and his nature. According to Sri Aurobindo the hearts of the children should be so developed that these should be full of love and sympathy. We should be considerate to all. This is real moral development.

Realisation of Self: To Sri Aurobindo, the real meaning of life is to rise above ego and become our true self i.e. to be conscious of our real being. To possess the self is the ultimate meaning of life on earth. Education should help one to realise his being-the self. Only that education is true which helps one to become actively conscious of supernatural and supreme being.

Spiritual Development: Spiritual development is yet another aim of education. In his own words, "The chief aim of education should be to help the growing soul to draw out that in itself which is best and make it perfect for a noble use".

Integral Curriculum : Sri Aurobindo and other researchers on him have listed the principles of integral curriculum:

(a) all life is education i.e. curriculum is not confined to a limited syllabus and a few text books.

(b) Curriculum should be interesting.

(c) It is a means towards an end, not an end by itself, the end being the development of integrated personality.

(d) Flexibility to meet individual needs is another important aspect of good curriculum.

(e) It should provide for leisure pursuits.

(f) Adequate funds are required for curriculum development.

(g) Curriculum should involve creativity of life and constructive activities.

The preceding discussion should give us an idea about the nature of integral curriculum. It is aimed at and includes subjects and activities for the development of an integrated personality. The different curriculum subjects which contribute towards different aspects of personality development are indicated below:

1. *Physical Education:* Games, athletics, acquatics, yogis aseans, first aid.
2. *Vital Education:* (a) Sense framing, (b) General science, (c) Aesthetic education, (d) Recreational activities, (e) Moral education.
3. Mental Education:

   (a) Languages.

   (b) Mathematics.

   (c) Social sciences including history.

   (d) Such other subjects contributing to mental development.
4. *Psychic and Spiritual Education:* The important thing is to be noticed is that curriculum is organised according to development aspects and not subject-wise.

He has given to us three cardinal principles of teaching which tell us about his method of teaching:

(a) The first principle of teaching is that nothing can be taught. The teacher is not an instructor or task master, he is a helper and guide. He does not actually train the mind. He only suggests or shows him how to perfect his instruments of knowledge and helps and encourages him in process. He does not impart knowledge but shows him how to acquire knowledge for himself. This is the fundamental principle of teaching.

(b) The second principle is that the mind has to be consulted in its own growth. The idea of hammering the child into shape denied by the parent or teacher is a barbarous and ignorant superstition. It is he himself who must be induced to expand in accordance with his own nature.

A question may arise in this connection-what has this principle to do with teaching? It can be very well seen that it has something to do with selection of subjects. The job consists in exploring and identifying the potentialities in the child and helping him in making the choice.

(c) The third principle is that child is best educated in an atmosphere with which he is familiar—the atmosphere of his own culture which includes his heredity and traditions.

The three cardinal principles make it clear that in the teaching learning process, learning is more important than teaching.

What then could be methods of teaching? Some principles are:

(i) Education through mother tongue.

(ii) Education through interest of the child.

(iii) Learning by doing.

(iv) Self-experience.

Place of Teacher : We have already said about it in the first principle of teaching. We repeat.

"The teacher is not an instructor or task master, he is a helper and guide. His business is to suggest and not to impose. He does not actually train the pupil's mind, he only shows him how to perfect his instruments of knowledge and helps him and encourages him in the process."

Education for Integration

Natural Education—education without strain-education which comes naturally and is easy and effective is called integral education. National reconstruction is to be achieved through it. Integral education is complete education.

The following points constitute integral education.

1. Mental and physical aspects have to be strengthened.
2. Education has five principal aspects—the physicals vital, mental, psychic and, spiritual. All these have to be developed together.
3. Four aspects of Truth—love, knowledge, power and beauty are to be developed.
4. Each aspect of Truth has a vehicle-four aspects have four vehicles:
   (a) Psychic for love
   (b) Mind for knowledge
   (c) Vital-power
   (d) Physical body for expression of beauty of a person-physical beauty of a person.
5. The aim, curriculum, methods of teaching are in the light of this concept of integral education.

The yogic principles of integral education are:

1. Truthfulness.
2. Right action.
3. Purity.
4. Remembrance.
5. Gratitude.
6. Humility.
7. Perseverance.
8. Faith.
9. Aspiration.
10. Devotion.
11. Sincerity.
12. Surrender.

New Trend

1. Aurobindo's system is child centred education.
2. Aims of education are based on idealistic philosophy of life.
3. He is a yogi. As such his philosophy is difficult to practise. It does not appeal to common man. It cannot be adopted
4. He believes in spiritualism. Whereas the world is 'full of materialism.'
5. He condemned western materialism but not of much avail.
6. He opened an ashram to practise what he preached. Overall Sri Aurobindo was one of the most eminent and distinguished educationists of our country.

The Pioneer

Sri Aurobindo was born in Calcutta on 15th August, 1872. His father Dr. Krishnadhan Ghosh had a fascination for western education and western life. Hence, he sent his son Aurobindo Ghosh to England for his studies when he was just seven years old. Aurobindo studied there at St. Paul School and Cambridge University. He appeared in the I.C.S. competitive examination and qualified in the written examination. But, he did not try to qualify in the horse riding test deliberately as he did not want to be a link of the foreign rule in India. He returned to India in 1893 and joined Baroda College. In 1905 emotionally stirred up by the Bengal Anti-Partition Agitation, he actively participated in the movement. He then shifted from Baroda to Calcutta as Principal of the National College. He wrote articles in the papers to motivate people to actively participate in the freedom movement of India. For one of these articles he was jailed also for one year. But, he could not continue in politics for long. In 1910 he left activism, came to Pondicherry and began to live a life of spiritualism. He founded an Ashram there known as Sri Aurobindo Ashram. He died in 1952.

Belief in Hinduism

Sri Aurobindo's philosophy was the philosophy of Vedanta and Yoga. The central point around which his thoughts were woven was attainment of Supreme Spirituality which to him, meant only realization of the Divine. In *The Human Cycle* (1949, p. 282) he said, "For accepting the truth of man's soul as a thing entirely divine in its essence, it will accept also the possibility of his whole being becoming divine in spite of Nature's first patent contradictions of this possibility". He further said, "It (the Spiritual Aim of life) will reveal to man the divinity in himself. It will show man the way to seek for the divine in every way of his being, *Sarvabhavena,* and so find it and live in it-live and act in that, in the Divine, in the Spirit, in the eternal Reality of his being" (The Human Cycle, 1949, p. 287).

Aurobindo's concept of Reality was very much similar to that of Sankhaya philosophy. He also saw existence as the grand manifestation of the Ultimate Supreme Power. He said, "Spiritual experience tells us that there is a Reality which supports and pervades all things as the Cosmic Self and Spirit." This can be discovered by the individual even here in the terrestrial embodiment as his own self and spirit as an infinite and eternal being. Thus, the ultimates of life, to Aurobindo, were spiritual which could be achieved only in the full light of the liberated self and spirit. He said that "it is the truth that all active being is a seeking for God, a seeking for, some highest self and deepest Reality,—a seeking for the hidden Divinity."

According to Sri Aurobindo every human being has in him something divine; every one is imperfect but has a chance of perfection. The goal of life must be to find it, develop it and use it. While living in the world, one can attain to "Life Divine". To achieve this objective Aurobindo suggested "Integral Yoga" as the means for which the most needed things were (i) Calm, (ii) Peace, (iii) Equality, (iv) Faith, (v) Aspiration and (vi) Surrender. "Opening personal consciousness to a higher spiritual consciousness based on a quiet mind was the first thing needed for this purpose. Peace is still more positive a condition. Sri Aurobindo said "To be able to receive the Divine Power and let it act through you in the things of the outward life, there are three necessary, conditions: (i) Quietitude, equanimity, i.e. not to be disturbed anything, (ii) Absolute faith, and (iii) Receptivity i.e., power to receive the divine force" (*Basis of Yoga,* p. 18). Yoga demanded, according to Sri Aurobindo "a total dedication to the spiritual life", "to surrender and to receive with joy whatever the Divine gives", "faith and reliance upon God". "opening of the being to the Mother's force and rejection of all egoism and demand and desire, all motives except the aspiration for the Divine truth," "to feel the Divine in you".

Sri Aurobindo strongly pleaded for the need of Spiritual Religion of Humanity which he thought was the hope of the future. He said, "A religion of humanity means the growing realization that there is a secret spirit, a Divine Reality in which we are all one—It implies a growing attempt to live out this knowledge and bring about a kingdom of this divine spirit upon earth." *(The Ideal of Human Unity, 1950, p. 378).*

The fundamental aspect of his philosophy in a nutshell may be said to be (a) to attain divinity in life, (b) through integral Yoga, (perfection of inner life) and (c) Dharma (the perfection of outer life).

Shri Aurobindo said that the true education is that which helps the individual, the nation and the whole of humanity to attain spiritual development. True education is that which brings out to full advantage all that is within the individual and that helps him to enter into his right relation with the life, mind and soul of the people, with the total life, mind and soul of the whole of humanity. *(On Education)*

The principle of moral training as suggested by Sri Aurobindo is "to suggest and invite, not command or impose. The best method of suggestion is by personal example, daily converse, and the books read from day to day and good company. The books to be read should contain for the younger students the lofty examples of the past given not as moral lessons, but as things of supreme human interest: and for the elder students these books should contain the great thoughts of great souls, the passages of literature which set fire to the highest emotions and prompt the highest ideals and aspirations. the records of history and biography which exemplify the living of those great thoughts, noble emotions and aspiring ideals (On *Education,* p. 16).

Another principle that Sri Aurobindo emphasized was that the mother tongue is the proper medium of education and therefore the first energies of the child should be directed to the thorough mastering of the medium.

Sri Aurobindo said that every child is a lover of interesting narrative a hero-worshipper and a patriot. Appeal to these qualities in him and through them let him master without knowing the living and human parts of his nation's history. Every child, he said, is an inquirer, an investigator, analyser, a merciless anatomist; appeal to these qualities in him and let him acquire without knowing it the right temper and the necessary fundamental knowledge of the scientist. He further said that every child has an insatiable intellectual curiosity and turn for metaphysical enquiry; so use it to draw him on slowly to an understanding of the world and himself. Every child has a gift of imitation and a touch of imaginative power; so use it to give him the groundwork of the faculty of the artist (On *Education, p.21).*

Sri Aurobindo strongly pleaded for perfect liberty for the child. He advised teachers not to be arbitrary, despotic, impatient and ill-tempered.

Sri Aurobindo also laid great stress on physical education. Sense improvement by practice, training of the mental faculties, training logical faculty and reasoning.

The Abode

Establishing an Ashram at Pondicherry is an immense contribution of Sri Aurobindo. The Ashram provides an environment of peace and harmony which is highly conducive to spiritual development of the inmates who are *poets,* musicians, artists, physicians. surgeons from different countries of the world. Located near the seashore, the Ashram presents "Ideal of Human Unity".

There is an Ashram school for the children of Sri Aurobindo's disciples. Also, there is an international center of education. It provides facilities for physical education, vital education, mental education, psychic and spiritual education, and international education.

Auroville : "The city of dawn" near Pondicherry was established in 1968. Representatives from 121 countries brought soils from their lands and poured into a lotus shaped urn symbolizing the unity of the human race.

QUESTIONS

1. Aurobindo suggested an educational philosophy in conformity with the Indian needs and culture. Discuss.

2. "That alone would be true and living education which helps to bring out to full advantage all that is in an individual man." Discuss.

3. Discuss the aims of education according to Aurobindo with special reference to moral and spiritual development of a child.

4. Aurobindo had designed curriculum for different stages of education. Elaborate highlighting is principles of curriculum construction.

17

Radhakrishnan

Life Sketch

Dr. Sarvepalli Radhakrishnan was born in 1888 in Tamilnadu, and got his schooling and college education there. After earning his degree in M.A. Philosophy in 1910, he was appointed professor of philosophy in Indian Universities for short periods, and then finally for 20 years in the Calcutta University. His career in writing was started during this period, and he continued to write very learned and perceptive works, which won him fame at home and in foreign countries.

Dr. Radhakrishnan was appointed at Oxford University in 1929 as a Professor of Comparative Religion and Philosophy, to be followed by his appointment at Andhra University in 1931 as Vice-Chancellor. He was later Vice-Chancellor of the Benaras Hindu University, and was invited to tour and lecture in China. Later he was appointed Chairman of the University Grants Commission, and led the first Indian delegation to UNESCO.

His association with UNESCO was the forerunner of Dr. Radhakrishnan's political career, and he was appointed India's Ambassador to the USSR. His impact in political circles was very great, and his learning and wisdom made him greatly respected. The Rajya Sabha elected him as the first Chairman and Vice-President, and his contribution to its functioning according to parliamentary and democratic standards was tremendous. He was appointed the second President of India in 1962. At the end of his term of office, he was awarded the highest national distinction, the Bharat Ratna, in 1967. Dr. Radhakrishnan's scholastic and literary career was brilliant, and this contributed to his stature in political circles as well. As an educational philosopher his contribution has been immense.

Published Work

Dr Radhakrishnan is known internationally for his prolific writings based on his original research in comparative religion and philosophy. His most renouned works are:

1. The Philosophy of Rabindra Nath Tagore.
2. Indian Philosophy.
3. The Hindu View of Life.
4. An Idealist View of Life.
5. East an West in Religion.
6. The Future of Civilization.
7. The Religion we need.
8. Gautama the Buddha.
9. Eastern Religion and Western Thought.
10. Education, Politics and War.
11. Bhagwad Gita.

12. Dhammapada.
13. The Recovery of Faith.
14. Brahma Sutra.
15. Fellowship of the Spirit.
16. On Nehru.
17. The Concept of Man.
18. My Search for Truth.
19. The Principle Upanishads.
20. Religion and Society.
21. Freedom of Culture.

The Ideology

Dr. Radhakrishnan believes that one's philosophy of life should guide the individual's life and action. Philosophy does not isolate one from life and reality, but should make us understand life and to face its realities. Dr. Radhakrishnan's philosophy is idealistic. He believes that life is meaningful, and has a purpose, and that ideals and values help one to realize those purpose and goals. These ideals and values are greater than man and society, and through a proper system of education, we must discover those values, and follow the pattern of life based on these values. This striving for perfection is inborn in man, and is based on man's inborn divinity. Because, everything that strives for perfection, in man, is a feeling for the Divine.

Spiritual Angle

There is a spark of divinity in every human being. If we do not recognize or utilize this divine element in us, then we surrender our humanity and we come worldly, materialistic and degraded. The spirituality in human beings can be strengthened and renewed through proper education, so that higher and nobler aims in life may be fulfilled. Man must not be allowed to become a robot, an unpersonal and unfeeling person and the divinity in him should be nourished and encouraged through religion, contemplation, reading and study of scriptures and through discourses. Matter is not the most important thing in life, and materialism is the worst enemy of the divine nature of man. Man's lower passions, greed and desire to accumulate worldly possessions and to dominate others, are the marks of materialism. However the true nature of man, and deep within him is a striving to overcome these desires, and to rise above them, to achieve true greatness through patience, study, tolerance and a love of mankind generate. The pursuit of knowledge, scientific truth and discoveries are important, but they should lead to humility and reverence for truth, not violence, distrust and domination of others.

Role of Religion

Based upon his concept of man's nature as being essentially divine. Dr. Radhakrishnan believes that religion is extremely important. Religion can establish values in man. However, doctrine and an ignoring of religions other than one's own, can lead to narrow sectarianism and bigotry.

A study of great religious works, meditation and discussion, can open one's mind and had to a desire to explore the essential divine spark within us. The purpose of all education is to help students to look within themselves, and religious study and meditation can stir them to view themselves and to discover their later spiritual nature. A close and reverent study of all religions, reaching of great books, discourses with noble and learned men, meditation and humility can lead to a discovery of the true spirit of man, which is the divinity within. This will ultimately lead to discovering also a harmony between the essentially great thoughts of great beings inherent an all religions.

Dr. Radhakrishnan stated that there is also the harmony between religion and science, which follows a close study of religion. Love of truth is the basis of a study of science, and this search for truth is also the aim of all religious quest. Hence religion and science should not be opposed to one another. Scientific study reveals the basis of all the power of matter, and the discovery of the laws of the physical universe. Scientific discoveries and inventions are based on dedicated study, meditation, experiment and very devoted and energetic work. Religious discoveries and insights also demand the same devotion and long hours of search and exploration. The attitudes of mind required of both are identical, and lead to humility, because man has much more to discover and to formulate in the fuss of science and religion. While Science educates and refines thinking and cognitive powers, religion strengthens and refines the feeling and affective processes. But both demand continuous striving and connative powers. Love of humanity, constructive amelioration of man's condition, compassion and justice should follow a study of Religion and Science, are what Dr. Radhakrishnan advocates. However, while scientific study and research should be promoted by the state and all religious studies should also be encouraged by the state, yet no one particular religion should be supported by the State. There should be no State religion as such. The State should not provide tax support for individual religions or religious institutions. No student should be required to take part in any religious ceremony or study of any particular religion in any institution against his own wish.

Concept of Education

According to the speeches and writings of Dr. Radhakrishnan, we have been able to draw out some of his invaluable ideas on education, which are briefly set forth below:

Education—*Training of the Mind and Spirit*: That education is complete which inculcates humanity in the students. It not only trains the intellectual powers, but also influences the heart, and refines the spirit of man. The intellectual training of the student is incomplete unless it has an impact on the heart and the spirit as well. In this education, compassion and kindness will figure, as they relate to the needs of those in distress and suffering. The welfare of human beings needs to be a primary concern in the education of people.

Education and Scientific Spirit—Education, according to Dr. Radhakrishnan should develop an enquiring mind, which is full of curiosity, and a desire to investigate and create. Traditional stereotyped ideas should be replaced by development of imagination and skills, students should explore new avenues of thinking and devote themselves to scientific studies. Prejudice and conservatism in thinking should give way to healthy ideas in accepting new ideas which scientific studies have discovered.

Education for Democracy—Education should instil in minds the worth of human beings. Each individual is free and should be allowed his freedom of thought, speech and action to a large extent within a social framework. The state should regard the freedom of the individual as important and provide an education accordingly. The masses of people should be given the opportunities of getting free education easily; and education should give every individual, however, poor or under-privileged, a chance to improve his existing material and social conditions. Education for the elite and privileged classes has been provided in our country for many centuries. However, Dr. Radhakrishnan advocates education for all, in a democratic set up.

Education and Self-discipline—Education should train us to control ourselves and to exercise reasoning and judgement in our actions. Whenever we act, we should not be hasty and quick but should wait and ponder, and discern, the true from the false, before being misled. All this requires a great deal of patience and self-control. We need to discipline ourselves, and education should train us accordingly.

Education for an Open Mind—Many scholars in India, after long years of reading and study have closed minds. They are not open to accepting any new ideas, nor ways of new thinking. Many beliefs have become old, outmoded and stagnant. The youth of today, should retain their spirit of youth, and adventure into new ways of constructive thinking, for the betterment of their own lives and the future of the country. The best from science and technology may be accepted, if it leads to a better life. Replacement of superstition, dogma and prejudice, by reasoning and thinking is essential and education should provide this. The ideas and ideals of ancient India should be kept alive by infusing in them the spirit of enquiry and adaptation according to the needs of today.

Education and Women—Dr. Radhakrishnan assigned an equal role to women, in his educational thoughts. Women should be given the same opportunities for intellectual development, equal rights and responsibilities in life, and should be regarded as citizens with the same rights and obligations.

Establishing Institutions

A university is a place where the intellectual, emotional and spiritual training of a man is of primary concern. If university man gains experience, but retains a spirit of adventure and exploration in whatever he learns. He forgets his own selfish desires, and studies with zeal and enthusiasm. The university prepares students to be dedicated and yet detached, casting aside worldly attachments in a pursuit of knowledge. Students, men and women gain not only knowledge but also acquire many skills and practical ability. A university fosters and encourages culture and refinement, and is not intended to stress memory and unintelligent repetition of passages from books on history or culture.

University Teachers—University teachers must be of the highest calibre, intellectuals, morally and culturally. They should be able to relate to young minds, in every way, be young in spirit, enthusiastic, and cheerful. Since they are to educate the leaders of the future, their words, their actions and their own lives, should provide living examples to young students.

A dull, introverted scholar, disinterested in anything outside of himself, is the worst type of teacher many of our universities are inflicted with. He may be learned, but he is incapable of making his students learn anything from him. The Guru or Acharya is a truly good and kind person, who relates to his students and attracts them to his teaching through his interest in each student. He has a desire to communicate with them through his life and actions in addition to his teaching. He can dispel their intellectual and spiritual ignorance accordingly.

The University teacher, selected for his intellectual, moral and spiritual stature, must also be paid suitably. He should be able to live comfortably, so that he can devote his time to learning, research and scholarship. Poorly paid teachers suffer from worry and uncertainty about maintaining themselves and their families, and may have to take up other jobs as well, to supplement their low salaries. This is a blow to the honourable profession of teaching. Dr. Radhakrishnan, himself having been a university teacher, was well conversant with the sad plight of many university teachers. He advocates proper salaries and provisions, to enable a teacher to live comfortably and to give his life entirely to his honourable profession of scholarly teaching and of total commitment to his students. Teachers should set the highest example of truth, goodness and noble ideas to their students.

Status of Students

The demands made by Dr. Radhakrishnan from University students are no less. Students are to dedicate themselves to the attainment of knowledge through disciplined pursuit of learning. They are to exercise self-discipline at all times. Students should be given opportunities and encouragement to participate in games, sports, National Cadet Corps etc. No university can exist unless there is ample provision for all physical activities, drama, music field strips and other activities to keep the youthful bodies and minds of students fully occupied and interested in a meaningful manner.

Belief in Hinduism

The goddess Saraswati according to Dr. Radhakrishnan should inspire in us the quality of discernment, or the separation of the good from the evil, of the corrupt from the incorrupt. The purity of the Swan on which Saraswati rides should guide us in our pursuit of knowledge and truth. Imagination, poetry, music and all the fine arts should be pursued by students at a university, at the same time the quest for truth, for self-discipline and restraint should not be abandoned.

Great Services

The most important thoughts of Dr. Radhakrishnan's are contained in the document based on detailed enquiry and study. The University Education Commission Report, of which he was President. This is in fact known as the Dr. Radhakrishnan Report on University Education, published in 1948. It has greatly influenced university education in post-independent India. It recommends 12 years of high school education for every student, to be followed by 3 years of education at a University. It proposed reforms, in the recruitment standards and salary conditions of university faculty. The commission has many recommendations regarding the goals and purposes of university education, and views religious education from a very innovative point of view. In conclusion, this Report has many new angles of approach to University education, emphasising ancient Indian ideals in a practical manner, humanitarianism, open-mindedness, faith in the power of peace and love justice and a devoted, endless search for truth through knowledge.

Noted Columnist S. Khushwant Singh once wrote about him :

If he had been living. Dr. Radhakrishnan would have been celebrating his 100th birthday next week. He was by any standard of reckoning a most erudite scholar whose genius lay in his ability to synthesise all he had read and create something new.

His critics claimed that he was not an original thinker but an interpreter of Hinduism in a language the West could understand. There was a sizeable lobby of envious, academics who tried to belittle his achievements. They have been cast in the dust heap of oblivion while Radhakrishnan's books continue to be read all over the world and his voice still echoes in the ears of those fortunate enough to have heard his spell binding oratory.

Radhakrishnan (born 5th September, 1888) in village Tiruttani (Andhra) was the second son of a clerk in the Tehsildar's office. It was at Madras Christian College that he attracted attention as a boy with a phenomenal memory and a gift of words. He was barely twenty when he wrote the Ethics of Vedanta as a part of his M.A. thesis. He had gone through college giving private tuitions and got his first job as teacher at no more than Rs. 60 per month. He did not abide by any rules. He came 20 minutes late for his class and ended 10 minutes earlier. He said all he had to say in 20 minutes. His students were more than happy with him.

Although in sympathy with the freedom movement, Radhakrishnan was not very impressed with Mahatma Gandhi when he first met him in 1915. He recalled the meeting later, "Gandhiji said to me: Don't drink milk, which is the essence of beef. I replied: In that case we are all cannibals. For we drink our mother's milk, which is the essence of human flesh."

Rabindranath Tagore impressed him much more than Gandhi. He wrote a book on the poet's philosophy which the poet admitted "surpassed his expectations." Radhakrishnan's professional career began in earnest at Mysore University. From there he went on to be the first King George V Professor at Calcutta University. He had a setback in his career when one of his students, Jadunath Sinha, took him to court for lifting passages out of his thesis and using them in his two volumes on Indian Philosophy without acknowledgment. Radhakrishnan denied the allegations and filed a counter suit of libel against Sinha. The cases were compromised. No one knows what the terms of compromise were.

The publication of the two volumes on Indian Philosophy opened up gates of all prestigious universities of the world for Radhakrishnan. Honorary doctorates. Memorial Lectures, and honours including a Knighthood were showered on him. Amongst those who attended them, were Bertrand Russell and H.N. Spalding who was so impressed that he instituted a Chair at Oxford University for Eastern Religions and Ethics and persuaded Radhakrishnan to accept it.

Pandit Nehru brought Radhakrishnan into the mainstream of the country's political life. He sent him as Ambassador to the Soviet Union. Stalin who had refused to meet Vijayalakshmi Pandit sent for him more than once and even allowed him to ruffle his hair and pat him on his cheeks. Nehru had elected him as Vice-President in the hope that on Rajendra Babu's retirement after the first terms, Radhakrishnan would become President. Rajendra Babu, despite noises he made of wanting to retire, refused to do so. And Radhakrishnan, despite noises he made that he would not serve another term as Vice-President, agreed to do so. The story was to be repeated when Radhakrishnan became President. When his term was about to end, despite protestations that he would like to return to academic life, he wanted a second term as President. Indira Gandhi who started off by being very enthusiastic about him had been soured by his criticism of her father and her corrupt ministers, finally forced him to make place for Zakir Hussain. No Indian quits the seat of authority willingly; Radhakrishnan was no exception.

This year a great deal has been published on this truly remarkable and loveable man. Most of it is entirely laudatory (and well he deserved to be lauded) and do not expose his warts. Radhakrishnan-His Life anal Ideas by K. Satchidananda Murty and Ashok Vohra (Ajanta) does refer to what his critics had to say about his greatness as preacher of sermons as well as his vaunting ambition, his dislikes (Krishna Menon being one) and promoting favourites. It is a very balanced and readable book.

Philosopher President Sarvapalli Radhakrishnan was born on September 5, 1888 at a small place Tirutani forty miles to the north-west of Chennai. He was the second child of Hindu parents who were conventional in their religious outlook. He did not have any advantage of birth or of wealth. The first 12 years of S. Radhakrishnan were spent in Tirutani and Tirupati, both famous as pilgrim centres.

S. Radhakrishnan loved loneliness. This is because he had a mediative frame of mind. He loved solitude. Books were his companions. He was not quite at home in the conventional social functions. In his own words, "While I am essentially shy and lonely, I pass for a social and sociable man. My withdrawn nature and social timidity have given me a reputation that I am difficult to know. Again, I am the opposite of it."

He had his schooling and college career in Christian Missionary institutions. He learnt new Testaments but his pride as a Hindu was roused by Swami Vivekananda. Radhakrishnan came to love Hinduism. He disliked the criticisms levelled by Christian Missionaries on Hindu beliefs and practices. This was a challenge and he decided to study Hinduism-what is dead in it and what is living in it. In 1908, he wrote his Master's thesis in Philosophy "Ethics of Vedanta." It was a great achievement at the age of just 20 years.

From 1909 to 1918, Radhakrishnan worked as assistant professor and then Professor of Philosophy, Presidency College, Madras. He remained engaged in the serious study of Indian Philosophy and religion. In his views Hindu religion cannot be regarded as worldly or other worldly.

In 1915, he met Gandhiji. In 1921, Radhakrishnan was appointed to the most important philosophy chair in India. King George V chair of Mental and Moral Science in the University of Calcutta. There he wrote systematic account of Indian philosophy at the initiation of Professor J.H. Mursheed. He remained at his post till 1931. In between lectured at Oxford and Harvard Universities in England. In 1928, Radhakrishnan met Jawaharlal Nehru.

From 1936 to 1939, he was Spalding Professor of Eastern Religion and Ethics at Oxford University and later on return a very successful Vice Chancellor of Banaras Hindu University from 1939 to 1948.

From 1948 to 1949, he was chairman of the University Education Commission. From 1944 to 1952 he was Indian's Ambassador to Russia. Radhakrishnan was received by Russian ruler J. Stalin a number of times. J. Stalin was always eager and willing to meet Dr. S. Radhakrishnan. It brought honour and glory to India.

From 1952 to 1962, he was Vice President of India and from 1962 to 1967, President of India.

Dr. S. Radhakrishnan died in 1976.

His works include: My Search for Truth, The Hindu View of Life, An Idealist View of Life, East and West in Religion, India and China, Religion and Society, The Principal Upanishads, Recovery of Faith and several other books.

Life Philosophy

Concept of Reality : The Upanishads raise the question- What is that reality which remains identical and persists through change? What is the world rooted in? What is that by reaching which we grasp as many objects perceived in the world round us?

The word used Upanishads to indicate the supreme reality is Brahman. It is realised from the root birth-to grow or to 'burst forth'. The derivation suggests gusting forth, bubbling over, ceaseless growth, brahttvam. There are other derivations of the word. For Madhva, Brahman is the person in whom the qualities dwell in fullness. The real is not pale abstraction, but is quickeningly alive, of powerful vitality. In the Rig Veda, Brahman is used in the sense of sacred knowledge or utterance, a hymn or incarnation." Brahman is mantra or prayer. Gradually it acquired potency of prayer. Brahaspati, Brahmaspati are interpreted as the lord of prayer.

In the Brahmasanas, Brahman devotes the ritual and so is regarded as omnipotent. He who knows Brahman knows and controls the universe. Brahman becomes the primal principle and guiding spirit of the universe. There is nothing more ancient or brighter than this Brahman.

In later thought, Brahman meant wisdom or Veda. As divine origin was ascribed to Veda or Brahman the two words are used with the same meaning. It began to be treated as creative principle, the cause of all existence.

The wish to know Real implies that we know it to some extent. If we do not know the Real, it is because the Real knows itself in us. The desire for God, the feeling that the reality of God, the feeling that we are in a state of exile, implies the reality of God within us. All spiritual progress is the growth of half-knowledge into clear illumination. Religious experience is the evidence for Divine-Religious experience is by no means diviner. God cannot be known experienced except through his own act. If we have a knowledge of Brahman, it is due to the working Brahman within us. The thinkers of Upanishads based the Reality of Brahman on the fact of spiritual experience, ranging from simple prayer to illuminated experience.

Taittiriya Upanishad mentions five levels of reality in the cosmic process-anna or matter, prana or life, manas or animal mind, vijnana or human intelligence and ananda or spiritual freedom. These are qualitatively distinct. Each level has its own governing principles or laws peculiar to it. The laws of the higher level do not displace of the lower but add something new or qualitatively distinct to them. Even the theory of dialectical materialism i.e. (present day communism) admits the fact of advance. History is a forward movement and not endless recurrence or repetition. The aim of the universe, for the Upanishad, is to produce beings in whom mind (manas) and intellect (vijnana) shall lead to spiritual excellence (ananda).

Brahman is not merely a featureless Absolute. It is all this world. Vayu or air is said to be manifest Brahman, pratyaksam brahma. The Svetasvatara Upanishad makes out that Brahman is beast, bird and insect, the tottering old man, boy and girl. Brahman sustains the cosmos and is the self of each individual. Supra-cosmic transcendence and cosmic universality are both real phases of the one Supreme. In the former aspect the Spirit is in no way dependent on the cosmic manifold; in the latter the Spirit functions as the principle of cosmic manifold. The supra-cosmic silence and the cosmic integration are both real. The two nirguna and saguna Brahman, Absolute and God, are not different. Jayatirtha contends that Samkara is wrong in holding that Brahman is of two kinds—brahmano dvairdgasya apramdnikatvat. It is the same Brahman who is described in different ways.

The personality of God is not to be conceived on the human lines. He is not to be thought of as greatly magnified person. We should not attribute to the Divine human qualities as we know them. We have (1) the Absolute, (2) God as Creative Power (3) God imminent in this world. These are not to be regarded as separate entities. They are arranged in this order because there is a logical priority. The Absolute must be there with slits possibilities before the Divine Creativity can choose one. The divine choice must be there before there can be the Divine imminent in this world. This is a logical succession and not a temporal one. The world spirit must be there before there can be the world. We thus get the four poises or statuses of reality, (1) the Absolute, Brahman, (2) the Creative Spirit, Isvara, (3) the World-Spirit, Hiranya-garbha, and (4) the World. This is the way in which the Hindu thinkers interpret the integral nature of the Supreme Reality. Mandukya Upanishad says that Brahman is catus-pat, four-footed, and its four principles are Brahman, Isvara, Hiranya-garbha and Viraj.

Concept of Man : From early times, religious thinkers tried to detect the vibrations of the individual, explore his secret movements, and follow his obscure preoccupations. Man remains a mystery to himself. Socrates felt it as Plato so impressively shows us in his Phaedrus. Man is always more than he is able to comprehend of himself. When he looks upon himself as an object, he is the subject which apprehends and knows itself. Thus man is forever transcending himself. The self goes beyond the perceptions of ideas, realisations of meanings and experiences of suffering and bliss. It is, however, an illusion to think that the human individual can understand himself as he really is. Plato makes fun of the philosophers who believed that they "like the goods can look down on human life from above."

Man is more than a physical being. Psychology is not a mere extension of physiology. There is a part in man's nature which is not merely objective; it is this non-objective aspect which gives man his uniqueness in the world of nature. Man is not merely a creature of instinct, not merely a centre of mind. His nature is not exhausted by that which he becomes as an object of physiology, psychology or sociology.

For the Indian thinkers, the problem of religion is bound up with man's intellectual nature, his distinctive way of knowing himself and the world in which he lives. Consciousness and choice distinguish men from other species. Consciousness leads to moral responsibility through choice. Man suffers from unawareness (avidya) which gives rise to selfish desire (kamd). Man is in a stricken of fallen condition. He has slowly evolved from the animal level and has developed self-consciousness which is an unhappy and divided consciousness. The Budha says that life is suffering. We live in a world governed by karma or necessity.

Concept of Mind : Radhakrishnan believed in Yoga. Yoga is the skilling of all mental activities. This skilling of activities lead us to the mind itself, which is the source and condition of all activity, in its original state.

There is a mind in man immeasurably superior to the ordinary mind. With the upper surface of the mind we articulate thoughts; deep down is the region where we meditate. We imagine that inspiration comes from above the soul; it comes from within the soul, from above conceptual reason. To get into the depths we must practice silent meditation. In that process we are alone but not lonely. In that solitude we perceive the power which gives confidence in spite of the presence of the negativities of existence. It is difficult to continue the practice of meditation for long. St. Gregory the Great refers to the passage in the Apocalypse: There was silence in heaven about half an hour and comments: "For heaven is the soul of the righteous. (When therefore the quiet of contemplation takes place in the mind, there is silence in heaven.....But because this quiet of the mind cannot be perfect in this life, it is not said that there was silence in heaven a whole hour, but about half an hour: because as soon as the mind begins to raise itself, and to be inundated with the light of interior quiet, the turmoil of thoughts soon comes back, and it is thrown into disorder from itself, and being disordered it is blinded."

The Yoga Sutra helps us to develop a single-minded concentration on the Supreme. It asks us to be still, to cease from struggle, to wait and let the light within shine forth. It assumes that the soul is the vehicle of the Spirit even as the body is the vehicle of the soul.

Learning Ideology

His theory of knowledge is intuitive knowledge, reason and mystical knowledge. He above all believes in intuition.

Intuitive knowledge is not opposed to intellectual knowledge as Bergson sometimes makes us believe. Intuition is not a reasonal thrill or an emotional debauch. Intuitive knowledge, intellect plays a considerable part. If intuition is not supported by intellect, it will lapse into self-satisfied obscurantism. Intuition assumes the continuity and unity of all experience. An intellectual search for the ultimate cause may lead us to an idea of God. Intuition tells us that idea is not merely an idea but a fact. The prophet souls, the religious seminars intuit cosmic truths which cannot be communicated except imperfectly. The intellectual creeds are such imperfect expressions and therefore sometimes seem to be conflicting one with another.

Intuitive knowing is immediate as distinct from the discussive and mediate knowledge. It is more immediate than sensory intuition, for it one comes the distinction between the knower and the known which subsists in sense intuition. Intuitive knowledge is perfect knowledge, while all other knowledge is incomplete and imperfect in so far as it does not bring about an identification between any subject and object. All other knowledge is indirect and has only symbolic or representative value. The only generally effective knowledge is that which penetrates into the very nature of things. But in lower forms of knowledge this penetration of the subject into the object is limited and partial. Scientific understanding assumes that an object can be known only if it is broken into simpler constituents. If anything organic is handled in this manner its significance is lost. By employing intuitive consciousness we know the object with less distortion and more actuality. We get close to perceiving the thing as it is.

Knowledge presupposes unity or oneness of thought and being, a unity that transcends the differentiation of subject and object. Such knowledge is revealed in man's very existence. It is unveiled rather than acquired. Knowledge is concealed in ignorance and when the latter is removed the former manifests itself. What we are, that we behold, and what we behold, that we are. Our thought, our life, and our being are uplifted in simplicity and we are made one with truth. Though we cannot understand or describe, we taste and we possess. We become new. When the beautific vision of Absolute Being has once dawned on the dazzled beholder, the savour of the phenomenal is gone for it is seen to be steeped in the noumenal.

Concept of Education

In order to understand more about knowledge, Vidya and Avidya (these are two concepts) have to be understood. In the words of Dr. S. Radhakrishnan, Vidya and Avidya are two ways of apprehending Reality. Both are forms of relative knowledge and belong to the manifested universe. Knowledge formulated logically is not equivalent to a direct and immediate apprehension of the Real. Whatever words we use, whatever concepts we employ, fall short of reality. The anubhava is beyond all manifestation and is complete in itself. Vidya stresses the harmony and interconnections of elements which make up the world; avidya the separateness, mutual independence and strife. Vidya helps us to appreciate intellectually the intelligible ideas about the nature of the Divine ground and the nature of the direct experience of it in relation to other experiences. It indicates the means by which we can attain Brahman. Such a system of theological doctrine points out that there is nothing intrinsically self contradictory about the postulate of religion viz. the divine reality, and that it is also empirically verifiable if only we are willing to submit to a discipline. The theological knowledge or vidya is different from the experience or anubhava of it. The experience is recorded as a pure and direct intellectual intuition in sruti. When we reflect on the experiences or their records and reduce them to a rational order we have smriti. While the first is the domain of metaphysical principles, the second applies these principles to individual and social conduct. Vidya is nearer the truth than Avidya.

But Vidya is also understood as jnana which is of the essential nature of the Divine Reality. It is then eternal wisdom which is not the knowledge possessed by any individual. It is the wisdom hidden beneath the sheaths of ignorance. It is one with the Supreme Self, which is self-evident and needs no proof, svatah-siddha, self-valid certainly.

Though intuitive wisdom is different from knowledge of the senses or anything we can achieve by logical reflection, it is not to be confused with occultism, obscurantism or extravagant emotion. It is not magical insight or heavenly vision, or special revelation obtained through supernatural powers. What we attain by vision; empirical or trans-empirical, belongs to the objective world. It is a distinction within the objective world, between the physical and the super-physical, between what we reach by the five senses and a sixth sense. Wisdom is pure reason, capacity for fundamental truth. It is the possession of the soul or it is the soul that penetrates into its own ground and depth and becomes essential being. It springs from it of necessity when it meditates on itself. This wisdom is eternal, universal and necessary for Samkara. It cannot be destroyed though it may be obscured.

All the same, the tradition of thought has been strong in the Upanishads. We lead up to experience through intellectual knowledge. For those who are incapable of integral insight, perception and inference are the only available means. Even men of experience do not contradict rational thought, though they go beyond it—From the Recovery of Faith.

Moral Aspects

Radhakrishnan is not interested in routine, mechanical and formalised rational ethics nor in "conventional good form" but in "creative good life." Radhakrishnan is interested in "moral heroes." The "moral hero" is an ideal who is marked out by an adventurous path and who is "akin to discoverer, who brings order into the scattered elements of science, or the artist who composes a piece of music of designs a building." All advances in moral life are due to such like moral heroes. The moral hero is one who is on the march to fulfil his spiritual destiny, he follows an inner rhythm which goads him on and he has the satisfaction of obeying his destiny, fulfilling his self." So conventional morality is out. It is moral hero who is in. Socrates refusal to escape from prison is one such example. Right and wrong are for him not just matter of opinion or of probability considerations; they are sure and certain knowledge which he possesses. Therefore, the best that lesser men are able to do is to imitate the moral hero; that will also be an education of conscience for them. And, ethical certainly requires a highest end from which all others are derived, an end which flows from the very self which also gives meaning and significance to the less general ethical ends. The moral hero automatically and by the very nature of his being knows the path of duty clearly. This certainty is not quite like the Categorical Imperative, because every man does not naturally know what he "ought" to do rather it takes a kind of moral superman, who paradoxically enough has also had the benefit of a rigorously educated and disciplined conscience, to gain automatically the knowledge of his duty.

On the surface, there is some similarity between Radhakrishnan's intuitive ethics and that of Richard Price, one of the earliest champions of this theory who extended Locke's notion of intuition to ethics. He spoke of an "immediate perception of morality without any deductions of reasoning". But there are differences. (1) For Price, moral intuition was an intellectual act containing its own evidence. Note that for him it is an intellectual act while for Radhakrishnan it is an act of integral insight, in which the whole personality dominated and controlled by mystical perception is involved. (2) Secondly, it is, for Price, a simple act which is within the power of man in his natural state in exercise, while for Radhakrishnan it is an integral act which requires a man of supernatural vision and perfect self-integration.

Radhakrishnan applies the method of integral insight to decide the question of good and right. It is very revealing to note that in Radhakrishnan "rightness", "oughtness", "the good", all apply not merely to general ethical judgments but also to concrete courses of duty.

Strictly speaking, Radhakrishnan's ethical theory is no ethical theory in the formal sense. His application of integral experience to the problem of moral judgment is designed to make moral heroes out of all men. He only tells us how the perfected behave. The realm of common morality for the natural man does not receive any positive attention from him. He develops no criteria for making ordinary judgments of goods and bad and right and wrong. As for the moral hero, he makes decisions as he intuits the truth, in the unique context of every life-situation. There is reason to argue that his moral hero is not just an ethical man but one who is guided by integral experience.

Educational Philosophy

Dr. S. Radhakrishnan was a pure philosopher and believed in Upanishads and Vedas. He talked of Vidya and Avidya in terms of knowledge and ignorance and not in formal terms of education. We are trying to derive the educational philosophy of Dr. S. Radhakrishnan from what has gone by.

Definition of Education : Dr. Radhakrishnan was Chairman of the University Education Commission in 1948-49. A definition of education is contained in this Report. This definition of education is in line with the thinking of Dr. S. Radhakrishnan. You can attribute this definition to Dr. Radhakrishnan.

"Education according to the Indian traditions is not merely a means of earning a living, nor it is only a nursery of thought or school for citizenship. It is initiation to the life of spirit, a training of human souls in the pursuit of truth and practice of virtual. It is second birth, "divitiyam janma."

Aims of Education : According to S. Radhakrishnan, the possible aims of education could be:

1. *To Know the Reality*—to know the pratman-to know the spirit. In his words:

   "The aim of education is neither national efficiency nor world solidarity, but making the individual feel that he has within himself something deeper than intellect, call it spirit if you like." Self-realisation is thus the aim of education along with knowing the Absolute.

2. To make an individual moral hero is yet another aim of education. The concept of moral hero has been discussed under 'Ethics/Values Building character thus is the second aim of education. Ethical preparation is insisted on. If we do not abstain from wrong doing, if we are not composed in our minds, we cannot attain to spiritual wisdom. Our moral being must be purged of all evil. The Svetasvatara Upanishad tells us that we should cleanse our natures to reach the goal, since even a mirror can reflect an image properly only if it is cleansed of its impurities. We must renounce selfish desire, surrender material possessions, become bereft of

egotism. The path is 'sharp as the edge of a razor and hard to cross, difficult to face'.

3. To promote democracy and to strengthen democracy in India is the third aim of education. According to Dr. Radhakrishnan, "Democracy is the way of life. It is more than a mere political arrangement."

4. To ensure justice—social, economic and political is yet another aim of education.

The Textbooks

Dr. S. Radhakrishnan was an idealist. His curriculum was similar to those of idealise. He suggested yoga, religion, morality, literature for the students. He is to make them moral heroes. It will be through these subjects. He was not very much for science as science believed in fragmenting an object and that deprived one of the thrill of knowledge. It is intellectual and moral activities which form base of Dr. Radhakrishnan's curriculum. Poetry, art, mathematics must be taught.

Approach to Teaching

Intuition is the source of knowledge. Self-knowledge is the source of knowledge. Reasoning is source of knowledge. Method of teaching cannot be lecture. It cannot be demonstration. It can be question-answer and discussion. Let people talk, reason out. And leave alone for self knowledge and for intuition.

Yoga and spiritual activities are not possible without proper discipline. Dr. Radhakrishnan believed in discipline. That only would lead to self-realisation.

Status of Teacher

He gave great importance to a teacher. He dedicated his birthday to the teachers. That is why every 5th September is celebrated as Teaching day all over the country. Radhakrishnan was responsible for getting many awards instituted for the teachers. The teachers are always beholders to him. So role of the teacher cannot be minimised

"A teacher who has attained the goal may help the aspiring soul. Truth has not only to be demonstrated but also communicated. It is relatively easy to demonstrate a truth, but it can be communicated only by one who has thought, willed, and felt the truth. Only a teacher can give it with its concrete quality. He that has a teacher knows, acaryana puniso veda. Only he must be a proper teacher who embodies truth and tradition. Only those who have the flame in them can stir the fire in others." "From Recovery of Faith".

The Evaluation

1. The philosophy of Dr. S. Radhakrishnan is different to understand.

2. The philosophy of Dr. S. Radhakrishnan is from Hindu point of view. It has its own plus and minus points. There are few interpreters of Hindi Philosophy. He is one of them. On the other hand we can say that it is narrow interpretation.

3. Dr. S. Radhakrishnan did not give any theory of Education. In later stages, he did write a book "Creative Education". But no theory was propounded in it. You can say that he was that original.

4. Radhakrishnan was a teacher himself. He gave great importance to teachers. We celebrate Teachers' Day on every 5th September.

5. But for Dr. Radhakrishnan Hindu Philosophy would here remain unknown.

Guru Purnima is the day traditionally reserved in India for expressing gratitude to teachers. All that teachers have done for us is remembered on this day. Teachers have taught us, trained us into various professions, enabled us to handle paradoxical pressures of the adult world and above all, as role models, shown us how to become better human beings. It is celebrated on the Purnima (full moon) of the month of Ashadha, corresponding to July-August. Over the centuries Indians have celebrated Guru Purnima with great enthusiasm, reverence and without any controversy.

September 5, a distinctly inauspicious day which, for too long now, has been a day of trouble and mourning. A few politicians and bureaucrats, with little sense of Indian culture, history and concerns, ordered that henceforth this would be the day for teachers. This government inspired idea does not seem to have found many takers. In colleges and universities this day is marked by complete indifference from students. Teachers on their part have chosen this day, for over a decade now, to wear black badges, take out morchas, easily inspired by government-sponsored symbolism. They go about organising functions in schools. How many of them do this with a sense of reverence, however, remains a moot point.

At the risk of sounding pedagogic and making an argument and hominem, we also need to take notice of the fact that Teachers' Day is organised to commemorate a Brahmin who spent most of his adult life in India as an educational administrator rather than as a teacher. His books, all of them in English, written for a western audience, were designed to give the West a brief glimpse, however inadequate, of a philosophical culture of India. Even there he was not able to identify significant elements of Indian philosophy such as aesthetics. His claim to fame, such as it is, rests on his beings an interpreter and not an original thinker. As to the morality of his personal life, of which we get a glimpse from his biography written by his son, S. Gopal, the less said the better. Little wonder that the symbolism of Teachers' Day associated with September 5 has fallen flat.

Isn't it high time that we scrap Teachers' Day and instead choose Guru Purnima to honour our teachers?

QUESTIONS

1. How did Dr. Radhakrishnan's early life and career influence his writings and philosophy?
2. Mention some of the most important reforms proposed by the Radhakrishnan University Education Commission?
3. Discuss Dr. Radhakrishnan's legacy to education in India.
4. What is Dr. Radhakrishnan's idea of a University? What according to him is the role of a teacher?
5. Discuss the aims and meaning of education according to Dr. Radhakrishnan.

18

Krishnamurthi

Life Sketch

Born in Madanapalli, Madras District in 1885, Juddu Krishnamurthi was placed by his father in the care of, and educated by Dr. Annie Besant, who had many brilliant tutors for him, at her Theosophical Headquarters, in Adyar, Madras. He travelled with her to many parts of the world, and had some of his higher education in England. As he grew up, his reading was wide and prolific. He became very philosophical and often went into mystical trances. From time to time he had unusual spiritual experiences and transformations. An unusual charisma enveloped him, which was noticed and felt by all who came near him. He gave up theosophy and became more deeply involved in philosophy. He learnt to speak French as well as Spanish, and was invited to speak to large gatherings in many countries of the world: England, Holland, Australia, North and South America. His profound utterances brought him many followers. He founded, with the help of his friends and followers, centres for philosophical study in England, Holland, Australia and North America. He wrote many tracts, articles and books. People listened to him with rapt attention, and many looked upon him as a World Teacher, a Buddha or as Lord Maitreya. He was deeply interested in education and in schools and the paragraphs following are extracts from 'Education and the Significance of Life. He founded eight schools in different parts of the world. He emphasized "Integral Education."

Educational present is simply accumulating knowledge and collecting information from books. It means acquiring skills, learning techniques which help in earning a living. This technique prevents us from understanding life. Emphasis on efficiency without understanding what life means, brings about misery and chaos in the world.

The exclusive creation of technique has produced scientists, mathematicians and engineers, who have no understanding of the process of life. Technical knowledge and technical progress do solve certain kinds of problems, but they do not resolve deeper issues, nor do they unravel our inner psychological conflicts. The man who can split the atom, but has no love in his heart, becomes a monster.

Any scheme of education which classifies children according to their aptitude or behaviour merely emphasizes their differences, and breeds antagonism. Governments control education because they need efficient technicians and workers, not human beings, because human beings can become dangerous to governments and religious organizations. Governments and religious organizations seek to control education and to control independent thinking.

Large impersonal schools with crowded classes and mass instruction cannot bring about the accomplishment of superior education; the careful study and understanding of children by teachers becomes impossible. Problems of discipline arise. Rewards and punishments are used to enforce discipline. Thoughtfulness and consideration for others is ruled out in such mass instruction which is based on strict discipline and the enticements of rewards, and the threats of punishments.

The present system of education depends upon authority and domination at all levels: the government, the headmaster and the teacher. All exercise their powers, and the pupil is at the lowest end, fearful and anxious. Fear thus generated, kills creativity; it can never foster cooperation, right relationships, and feeling for others. Shaping the child according to a rigidly organized system is one of the pitfalls in our education today. Fear prevents intelligence from functioning. Children are curious, but their curiosity is curbed and brushed aside; teachers are apprehensive of what may be asked of them, and pupils are often asked to accept statements and judgments without any questions. Text books are followed rigidly.

Existing social values, traditions, forms of government and religious beliefs in many schools, have to be accepted by the youthful mind, unquestioningly and he is not allowed to discuss or challenge any of them. Curiosity and dissent amongst pupils are not allowed in many schools, because these bring about disorder in the classroom and school. Pupils are persuaded to accept the existing order of things. Priests and politician who often control educational systems are not interested in helping the students understand life but only in perpetuating existing beliefs, and the social order. Authority and rigidity control our educational systems. Large schools and mass education, in overcrowded classrooms, prevent the individual pupil from asking questions or discovering truths. Covering the syllabus of instruction is more important for the teacher and for the school.

Objectives and Aims

Education in the true sense in helping the individual to be mature and to flower in love and goodness. Love and understanding should be fostered so that these can bring about instant communication among human beings. The purpose of education is to create right relationships, not only between individuals, but between the individual and society.

There are instinctive fears in every child, and as he grows up, they dominate his attitude and judgment and create many

reality principle develops in him which permits him to take into account both the present facts and the future possibilities of a situation. As the individual grows the 'Super-ego' develops in him. The urges which take the rise in super-ego motivate individual for idealistic behaviour. Freud explains every type of behaviour by the help of these three basic motives. These three types of urges determine different types of behaviours. If ego is strong the behaviour will be according to the demands of reality.

Freud makes one more assumption. Every living being is born with a great amount of energy 'Libido'-energy of sex instinct. Any kind of urge that takes rise in organism is a part of Libidinal energy. The attachment of Libidinal energy to a given object, situation or person is called 'Cathexes'. So, Libido is also a source of behaviour which motivates the individual to act..

Freud and Jung, have same views about motivation but, Adler doesn't believe in Libido. According to him the whole behaviour of individual is governed by the 'Master Motive' or 'Power Motive'. According to his views every child at the time of birth has a strong motive force in himself- 'Sense of Superiority'. Just after birth the child wants to master each and every situation. But, as he grows he experiences clashes between self and environment. He develops an inferiority complex from which he gets pain. But, a person can not live with pain for a long time, so he develops a 'style of life' which is socially acceptable. So, Adler's theory of human motivation emphasizes social factors and opposes biological factors.

Behaviouristic Theory of Motivation: The propounder of this theory is Watson. To him conditioned response, formation of habit or behaviour is stimulus-directed; the stimulus may come from within the organism or outside the organism. Motivation is defined as the urge to act which results from a stimulus. Since behaviour is stimulus directed, it is not related to purpose of any kind. An associationist's theory of motivation has important implication for, education. According to his view point, a child does not have 'want' to learn Maths in order to learn it. He does have to be persuaded to study it, to repeat calculations which he associates with a knowledge of Maths. Any one can learn anything of which he is capable, if he will only allow himself to be put through the pattern of activity necessary for conditioning to take place. Thus, the behaviourist engages students in activity and assumes that activity with reinforcement automatically will result into learning.

So, the cause of motivation are those results that work as reward or satisfaction.

Further, this theory is based on Pavlov's conditioning. In our daily life we observe so many examples of conditioning. No sooner does the bell go, then the students move towards the mess. In fact it is natural act to move towards mess on account of hunger and here the bell is associated with the mess. Here, the feeling for hunger is an unconditional stimulus and the ringing of bell is conditioned stimulus. Similarly, a kiddy does not like a doctor because the latter injects the former. First, he cries on account of being injected, after sometimes he weeps at the approach of doctor and even later he begins to do so as soon as he reaches the doctor's clinic and finally he does the same either at the corner of the street leading to the doctor's clinic or at the time of his father's taking the phial for the medicine. Getting injected on the part of the kiddy was conditioned stimulus and crying over it was reflex action or conditioned response. With the help of the principle of conditioning we better understand child's learning. In teaching this principle of transfer of stimulus and crying over it was reflex action or conditioned response. With the help of the principle of conditioning we better understand child's learning. In teaching this principle of transfer of stimulus should be kept in mind. In Hull's view drive, cue, response, reward is must for learning. Let, a child interested in sweets be left in library to eat it with the remark that the sweet is placed somewhere behind the row of books. Here desire for sweet is, 'drive', behind the row is 'cue', attempts to trace sweet is 'response' and allowed to eat is 'reward'. Next time the child will take less time in tracing the sweet. This is all learning.

Gestalt View of Motivation : A Gestalt-Field psychologist regards motivation as a product of disequilibrium within the life space. A life space includes goals and often barriers to the achievement of these goals. When a barrier i.e., any obstacle appears, a person feels tense. He tries to relieve tension by surmounting the barrier. The tendency to release tension by proceeding towards a goal, including the over-comming of whatever barriers are in the way, is motivation. A teacher who accepts the Gestalt-Field concept of motivation sees that personal goals of the students should always be relevant. He will try to help them to rethink their goals and discard those which are trivial and whimsical. Most of the time he will attempt to arrange the teaching-learning situation so that students will adopt goals entirely new

problems. The right kind of education must take into consideration this question of fear, because fear warps our whole outlook. To be without fear is the beginning of wisdom.

True education is concerned with individual freedom which alone can bring about cooperation with the whole and with the many. But this freedom is not achieved through the pursuit of one's own aggrandizement and success. Freedom comes with self-knowledge. It is the function of education to help each pupil to discover his own inner psychological resources and to develop his own individual strengths, as well as to realize his weaknesses, without imposing upon him the teachers, notion of what he should be.

Education for Integration

Education is at present concerned with outward efficiency and develops the external part of man. To educate the student rightly is to help him understand his total being, for it is only when there is integration of the mind and the heart in everyday action that there can be intelligence and inward transformation. While imparting information and technical knowledge, education should above all encourage an integrated outlook on life. It should help the student recognize and breakdown in himself all social distinctions and discourage the acquisitive pursuit of power and domination. Education should encourage self-observation and the experiencing of life as a whold, not to "me" and "mine" but to go above and beyond to discover the real.

In imparting integral education there can be no fanatical or unreasonable emphasis by the teacher on any one phase of life. It is the understanding of the whole process of existence that brings about integration. Human beings must be integrated if they are to survive after any crisis. The teacher must himself be a properly integrated human being. Another function of education is to create new values and not merely to implant existing values in the mind of the child or to make him conform to ideals without his intelligent discussion or questioning.

Status as Educationist

True education is intimately related to the present events in the world, and the educator who sees the causes of universal chaos should ask himself how to awaken the students intelligent understanding so that he may be helped to avoid future conflicts and disaster in the coming generation. The educator has to be careful, thoughtful and affectionate in the creation of the right environment for the development of understanding to enable the child to deal intelligently with human problems. In order to achieve all this, the educator needs to understand himself, instead of relying on ideologies, systems and beliefs. Let the educator not be concerned in terms of principles and ideals, but be concerned with things as they are. The teacher will not depend upon a method, but will study each individual pupil. In his relationship with young pupils and children, the teacher is dealing not with mechanical devices, but with human beings who are impressionable, volatile, sensitive, afraid and affectionate. In order to deal with them, a great of patience and understanding are needed.

Parents and teachers try to shape the pupils' ways of thinking and feeling and mould them in accordance with their own cravings and intentions. Many parents and teachers often seek to fulfil themselves in their children, and build walls around them, conditioning them by their own beliefs and ideologies, fears and hopes. But the right kind of teacher helps each individual pupil to become aware of himself and the influence around him. If the teacher is merely an instrument for imparting knowledge, there can be no respect for him from his pupils. In order to obtain respect from his pupils, he must respect his pupils first, and treat them as intelligent beings otherwise he can only get indifference or even disrespect from them.

The best teachers are those who become teachers by their own choice, and not by persuasion or selection by others. Dedication and vitality are needed in all teachers. The teacher should discuss matters relating to the classroom and well-being of the students, with them. Delegation of many kinds of responsibilities to students in the classroom should form an important part of the educative process. The teacher should encourage students to be considerate and to understand the moods and peculiarities of their classmates, and to be helpful, kind, thoughtful and patient in their relationships with their classmates and other schoolmates. Discouraging pupils from merely accepting statements from books, and formulae, and exercizing their critical thinking and judgment, questioning and skepticism, need to be part of the educative process in the classroom. Creative intelligence is thereby being encouraged by the teacher.

The teacher will not guide the student to any particular vocational goal, because that impairs creativity. He can help the student to discover what he is most interested in, so that he may be able ultimately to find his own vocation. An educator is not merely a giver of information, he is the one who points the way for his students to attain wisdom and truth, because he does not teach pupils what to think, but how to think. The true educator is inwardly rich and should be given the highest place in an enlightened society.

Teaching Institutions

A school which is successful in the wordly sense is more often than not a failure as a centre of education. A large and flourishing institution in which hundreds of children are educated together, with all its accompanying show and success can produce bank managers, super-salesmen, industrialists and engineers—superficial people who are technically efficient. There is hope only in the integrated individual, which only small schools with a limited number of pupils, and where there are small classes, not schools on a large scale. Nothing of fundamental value can be accomplished through mass education. True education needs careful study and understanding of the difficulties, tendencies and capacities of each pupil, by the educator. Those who want to help the young, should come together and start a school to help the child to become integrated and intelligent. One can be a true teacher at home, as a parent. Those who love their own children as well as the children around them, and are in earnest, will see to it that a school is started somewhere around the corner. To maintain a small school of the right kind is of course financially difficult; it can only flourish on self-sacrifice and not on a fat bank account. The institution however, should not be more important than the child.

If parents really love their children, they will try to bring about legislation and use other means to establish small schools, staffed with dedicated teachers. Being absorbed in their own problems, many parents shift to the school the responsibility for the well being of their children, hence the school and the educators should take an interest in educating the parents as well. Educators must talk to the parents, and have discussions with them, explaining what they are attempting to do for their children. The school must gain the confidence of the parents, and teachers should discuss individual pupils' difficulties, aptitude, abilities, interests and temperament. The parents trust provide feed-back regarding the home life of the child. Enlightened teachers in a good school can create an enlightened community, and work our the strategies and means of how best to bring up children. Experiments along these lines can be undertaken by the school with the help and cooperation of parents.

The Principal of a school should work through his enthusiasm and energy and not through domination and authority. Let him give freedom to the teachers in their classroom work, treat them with equality, gain their cooperation and goodwill through mutual respect. Faculty meetings should not be occasions for giving orders to the teachers. Problems and issues should be brought forward by the teachers, and free as well as frank discussions held on solutions to them. The faculty should have no fear, and no feelings of superiority should be expressed by Principal or senior faculty members during a faculty meeting. Fair and just distribution of workloads, and no possibility of over work or piling of extra work for certain teachers, means a lot in the administration of a school.

The school should promote student-councils and student representation on committees whenever any matters relating to the schools' and students' well-being are discussed. Students may be delegated many responsibilities in the daily running of the school, thereby giving them true learning experience and preparing them for life.

Discipline in the school should be self-discipline, based on understanding and cooperation among teachers, and pupils as well as among the pupils themselves. Rewards as incentives and punishments as threats should find no place in a school where there is self discipline. Small size classes, and attention to the individual pupil, characterize a good school.

QUESTIONS

1. Discuss some of the shortcomings of the present educational system, as pointed out by Krishnamurthi.
2. How does Krishnamurthi justify his statement that the true educator is inwardly rich and should be given the highest place in an enlightened society?
3. According to Krishnamurthi, a school which is successful in the worldly sense is often a failure as a centre of education. How does he substantiate this view?
4. Are there any common characteristics between the views of Rousseau and Krishnamurthi on the child and his education? Discuss some of them.

Bibliography

Aggarwal, J.C., *National Policy on Education*, Arya Book Depot, New Delhi, 1979.

Alva Myrdal, *Education in World Perspective*, Lancer Books, New York, 1965.

Biswas, Dutt Sunnittee and R.P. Singhal, *The New Educational Pattern in India*, Vikas Publishing House, Delhi, 1916.

Cattell, B.B., *Abilities: their Structure, Growth and Action*, Houghton Mifflin Co., Boston, 1971.

Charles Jeffries, *Illiteracy : A World Problem*, Pall Mall Press, London, 1967.

Crow, Lester D., and Crow, A., *An Introduction to Guidance Principles and Practices*, Eurasia Publishing House, New Delhi, 1962.

Erickson, Clifford, E., *A Basic Text for Guidance Workers*, Englewood Cliffs, Prentice Hall, 1955.

Gandhi, M.K., *My Views on Education*, Bharatiya Vidya Bhavan, Bombay, 1970.

Garret, A., *Interviewing: Its Principles and Methods*, Family Service Association of America, New York, 1942.

Gaur, J.S. and Saraswat, R.K., *Occupational Literature: An Annotated Biblography*, NCERT, New Delhi, 1978.

Gopinathan, Nair, P.R., *Primary Education, Population Growth and Socio-economic Change*, Allied Publishers, New Delhi, 1981.

John, Vaizey, *Education for Tomorrow*, Penguin, London, 1966.

Joshi, R.N., *Education—Elsewhere and Here*, Bharatiya Vidya Bhavan, Bombay, 1979.

Kamat, A.R., *The Educational Situation and other Essays on Education*, People's Publishing House, New Delhi, 1973.

Kidd, J.R., *Education for Perspective*, Indian Education Association, New Delhi, 1969.

Kochhar, S.K., *Pivotal Issues in Indian Education*, Sterling, New Delhi, 1981.

Lakshmana Swamy Mudaliar A., *Education in India*, Asia Publishing House, Bombay, 1960.

Majid Rahnema, *Educational Strategies in Developing Countries*, Sterling Publishers, New Delhi, 1976.

Naik, J.P., *India Since Independence*, Vikas Publishing House, New Delhi, 1977.

Rudolph & Rudolph, *Education and Politics in India Studies in Organisation, Society and Policy*, Harvard University Press, Cambridge, 1972.

Satya, R.N., *Innovations and Latest Trends in Education*, The Associated Publishers, Ambala Cantt., 1976.

Saxena, Sateswari, *Education Planning in India : A Study in Approach and Methodology*, Sterling Publishers, New Delhi, 1974.

Shipman, M.D., *Education and Modernisation* : Faber and Faber, London, 1971.

Siqueira, T.N., *The Education of India-History and Problems*, Oxford University Press, London, 1952.

Tiwari, D.D., *Education at the Cross Roads*, Chugh Publications, Allahabad, 1975.